READERS THEATRE HANDBOOK

A DRAMATIC APPROACH TO LITERATURE

Readers Theatre Handbook

LESLIE IRENE COGER
Southwest Missouri State College

MELVIN R. WHITE
Brooklyn College of the City University of New York

SCOTT, FORESMAN AND COMPANY

Library of Congress Catalog Card No. 67-21192
Copyright © 1967 by Scott, Foresman and Company, Glenview, Illinois 60025.
All rights reserved. Printed in the United States of America.
Regional offices of Scott, Foresman and Company are located in
Atlanta, Dallas, Glenview, Palo Alto, and Oakland, N.J.

With reference to the sample scripts, we emphasize that authors and publishers
have permitted the inclusion of copyrighted material with the explicit
understanding that such material may be used *only* for study and instructional
purposes and for classroom discussion and/or presentation and may not be
reproduced or presented without written permission of the copyright owner. For
other uses, application should be made to the copyright holders listed with the
scripts themselves.

Permission to reprint the following pictures is gratefully acknowledged: *To Kill
a Mockingbird*, courtesy of Robert Wilhoit, Drury College; *The Mikado*,
courtesy of Preston Magruder, University of Arkansas; *Abraham Lincoln*,
courtesy of Duane Hunt and Preston Magruder, University of Arkansas;
Mary Poppins, University of Missouri's production, directed by Charles
Closser, Jr.; *Skin of Our Teeth*, courtesy of Brooklyn College of the City
University of New York; *Mother to Son*, *James and the Giant Peach*, *Maria*,
Chitty-Chitty-Bang-Bang, *The Children's Story*, *Happily Sedated*, *Passionella*,
and *The Murder of Lidice*, courtesy of Southwest Missouri State College. The
photograph on p. 128 is by Wayne Schiska.

PREFACE

ECHO FOR THREE VOICES.	Readers Theatre . . .
	Readers Theatre . . .
	Readers Theatre . . .
VOICE ONE.	What is it?
VOICES ONE AND TWO.	It is theatre:
VOICE THREE.	Theatre with a script.
VOICE ONE.	Theatre of the Mind,
VOICE TWO.	Creating with words
VOICE THREE.	People who are alive,
VOICE ONE.	Who think and feel,
VOICE TWO.	Who know the enjoyment of life.
VOICE THREE.	Fun!
VOICE ONE.	Excitement!
VOICE TWO.	Entertainment!
VOICE THREE.	Magic!
ALL VOICES.	*(After a pause.)* Presenting with our voices . . .
VOICE ONE.	A realistic impression,
VOICE TWO.	A mental picture,
ALL VOICES.	To occur in your minds.
ECHO FOR THREE VOICES.	Readers Theatre . . .
	Readers Theatre . . .
	Readers Theatre . . .
VOICE ONE.	A vocal message,
VOICE TWO.	A mental vision,
VOICE THREE.	People living events of sadness,
VOICE ONE.	Happiness,
VOICE TWO.	And love.
VOICE THREE.	Authors . . .
VOICE ONE.	Telling the human story,

VOICE TWO.	Satirizing man's frailties,
VOICE ONE.	Relating his bias,
VOICE THREE.	Creating worlds of fantasy,
VOICE TWO.	And telling the humor of being human.
ALL VOICES.	Birth . . . Life . . . Death . . . Readers Theatre!
VOICE TWO.	An intimate sharing of literature
VOICE THREE.	Between an audience and the readers.

In this way a group of readers might introduce to an audience the purposes and techniques of Readers Theatre.

In the past few years there has been much experimentation on and off Broadway, as well as on campuses across the country; and the very rapid increase in the use of Readers Theatre indicates that even more experimenting will be done in the future. With so much activity, the need for a textbook in the field has become evident, and *Readers Theatre Handbook* attempts to fill this need. In this Handbook we will investigate the origins and history of this medium, examine the forms it has taken in the past few years on both the professional and educational stage, and consider some of the dynamics and procedures involved in its presentation.

In Part I, some fundamental principles of this interpretive art form are delineated, with particular emphasis upon a key premise that there is no *one* way of presenting literature in Readers Theatre. From first to last we take the view that it is essentially the material itself which should guide and shape the way it is to be handled. While guidelines are suggested from time to time, we believe that rules or rigid formulations tend to hamper creative development. We encourage the use of creative imagination. In the first five chapters of Part I, the aesthetic appeals and educational values of the medium are explored, and an attempt is made to provide useful ideas and instruction pertinent to selecting, cutting, adapting, directing, and presenting literary materials of various kinds. Attention is also given to the means for achieving vivid line-reading and for correcting faulty interpretation of the spoken word. The last chapter is devoted to Readers Theatre for children. Throughout Part I, we hold to the conviction that in Readers Theatre—as in any other art form—all elements must be carefully synthesized into a cohesive whole.

In Part II, we present a series of brief, summary descriptions of actual Readers Theatre productions in order to stimulate the use of this interpretive medium by many different groups under widely diverse circumstances. Instead of saying, "This is *the* way to do it," we try to follow the more factual, objective approach of "This is the way it was done." In addition to offering a wide variety of reports on specific presentations, this Part reflects—as does the entire book—the concept of the continuum that exists between conventional theatre and Readers Theatre. Similarities exist; differences exist; and with respect to any one of these likenesses or dissimilarities, it is difficult to assert arbitrarily that "This is the point at which one stops and the other begins." Such a continuum can, nevertheless, provide a helpful perspective. For instance, some performances of Readers Theatre are very close to conventional theatre in that they employ lights, costumes, a combination of onstage techniques with off-stage focus, and physical movement. Other Readers Theatre presentations are near the opposite end of the continuum, since nothing but the readers, their in-hand scripts, and possibly stools and lecterns are visible to the audience. Examples of these varied productions are provided in this Handbook.

Part III, Sample Scripts, offers a fairly broad range of literary-dramatic materials. These were chosen to demonstrate—especially for the uninitiated—the varied types of materials and formats which may be employed in preparing actual scripts for Readers Theatre and to stimulate the imagination and offer a possible point of departure for those teachers and directors desiring to develop their own materials. These sample scripts are intended to show how a working manuscript *might* be prepared, not how it *must* be developed, and to demonstrate that there are no fixed rules to be followed.

To broaden the scope of the book, in Part IV we have reprinted articles about multiple reading from our earlier book, *Studies in Readers Theatre* (now out of print), as well as other materials on Readers Theatre from recent professional periodicals. Following Part IV is a Selected Bibliography for the benefit of those who wish to carry their study of this interpretive medium beyond the horizon of this book.

Readers Theatre Handbook should prove of special value as a college-level textbook, which can be used for basic courses in Readers Theatre and oral interpretation in which group reading is taught and also for supplementary study in such courses as directing, acting, and scriptwriting. It should also be of service to the teacher of English who wishes to vitalize his teaching by approaching literature orally and to stimulate his students not only to analyze a text but to experience it by vocally and physically embodying it. Toward this end, Readers Theatre techniques are being introduced at all educational levels. It should also serve conveniently, we believe, as a sourcebook and reference for all those who conduct seminars and workshops and who direct presentations in Readers Theatre, at whatever level and in whatever circumstance. Our aim has been to structure our materials and to express our ideas in such a way that this Handbook can serve both as a practical guide to the beginner in the field and as a stimulating text and adjunct for the experienced practitioner of the art.

Although, as co-authors, we have both contributed to the ideas and materials appearing in this work, Dr. Coger is primarily responsible for Part I, and Dr. White for Parts II and IV. Part III contains scripts prepared by both of us, working independently.

We wish to express our grateful appreciation to all those who have so generously allowed us to quote from their writings, and who have so graciously permitted us to include summaries of ideas and materials evolved from their productions and to reproduce descriptions and illustrations from their presentations. We are deeply indebted and most grateful to Verne Powers of Scott, Foresman and Company for his tremendous contribution. To him we owe our profound thanks, as we owe appreciative gratitude to Janet Strening for her considerate editing. We also wish to give thanks to Jerry Darnall for his help in preparing the drawings to illustrate the concept of focus in relation to Readers Theatre and to Richard Hieronymus for his assistance in writing the brief introductory script for the Preface.

Leslie Irene Coger
Melvin R. White

Table of Contents

PART THREE / SAMPLE SCRIPTS FOR READERS THEATRE

PART FOUR / SELECTED ARTICLES FOR FURTHER STUDY

PART ONE

Origins, Concepts, and Precepts

CHAPTER ONE

Readers Theatre:
An Introduction

Alfred North Whitehead, discussing the aims of education, said, "Above all, the art of reading aloud should be cultivated."[1] In this cultivation, the oral art of Readers Theatre can play a unique and useful role. In Readers Theatre, the director's goal is to present a literary script with oral readers using their voices and bodies to suggest the intellectual, emotional, and sensory experiences inherent in the literature. The readers may or may not be aided in their interpretive function by lighting, music, sound effects, simple costuming, and nonillusory staging. From this it may be correctly inferred that Readers Theatre is an effective stimulant for understanding literature, for developing skills in reading aloud, and for adding to the cultural enrichment of the readers and their audiences. It contributes to a greater mastery of voice and body. It develops creativity and sensitivity.

VITALIZED LITERARY STUDY

A group of English and Speech teachers would undoubtedly be excited if someone were to announce: "I have a means whereby students can be influenced not only to love good literature but also to become tremendously excited over it, to analyze the meanings and style with avid interest, to want to share their enthusiasm with other students and with parents and friends." Readers Theatre is such a means.

Increasingly, teachers are recognizing the exciting possibilities of this approach in developing an appreciation of the best that mankind has written. An increasing number of colleges and universities offer courses in Readers Theatre, while numerous others make Readers Theatre a part of classes in oral interpretation. Readers Theatre is also used in regular English classes as a way of vivifying the literary text. Growing out of

---

[1]Alfred North Whitehead. *The Aims of Education and Other Essays* (New York: The Macmillan Company, 1929), p. 78.

these academic studies are a great many extracurricular performances. The widespread use of this popular form of theatre is clearly evident in the annual listing of productions prepared by the Bibliography Committee of the Interpretation Interest Group of the Speech Association of America and in the reports of performances enumerated in the *Educational Theatre Journal.* Not only is Readers Theatre employed extensively on college and university campuses, but it is also used meaningfully on the secondary school level. It is recommended strongly in the new course of study for high school speech teachers which was prepared by a curriculum committee of the American Educational Theatre Association. The large school system of Fullerton, California, approaches the study of literature through Readers Theatre. Greenwood High School, the training center for Southwest Missouri State College, uses it to enrich the teaching of literature as well as to encourage better speech habits and to permit a large number of students to participate in a self-expressive activity before an audience—a much larger number than can take part in the one or two annual plays presented by the school. These are but a few examples of how Readers Theatre is being used across the nation to create an appreciation of literature.

When literature becomes an enjoyable, personalized experience, it takes on a significance, a new excitement. The study of the written page becomes fun when it prepares the reader for sharing literary material with an audience. And reading literature aloud deepens the reader's understanding of the text; for in giving it voice, he experiences the writing more completely, more comprehensibly, than he does in silent reading. Not only must he discern and understand the attitude of the author, but he must express that attitude with his voice and his body. In this sense, the oral reader re-embodies the original speaker or the creator of the text. Not only must he recognize the tone[2] of the poem, but he is stimulated to *reproduce* the tone.

Oral reading, as used in Readers Theatre, is one of the best ways to know and to feel the full meaning of literature because, audibly expressed, it appeals not only to the mind but to the whole range of the senses. If a student is to understand and enjoy a literary text, he will first, as Henri Bergson said, " . . . have to reinvent it, or in other words appropriate to a certain extent the inspiration of the author. To do so he must fall into step with him by adopting his gesture, his attitudes, his gait, by which I mean learning to read the text aloud with the proper intonation and inflection."[3] Working from such a highly personalized viewpoint, the student comes to realize that if he is to read the material aloud properly, he must understand not only what the author has said but also the structure of the literary piece: its "builds" and climaxes, its forewarnings, and its

---

[2]For a detailed discussion of tone, see pages 42-43.
[3]Henri Bergson, *The Creative Mind,* trans. Mabelle L. Andison (New York: Philosophical Library, Inc., 1946), pp. 101-102.

character relationships. The student is thereby stimulated to make the close textual study of the literature needed to comprehend the material thoroughly. When he understands it, he almost invariably enjoys it.

PERSONAL DEVELOPMENT

Not only does Readers Theatre enrich the study of literature, but it also contributes significantly to the personal development of the participants. Since the readers have only their voices, the muscle tone of their bodies, and their facial expressions by which to convey the ideas, the emotions, and the attitudes expressed in the literature, they are motivated to develop rich, flexible, expressive voices and to free themselves from muscular tensions so that they can respond vocally and physically to the content of the literary material. For example, read the following poem "High Flight" by John Gillespie Magee, Jr.

> Oh, I have slipped the surly bonds of earth
> And danced the skies on laughter-silvered wings;
> Sunward I've climbed and joined the tumbling mirth
> Of sun-split clouds—and done a hundred things
> You have not dreamed of—wheeled and soared and swung
> High in the sunlit silence. Hov'ring there,
> I've chased the shouting wind along and flung
> My eager craft through footless halls of air.
> Up, up the long delirious, burning blue
> I've topped the wind-swept heights with easy grace
> Where never lark, or even eagle flew;
> And, while with silent, lifting mind I've trod
> The high untrespassed sanctity of space,
> Put out my hand, and touched the face of God.[4]

In the poem, the reader can experience the exhilaration of flying: he slips, dances, climbs, wheels, soars, hovers, chases, and flings himself through the blue with the pilot. He senses the laughter-silvered wings, tumbling mirth, sun-split clouds, shouting wind, the eager craft, the delirious burning blue, and windswept heights as the author describes them. Through his muscles surge the vestigial movements of the wheeling, soaring, and dancing of the poem. His face reflects the pleasure of the speaker-in-the-poem; his voice quality conveys the emotion of the pilot and reconstitutes the tumbling mirth and the shouting wind. In giving the lines full meaning and vitality and thus projecting the life of the poem to the audience, the reader learns self-discipline. Anything he does to disrupt the audience's mental participation will break their empathic re-

---

[4]Pilot-Officer John Gillespie Magee, Jr., RCAF, "High Flight," reprinted from *New York Herald Tribune,* February 8, 1942, by permission of Mrs. John G. Magee and the *World Journal Tribune,* New York.

sponse to the literary material. Since an effective reading demands close attention to details, the reader must concentrate wholly on the meanings to be expressed and, in turn, must cause the audience to concentrate. Also, the student has the opportunity to portray a variety of roles within a single script; sometimes, for instance, he may be called upon to interpret three or four different characters within a few minutes—a challenge to his skill.

When students experience literature that gives them insight into their fellow human beings—their desires, their aspirations, and their frustrations—they gain a clearer understanding of the problems of others and are helped thereby to comprehend their own quandaries, to know themselves. *The Diary of Anne Frank,* the biography of Helen Keller, *Kon-Tiki,* the poetry of Theodore Roethke will open fascinating doors and windows to the young and to the young in spirit.

Because it requires little, if any, scenic elaboration, Readers Theatre can be presented effectively in student centers, in banquet halls, in living rooms, around campfires, and in other places having no formal stage. This suggests its usefulness to those who work in churches, temples, summer camps, clubs, parent-teacher associations, and other community-centered groups, whether their purpose be religious, social, or recreational. Functioning from such a broad base and with so much potential for performing, Readers Theatre stimulates the student to master the techniques of effective oral reading in various situations, making him more confident, flexible, and creative.

CULTURAL ENRICHMENT

In a wide variety of ways, Readers Theatre can add to the cultural enrichment of the individual and the group. It appreciably enlarges the dramatic fare because it is possible for an interpreter to read aloud many plays for which a fully staged production would be too costly, or to read aloud individual scenes as the students study the plays in literature classes. In fact, the medium can broaden the entire literary spectrum, for it makes use not only of plays but also of poetry, narratives, letters, diaries, biographies, and other forms of literature.

Students at both university and secondary school levels enjoy participating in Readers Theatre and often arrange programs on their own initiative. Working alone or in groups, they adapt scripts from both serious and comic materials in their literature texts and from their outside reading, which not only exposes them to various types of literature but also forces them to study, analyze, and compare the selections they consider.

CREATIVITY

Especially important among the many values to be derived from Readers Theatre is the *creativity* it helps to generate in students, the outlet it provides for their originative talents. This is particularly true when they are called upon to develop a script from more than one source. Combining the materials and effecting transitions allows them to be creative. Performance of the scripts also presents the readers with an opportunity to create—to create a believable character, a mood, or an emotion.

These, then, are some of the benefits of participating in Readers Theatre: It is a stimulus for a close reading of literature which, in turn, leads to a fuller understanding and a keener enjoyment of the best that has been written. This approach to the study of literature results in a deeper understanding of life as a whole, an appreciation of human needs and desires, and a more penetrative self-knowledge. Readers Theatre provides, moreover, a strong and enduring incentive for mastering the skills of effective oral interpretation. Working in this medium the interpreters develop more flexible, resonant voices and better diction as they strive to "read out" the full meaning and import of the literature; and they gain poise as well as agile, expressive bodies. They have a creative outlet. They become more sensitive in their responses to literature and to life.

Audiences, too, derive substantial benefits from their participation in Readers Theatre. For them, it provides the opportunity to explore the wide horizons of literature—great novels, memorable short stories, stirring poetry, and distinguished plays seldom produced in the theatre—and it challenges them to participate in the literary experience. In a very special sense, the audiences of Readers Theatre are also "readers"—those who love to read. Clearly, this oral-interpretational art performs a threefold service: for the reader, for the audience, and for the literature itself.

Having considered some of its benefits, let us now move in for a closer examination of Readers Theatre, a somewhat more detailed perspective in which we devote special attention to its definition and origin, its parallel development at both the professional and educational levels, and to some of the playwrights who have experimented with ways and means of creating performer-audience relationships which are similarly direct and participatory.

CHAPTER TWO

Readers Theatre:
Theatre of the Mind[1]

This art form has a varied nature and a dual origin; thus many labels have been used to identify this way of presenting literature to an audience. Although now designated as Readers Theatre in the *Educational Theatre Journal* listing of productions, it is also called Interpreters Theatre, Platform Theatre, Concert Reading, Group Reading, Multiple Reading, and Staged Readings.

DEFINITIONS OF READERS THEATRE

Basically, Readers Theatre is a medium in which two or more oral interpreters through their oral reading cause an audience to experience literature. Definitions of Readers Theatre vary somewhat, yet agree on basic principles. Johnnye Akin of Denver University has called it "a form of oral interpretation in which all types of literature may be projected by means of characterized readings enhanced by theatrical effects."[2] Keith Brooks of Ohio State University has said, "Readers Theatre is a group activity in which the best of literature is communicated from manuscript to an audience through the oral interpretation approach of vocal and physical suggestion."[3] Wallace Bacon of Northwestern University, in enlarging upon these concepts and adding some specifics, has stated:

> Readers Theatre, in our discussion, embraces the group reading of material involving delineated characters, with or without the presence of a narrator, in such a manner as to establish the focus of the piece not onstage with the readers but in the imagination of the audience. The reading of expository prose by a group of readers would not, therefore, be included in our definition. The reading of Biblical psalms by a group would not be included. But the reading

---

[1]Revised from Leslie Irene Coger, "Interpreters Theatre: Theatre of the Mind," *Quarterly Journal of Speech*, XLIX, No. 2 (April 1963), 157-164.

[2]A Denver University brochure announcing a contest for Readers Theatre scripts (1962).

[3]Keith Brooks, "Readers Theatre: Some Questions and Answers," *Dramatics*, XXXIV, No. 3 (December 1962), 14.

of Browning's "Pied Piper of Hamelin," with the readers taking the parts of the Mayor, the Piper, and the Little Lame Boy, would be, provided that the locus was offstage. And clearly a reading of *King Lear* by a group of readers would be—again provided that the locus was not onstage.[4]

In his definition of oral interpretation, which lies at the heart of Readers Theatre, Don Geiger of the University of California at Berkeley has singled out certain considerations which are particularly pertinent to the latter: " . . . oral interpretation, then, is an unformulable amalgam of acting, public speaking, critical reaction, and sympathetic sharing. . . . [It] presumes to be, like other kinds of literary interpretation, a critical illumination publicly offered in behalf of literature."[5] These writers, as well as most of the others who have expressed their ideas on the subject, all seem to agree that the essence of Readers Theatre is creative oral reading which calls forth mental images of characters enacting a scene that exists primarily in the minds of the participants—both the readers' and the audience's.

READERS THEATRE AND THE STAGE

A Readers Theatre presentation differs from a conventional play in that it demands stricter attention to the aural elements of the literature. The interpreter must express the emotions, the attitudes, and the actions of the characters by economically using his face, his voice, and his body as vocal and physical clues to meaning. Nothing he does should distract the audience's attention from the characters, the scene, and the action within the literature. Overdoing these clues is "ham" acting and bad interpretation. Obtrusive gesturing is not acting as opposed to interpretation (it would be equally bad on the part of the actor); it is a lack of selectivity and the use of meaningless gestures on the part of the interpreter.

A Readers Theatre production also differs from a conventional play in the type of participation which Readers Theatre requires of its audience. The oral interpreter gives to the audience, as does the actor in a play, the text and subtext of the literature—its inner essence; but the audience must generate its own visualization of the scenery, the costumes, the action, the make-up, and the physical appearance of the characters. In a play these components are usually presented tangibly on the stage.

In Readers Theatre, then, the majority of the action does not occur onstage with the interpreters but rather in the imagination of the audience. Through the artistry and skill of the readers, the audience is stimulated to experience the emotional impact of the literature as well as its intellectual content; and since so much of the performance depends upon

---

[4]Wallace Bacon, *The Art of Interpretation* (New York: Holt, Rinehart & Winston, Inc., 1966), p. 311. Reprinted by permission.
[5]Don Geiger, *The Sound, Sense, and Performance of Literature* (Glenview, Ill.: Scott, Foresman and Company, 1963), p. 86 and the Preface.

the mental creativity and contribution of the audience, Readers Theatre may well be called the Theatre of the Mind.

ORIGIN AND HISTORY

The form taken by this oral art is not altogether new, but the impetus of its revival and resurgency is comparatively recent. The roots of Readers Theatre can be traced to the dramatic practices of fifth-century Greece. According to Eugene Bahn of Wayne State University:

> There . . . arose in Greece . . . a recitative art. This was carried on by wandering minstrels known as "rhapsodes." The rhapsode spoke, in a measured recitative, portions of the national epics. Sometimes he read to the accompaniment of a lyre or other primitive musical instrument. . . . [T]here was a form of dialogue carried on between two characters, read by two rhapsodes. One would read, in the first book of the *Iliad,* up to the quarrel of the princes; then a second reciter would step forward and declaim the speeches of Agamemnon while the other read the part of Achilles. . . .
>
> The rhapsodes did not always confine themselves to the epic poems. They also read the didactic and gnomic poetry of such writers as Hesiod. . . . When these poems, which were read by one person, had more than one character in them, a type of activity which approaches the art of the interpretative reading of plays was developed. When . . . two characters were read by two different individuals, the drama began.[6]

One might add that when these two characters were read by two different individuals, Readers Theatre began. Bahn also referred to other Grecian activities which are incorporated in Readers Theatre today. Writing of the dithyramb, the hymn sung to Bacchus and accompanied by dancing, he remarked:

> The dithyramb was performed by a chorus, and after it had sung a hymn in honor of Bacchus, Thespis stepped forward, out from the chorus. He came in front of the chorus, placed himself on an elevated stand and recited one of the religious stories or historical myths, just as any rhapsode would have done. When he had finished his reciting, the chorus again continued with its singing and dancing, and the rhapsode again disappeared. As time went on, the chorus began to take a part in the story of the rhapsode, giving an exclamation, offering an answer, or asking a question. . . . In this new art there was a combination of the arts of dancing, music, song and interpretative reading. However, the first three were always subordinate to the last, the element of speech.[7]

Drama and interpretive reading sometimes were united in medieval times too. Church liturgy was amplified by the addition of mimetic action, symbolic costume, and the suggestion of dialogue through antiphonal

---

[6]Eugene Bahn, "Interpretative Reading in Ancient Greece," *Quarterly Journal of Speech,* XVIII (June 1932), 434-437, Reprinted by permission of the author.
[7]Ibid., 438.

chant. While this would seem to describe the drama more than it does the Readers Theatre, it should be remembered that the Easter *trope* was at first "a simple chanted colloquy between voices of the choir, signifying the two Maries and the responding angel."[8] Viewed in this way, the *trope* and Readers Theatre have certain elements in common, and one can thus discern the two forms emerging from the same source.

From this and similar scholarly research, it can be seen that theatre and interpretive reading have a common background. In Readers Theatre they come together again. Today, artists in both theatre and oral interpretation are turning to this unique and challenging medium, experimenting with its possibilities, exploring its many facets. This dual approach to Readers Theatre is the source of some controversy regarding the form a particular presentation should take. Those teachers and directors who have an oral interpretation orientation usually require their readers to carry a written script and read aloud from it, whereas theatre-orientated directors agree on memorization of lines as the natural approach. Similar arguments arise over whether the readers should relate directly to one another and look at each other on the stage, and whether music, movement, and lighting should be used.[9] Fortunately for the medium, there is no final arbiter on these questions, and lively experimentation is continuing.

PROFESSIONAL READERS THEATRE

As another basis for discussing the nature of Readers Theatre, one may observe the form it has taken on the professional stage, both as to production methods and as to the literary material used.

In 1951, a *Don Juan in Hell* production was given by a "drama quartet" which featured four well-known actors: Charles Boyer, Sir Cedric Hardwicke, Charles Laughton, and Agnes Moorehead. These artists sat on stools and appeared to read from scripts placed on lecterns even though it was obvious they had memorized the material. In this seldom-staged third act of Shaw's play *Man and Superman,* the readers sometimes shifted their positions on the stools but in general used little movement.

In 1952 Stephen Vincent Benét's long narrative poem *John Brown's Body,* adapted and directed by Charles Laughton, was presented by three readers and a chorus of twenty. Raymond Massey, Judith Anderson, and Tyrone Power read the various roles. In contrast to *Don Juan in Hell,* in which each reader read the lines of only one character, each actor in

---

[8]Felix Schelling, *Elizabethan Playwrights* (New York: Harper & Brothers, 1925), p. 7.

[9]Wilma H. Grimes and Alethea Smith Mattingly, in their book *Interpretation: Writer, Reader, Audience* (San Francisco: Wadsworth Publishing Company, Inc., 1961), pp. 333-336, discuss the use of costuming, lighting, and other aspects of this medium under the heading "Readers Theatre." See also Karl Robinson and Charlotte Lee, *Speech in Action* (Glenview, Ill.: Scott, Foresman and Company, 1965), pp. 475-476.

John Brown's Body read many different parts. The chorus—which chanted, hummed, and produced other vocal sound effects—and a musical accompaniment composed by Walter Schumann were used not so much for background as for helping to carry the dramatic action forward as the chorus did in Greek drama. Considerably more movement was used in this production than in *Don Juan in Hell.* For instance, in the ballroom scene Miss Anderson moved about as if she were dancing. The only property was a three-foot-high railing used both as a place to pray and as a place to hide from the enemy. Occasionally, the readers sat on or leaned against this railing. Lighting was used to enhance the mood.

Raymond Massey's account of his experience in this production demonstrates some of the striking and occasionally unexpected ways in which this art elicits audience participation:

> Thirty years of stage work before audiences prepared me in no way for what happened out front with *John Brown's Body.* It's frightening. They are so still. Nobody out there sees the same show. . . . Steve Benét's words do, indeed, cast a spell. Those people are enchanted. The quiet of our audience is an awesome thing. But the audience is not just sitting there, allowing itself to be entertained. We seem to have brought to them the key to that too-long-locked room where they had put away their own ability to imagine—to see, to do, to share.[10]

Massey mentioned Cyrus Drugin, a western critic, who in his critique described in detail a white picket fence. There was, of course, no fence of this kind on the stage; but he had been stimulated to see it so vividly in his mind's eye that he was positive that such a fence actually existed. According to Massey, Drugin remarked: "I daresay that no two people in the capacity audience formed just the same mental picture of what was going on in the drama of *John Brown's Body.* You formed your own image according to your imaginative resources and accordingly you were moved, amused, excited, enthralled."[11]

William Hawkins, in the *New York Mirror,* February 16, 1953, wrote of the same production: "The work is staged so nothing interferes with the poet's phrases, in their primary function of inciting you, the listener, to create image after image of your own." These comments by Hawkins and the others further emphasize the unique nature of the audience's role in Readers Theatre: that of creative participation in the production.

There have been many other professional productions which have employed the concepts and techniques of Readers Theatre and which have, in turn, made significant contributions to this medium of interpretive art. For instance, Paul Shyre, a New York producer, used it to present three volumes of Sean O'Casey's six-volume autobiography. In his

---

[10]Raymond Massey, "American Classic: *John Brown's Body* Is a Vivid Reminder of Our Heritage," *New York Herald Tribune* (February 8, 1953), Sec. 4, p. 3.
[11]Ibid.

first two productions, *Pictures in the Hallway* and *I Knock at the Door,* he employed six readers sitting on stools before lecterns, reading in concert style. Each participant read many different parts. In planning his production of the third volume, Shyre decided to change the style of presentation:

> *Drums Under the Windows* will be staged as a sort of narrative panorama rather than as a formal reading with actors reciting from scripts. The actors will not sit behind lecterns this time; more characters will be represented, and there will be a lot of action. A narrator will link thirty-two scenes in which seven actors will play sixty roles. They will use the entire bare stage back to the brick wall. . . . *Drums Under the Windows,* which deals with O'Casey's intellectual and philosophical development in his twenties, called for a new form of presentation. The first two volumes concerned O'Casey and his family and were more sentimental. In this one, there is more Dublin and less O'Casey. It goes into the influences of Yeats, Shaw, and Darwin and incorporates a great deal of fantasy and tells the story of the 1916 Easter Rebellion. I don't think I could cope with all of this in a conventional reading which in itself imposes restrictions.[12]

For this project Shyre felt the need for movement and the accommodation of the entire stage space, but since he used a "bare stage back to the brick wall," the scene still had to be imagined by the audience.

Gene Frankel, in directing the New York production of *Brecht on Brecht,* used stools and lecterns but moved his six actors about a platform that had a large picture of Brecht hanging from the ceiling. Also, a few placards were lowered on ropes at various times during the performance. The program consisted of two parts. Part I, called "Life," was made up of poems, songs, letters, essays, and stories revealing the life of Brecht. Part II, called "Theatre," consisted of long speeches, songs, and scenes from some of Brecht's plays.

Another professional production, John Dos Passos' *U.S.A.,* was presented by a chorus of six readers who, as they stood in line before an abstract background, delivered expository comments from the book in the form of news flashes.[13] From their initial positions the readers moved into localized areas with simple properties, such as chairs and tables,

---

[12]Arthur Gelb, "Campaigner in the Cause of Sean O'Casey," *The New York Times* (September 25, 1960). Sec. D, p. 1.

[13]This production had elements of a form of theatre called Chamber Theatre. Its originator, Robert Breen of the School of Speech, Northwestern University, defines it in "Suggestions for a Course of Study in Theatre Arts at the Secondary School Level," presented at the Secondary School Theatre Conference, August 21, 1962, Eugene, Oregon: "Chamber Theatre may be defined simply as a method of preparing and presenting undramatized fiction for the stage, as written, the only changes being those to accommodate the limitation of time, physical stage set-up, or number of actors. . . . What an audience sees in a Chamber Theatre production bears some resemblance to a traditional play— there are characters speaking dialogue, expressing emotions in a plotted action, and giving all the evidence of vital immediacy. What distinguishes the production from a conventional play, however, is the use of the author's narration to create setting and atmosphere and, more important, to explore the motivations of the characters at the moment of action." See also *Course of Study in Theatre Arts at the Secondary School Level* (Washington, D.C.: American Educational Theatre Association, 1963), pp. 50-52.

and acted out scenes dramatized from the novel. One or two long sections were given in a narrative manner directly to the audience.

Other Readers Theatre materials have been developed for and at the professional level: Dylan Thomas wrote a script, *Under Milk Wood,* which he subtitled *A Play for Voices;* Lewis John Carlino created a "collage for voices" entitled *Telemachus Clay;* Jerome Kilty adapted the correspondence of George Bernard Shaw and Mrs. Patrick Campbell into a script for two which he called *Dear Liar;* a multiple reading of the compiled script, *Chekhov's Stories,* was presented off-Broadway with the readers using stools and lecterns; *Adam's Diary* and *Eve's Diary* were given as one part of a program at Town Hall in New York; and *The World of Carl Sandburg,* a program made up of his prose and poetry, was presented in New York and on the road. Recently *Spoon River Anthology* and *In White America,* presented professionally, have won success and acclaim in New York as well as across the country.

The Hollow Crown, presented by the Royal Shakespeare Company of London, used four readers sitting informally at a coffee table located on one side of the platform; on the other side, a pianist sat at a piano, with a harpsichord close by. According to the program, *The Hollow Crown* is ". . . an entertainment by and about the kings and queens of England—music, poetry, speeches, letters, and other writings from the chronicles, from plays, and in the monarchs' own words—also music concerning them and by them." Some of the material was read while the actors were seated, but for most of the program, the actors moved about and took different positions on the stage. At times, two actors engaged in dialogue; at other times, one walked forward and told a story, read a poem or letter, gave a speech directly to the audience, or leaned against the piano while singing a song. In *The Rebel,* another presentation by the same company, the program was unified by the idea that the rebel is the man who says no. It was composed of prose, verse, and song—all expressing defiance of authority by the individual. *The Golden Age,* similar in format, presented the Elizabethan age in prose, poetry, and drama. In all three of these performances, the readers wore formal attire.

A Readers Theatre type production presented on Broadway during the 1966-1967 season was *The Investigation* by Peter Weiss, a cold and impersonal digest of the court record of the men tried for participation in the destruction of four million people at the German concentration camp, Auschwitz, 1941-1945. The play is a distillation of the facts and words of the witnesses, the accused, the prosecution, and the defense during the Frankfurt, Germany, trial in 1964 and 1965, "a selective transcript, an evening of edited fact," as Walter Kerr described it. In the production, thirteen men played the roles of the accused, each maintaining his own identity throughout. The seven witnesses each played a variety of roles—all of them prisoners spared from death, but each representing a composite of hundreds of witnesses. The lines were memorized. The narration was provided by three actors portraying the judge, the defense attorney, and the prosecuting attorney, who sat at a table in the built-up orchestra pit area. The questions of the presiding judge moved the story along. The accused and the witnesses stood as they gave testimony; the judge and the attorneys either remained in their seats at the table or stood near their seats. The play had no conventional plot, a modicum of gesture, but had many dialogue-like speeches. The prisoners and witnesses sat in cubicles on the stage, each tier of cubicles elevated above that in front of it. The houselights remained on throughout the performance, and the audience intermission was announced to the courtroom as a ten-minute recess in the trial. In short, *The Investigation* was dramatic use of essentially nondramatic materials.

It is significant that these professional productions ranged in composition from four actors who used stools, lecterns, and written scripts to a much larger group of readers who memorized their lines, utilized tables and chairs as needed, and, in some instances, employed movement and physical action to develop or enhance their interpretation. Viewed collectively, these productions clearly indicate that (1) professional Readers Theatre is experimental, (2) it has no one established form of presentation, and (3) it uses all types of literature.

NONPROFESSIONAL READERS THEATRE

The imaginative approach, the courage to experiment with new elements and techniques, and the eagerness to interpret a challenging variety of literary materials which have characterized the professional producer of Readers Theatre are also evident in his academic counterpart. In educational institutions the vision and energies of teacher-directors have also produced exciting and noteworthy results. In addition to developing in their students oral interpretive skills, they have used techniques of Readers Theatre in the teaching and learning processes and are involving their audiences in the experiencing of "live" literature. Often, their progress has paralleled but in no sense imitated that of their Broadway counterparts. At the college and university level, Readers Theatre programs have ranged from the simplest forms of oral reading with little or no movement by the interpreters to more elaborate, even somewhat theatrical, presentations. Since Part II of this book contains summary-descriptions of many of these educational productions, a full-scale discussion of them will not be provided here. However, to suggest something of the energetic experimentation being carried out on campuses across the country and the freshness and originality with which these efforts are being infused, it may prove helpful to cite a few typical productions.

At the 1957 Joint Convention of the American Educational Theatre Association and the Speech Association of America, Helen Hicks of Hunter College presented Book I of *John Brown's Body,* with readers using scripts as they sat behind lecterns. At a subsequent meeting of the Speech Association of America, Wallace Bacon of Northwestern University, Albert Martin of DePaul University, and Natalie Cherry, a former Northwestern student, presented Henry James' "The Beast in the Jungle" in a similar manner. At the 1960 Convention of the Speech Association of America, Southwest Missouri State College presented Ray Bradbury's novel *Dandelion Wine,* with six readers using stools, lecterns, and scripts, and employing some movement. For "Imagination '62," a festival sponsored by the University of Kansas, this same group produced a script, *Ebony Ghetto,* compiled from a narrative by Frederick Ramsey interspersed with poems by Langston Hughes and Fenton Johnson and interwoven with ballads by a folk singer. The physical arrangement consisted of one stool, two lecterns, and a bench. The storyteller sat on the stool while three other readers moved into a succession of different positions that suggested the changing relationships and moods of the characters. All but one of these readers carried scripts in small, easily managed notebooks; the guitar-playing folksinger rested his material on a lectern. Other productions given at national professional conventions include *The Battle of the Sexes,* presented by Central Michigan University; Camus's *The Stranger* by Southern California University; Fielding's *The Tragedy of Tragedies: Or the Life and Death of Tom Thumb the Great* by Northwestern University; and *Readers Theatre for Children* by Southwest Missouri State College.

As a further reflection of the interesting and extensive interpretive activity being carried on at the campus level, it should be noted that the Interpretation Interest Group of the Speech Association of America periodically prepares a report of college and university research in this field. In one of their most recent summations, the Interpretation Interest Group (IIG) categorizes twenty-one articles, dissertations, and theses written on various aspects of Readers Theatre and lists more than two hundred specific literary selections—prose, poetry, and plays—which have been presented in group reading from coast to coast.[14]

From this brief overview, it should be evident that earnest experimentation and creative effort are continuing and expanding on both the professional and educational stage. Although professional producers and directors, being more strongly oriented toward the theatre, tend to make greater use of memorization and physical movement, both groups are striving vigorously toward a mutual goal: to create for the widest possible audience the opportunity to experience a "living" literature—a literature that is emotionally and intellectually invigorating, that can probe man's interrelationships and interdependencies in new and revealing ways, and that can revitalize the human spirit.

---

[14]Clark S. Marlor, ed., "Readers Theatre Bibliography: 1960-64," *Central States Speech Journal,* XVII, No. 1 (February 1966), 33-39.

The statement is occasionally made, and with some justification, that the writing which has been produced for Readers Theatre is adaptive rather than original. Certainly, very few original scripts have been written exclusively for performance in this medium. The originality of the scripts lies rather in the selection and arrangement of the materials and the ways in which they can be made to invoke a special and direct relationship with an audience. While there are similarities between Readers Theatre and a stage play, there are also significant differences. Readers Theatre is not like a conventional play, nor is it like a revue; it is, as we have seen, an art form that seeks a more direct relationship between audience and readers. In realistic drama, playwrights worked to maintain what has been termed *a fourth wall* between those who were enacting their story ideas and those who were witnessing them. This indirect relationship between actors and audience was thought to be essential for a proper balance between the subjective and objective appreciation of the dramatic form. Put another way, the audience was "looking in" upon the actors, but the actors were not "looking out" at the audience.

Breaking the mold: Wilder and others
In recent years, several modern dramatists have been trying to break out of this mold and have been seeking means of creating actor-audience relationships which are much more direct and participatory. It is in this aspect of play-writing that creators of Readers Theatre scripts and the modern playwrights have a similar goal. Among the foremost of these experimenters is Thornton Wilder. In his play *Our Town*, Wilder used a narrator to unite scenes which lacked conventional settings and which used only the unadorned rear wall of the theatre as background and only such necessary properties as tables, chairs, and ordinary stepladders. In *Skin of Our Teeth*, he employed direct actor-audience contact. Archibald MacLeish used this principle of actor-audience contact in *J. B.*, and Robert Bolt employed it in *A Man for All Seasons*. Bertolt Brecht also sought forms and devices that would break with traditional staging in order to develop a new relationship with the audience.

The Brechtian impetus
Since they have striking similarities, an understanding of Brecht's Epic Theatre may help one understand more fully the form of Readers Theatre, or Concert Theatre[15] as he called it, although his reasons for turning to a new form differ quite radically from those of the directors of

---

[15]That Brecht was deliberately bringing the quality of a concert into his presentation is attested in a statement he made to Mordecai Gorelik about the set for *The Mother*. Said Brecht, "We'll place two grand pianos visibly at one side of the stage; the play must have the quality of a concert as well as that of a drama." See Mordecai Gorelik, "Brecht: I am the Einstein of the new stage form," *Theatre Arts*, 41 (March 1957), 73.

Readers Theatre. Brecht invented or evolved his Epic form because he wanted his audience primarily to *think,* to become—above all else—intellectually involved. He wanted to prevent his audience from becoming so emotionally involved in the characters that they no longer evaluated the significance of the thoughts being presented. Readers Theatre likewise demands a thinking audience, but it also demands an emotionally involved audience.

William Menze of the University of Minnesota has pointed out, in mimeographed material distributed to his students, that Epic drama is a hybrid form of drama employing epic, dramatic, and lyric elements; and he added that, according to Brecht, Epic drama is "a narrator of events," operating from a stage that serves as a platform. To prevent emotional involvement by the audience, Brecht introduced what he called *alienating devices.* These bear a striking resemblance to methods used in Readers Theatre, the goal of which is total involvement, both mental and emotional, on the part of the audience. One means of alienation advocated by Brecht is a narrator or storyteller who talks directly to the audience and who interprets and comments on the events and incidents. This narrator verbally changes the scene, a device which is also used in Readers Theatre. Moreover, in Brecht's theatre there is an avoidance of the concept of the *fourth wall,* a convention commonly avoided in Readers Theatre too.

Brecht also had his actors shift roles and play more than one character, as was done in *John Brown's Body, I Knock at the Door,* and other Readers Theatre performances. An example of Brecht's role-shifting technique can be seen in his play *The Experiment,* in which three comrades return from China and report on their activities there. With the help of a chorus and an orchestra, they tell their story by acting it out. The three comrades play the roles of all those who enter into the narrative. This closely approximates the form followed by Charles Laughton for *John Brown's Body,* even to the use of a chorus.

Another alienating device used by Brecht was to have an actor step out of the scene to sing directly to the audience a song that comments on the action. He also made use of such devices as the projection of pictures, printed comments, and similar information onto a background screen; and he characteristically employed bare stage walls and minimal properties to keep the audience continuously aware of differences between real life and the stage.

Many of Brecht's dramas are made up of a succession of several scenes, each existing for itself instead of being linked to subsequent scenes. In short, Epic drama tends to consist of a series of relatively independent segments which, when taken together, present a broad overview of a sequence of events. This compositional form is similar to that found in *The World of Carl Sandburg* and in *A Thurber Carnival.* The latter, incidentally, consists of short dramatic sketches on an uncluttered stage, with blown-up Thurber drawings projected onto a screen, storytellers narrating directly to the audience, and dancing couples who suddenly "freeze" and fling out Thurberisms.

Thus Brecht, in searching for a new relationship with his audience, used many of the compositional and presentational elements employed in Readers Theatre: he utilized a narrator to tie segments together, to verbally set the scenes, to comment upon and interpret the action; his actors portrayed more than one role; and his stage was a platform with few properties. Each scene existed for itself; but when the scenes were taken together, they presented a broad overview of a major premise. He, too, demanded a thinking audience; but contrary to the aim of Readers Theatre, Brecht sought to avoid emotional involvement on the part of the audience.

Key characteristics: a summation
What, then, are the unique and distinguishing characteristics of Readers Theatre? In most of the professional and educational productions surveyed in this chapter, certain elements have recurred frequently enough to be considered typical: scenery and costumes are not used or are only selectively implied; action or physical movement is merely suggested by the interpreter and is visualized in the minds of the audience; a narrator, speaking directly to the audience, usually establishes the basic situation or theme and links the various segments together; a physical script is usually carried by the reader or is at least in evidence somewhere; and, probably most important, there is a continuing effort to develop and maintain a closer, more personalized relationship between performer and audience—a relationship which, in Readers Theatre, requires a decidedly different kind of participation from that demanded by the conventional theatre. Specifically, the emphasis in Readers Theatre is upon the aural appeal, and the audience's attention is concentrated upon the literature. In both theatres, the subtext of the material—the meaning underlying the words—is shared with the audience to the fullest extent possible; and, Brecht notwithstanding, the audience is emotionally involved.

The possibilities of this medium have not yet been fully realized or exploited. Relatively new on the contemporary scene, Readers Theatre is free for experimentation and open to the use of imaginative techniques for bringing literature to an audience. As Allardyce Nicoll has said, "Almost always we find dramatic genius flowering when a particular land in a particular age discovers a theatrical form that is new, adjusted to its demands, and hitherto not fully exploited."[16] Readers Theatre, it must be reiterated, is not a substitute for conventional theatre and is not intended to be. It is a different form, with a focus on the written word. With few outside trappings, it centers the audience's interest on the author's

---

[16]Allardyce Nicoll, *World Drama* (New York: Harcourt, Brace & Company, 1950), p. 933.

text. Since it is not limited to the play form, it can bring to the stage a far greater range of literary materials than conventional theatre. Whether playwrights create new material, as did Dylan Thomas in *Under Milk Wood,* or adapters arrange scripts from plays or other literary sources, they are seeking to stimulate the audience and are demanding of the audience a special type of creative participation. This, then, is the essence of Readers Theatre, which may properly be called Theatre of the Mind.

CHAPTER THREE
Selecting and Adapting Material for Readers Theatre

The range of literature suitable to Readers Theatre is limitless. As we have noted, plays, novels, short stories, letters, diaries, poems, and even some essays have been used successfully. Both serious and comic materials have been adapted. From the following list we can glimpse the infinite variety that is possible: Robert Frost's poem "The Death of the Hired Man"; James Thurber's short story "The Secret Life of Walter Mitty"; Mark Twain's *Adam's Diary* and *Eve's Diary* (see pp. 174-181); Norman Corwin's radio script *Mary and the Fairy;* Oscar Wilde's play *The Importance of Being Earnest;* James Purdy's novel *Malcolm;* Addison and Steele's essays *The Spectator Papers;* the letters exchanged by Jane Welsh and Thomas Carlyle; and even the comic strips of Jules Feiffer.

This wide range of appropriate materials places a challenging and somewhat complicated responsibility upon those who would prepare scripts for Readers Theatre. This preparation is basically a two-step process which involves, first, selecting materials with high literary values and strong dramatic potential and, second, adapting these selections for a script which—through its aural appeals—will secure the desired emotional and intellectual response from the audience. The task is not, however, as formidable as it may appear at first glance. Experimentation and experience have singled out certain qualities that the selector-adapter can look for as he goes about the job of finding and choosing his materials and certain precepts that will aid him in adjusting and fitting the components together into a unified and fluid whole.

SELECTING SCRIPT MATERIALS

Certain qualities should be looked for in any subject matter and style of writing that is being considered for Readers Theatre: *evocative power, compelling characters, action, enriched language,* and *wholeness.*

Evocative power

Literature with a strong evocative power—the kind encountered, for instance, in John Steinbeck's short story "The Promise"—is one important requisite for a successful Readers Theatre script. Such writing has the power to stir the imagination, the emotions, and the mind of the listener. It evokes a definite response from the audience; it makes them shiver, makes them cry, makes them happy. It provides a memorable moment. Such material usually expresses a "moment of truth" (Chekhov's "How Much Land Does a Man Need"); provides a flash of insight into a fellow human being (Marjorie Kinnan Rawlings' "Mother in Manville"), into a complex problem (James Clavell's "The Children's Story"), into man's relationship with a higher being (T. W. Turner's "Christ in the Concrete City"); or delineates a meaningful relationship with nature (Hamlin Garland's "Under the Lion's Paw") or with society (Gerhart Hauptmann's *The Weavers*).

Interesting characters

Literature with interesting characters in action is especially good material for Readers Theatre. One of the major ingredients needed in any type of theatre is interaction among characters, and literature containing no element of characterization lacks an element vital for a good Readers Theatre script. That is why many essays cannot be successfully adapted to this medium and why literary material containing only one character would resemble solo acting more than true theatre. Our interest is aroused by characters who are not only interacting but who are so familiar that we may identify with them, are so different that they are unique, or are capable of "surprising us convincingly." A familiar character in an unfamiliar situation is intriguing. An example is the heroine in *Alice in Wonderland;* Walter Mitty is another. Lady Macbeth, the monk in Browning's "Soliloquy of the Spanish Cloister," Yank in O'Neill's *The Hairy Ape,* and the delightful detective Christophero in Peter Shafer's *The Private Eye* are all strongly drawn, interesting characters, each distinctive yet capable of being understood. They are attention-holding in themselves. And although not people in the ordinary sense, the characters in Roald Dahl's *James and the Giant Peach* are fascinating, especially the Earthworm and the Centipede.

Action: outward and inward

In a script worthy of Readers Theatre, the characters need to be seen in action—action that is provocative, intriguing, stirring. This action need not be physical; a character thinking or feeling is a character in action, especially if the thinking or feeling is directed against a counter sentiment or force. The conflict which induces dramatic action, then, may be either outward or inward. Action can be the result of a conflict between two or more people, as shown in the gang wars of *West Side Story;* or an individual may engage in conflict with society, as in Ibsen's *An Enemy of the People,* where Dr. Stockman is in conflict with all the people in his town. The conflict may also be with a force in nature. In Jack London's "To Build a Fire," a man is trying to cope with the freezing cold. Or the conflict may be an inner one—for instance, a man in doubt, fighting his own conscience or making a difficult choice. This is the conflict in Hamlet, Macbeth, and the character in Frost's poem, "The Road Not Taken." This element of man-in-action—be it inner or outer—is imperative in the material chosen for Readers Theatre. It should not be random or aimless; action is more interesting if it has a "going somewhere" quality. As Bacon and Breen point out in *Literature As Experience:*

> No piece of prose fiction lacks *an action*—that is, a progression from one posi-
> tion or one point of awareness to another. Someone must undergo a change
> in awareness because a story *cannot be* (though a poem *may be* and a pure lyric
> poem *is*) in this sense static. The change in awareness may or may not be in
> a character or characters within the story; it may be produced within the
> reader alone, while the characters remain unaware. But it is this revelation . . .
> which is basic to the life of the story and which constitutes its design, its action.[1]

Since the action in a Readers Theatre production is usually suggested rather than literal, the written material must contain clear and vital action that the audience can visualize in a succession of mental images. This action must be concretely phrased, couched in vivid, mimetic terms; and since it is often suspense-filled, it should build to an unmistakable climax.

Enriched language

Not only should material be thought-provoking, provide a memorable emotional experience, and present interesting characters in provocative action, but it should also be written in language rich in evocative overtones, in language with a poetic cast. Auditory effectiveness is achieved, for the most part, through repetition of various sounds. Though found most frequently in poetry, this repetition is also found in prose having a poetic quality. Alliteration, assonance, and onomatopoeia are among the more common forms; they are readily identifiable in the following brief illustrative passages:

Alliteration:	The *r*umble of *r*everberation *r*ose to a *r*oar.
	The *b*lazing *b*rightness of her *b*eauties *b*ecame. . . .
Assonance:	A g*o*lden gl*o*w suffused the d*o*me.
	The l*o*wing herd wind sl*o*wly *o*'er the lea.
Onomatopoeia:	The hissing of the skates on the slick ice.
	The moan of doves in immemorial elms,
	And murmur of innumerable bees.

---

[1]Wallace Bacon and Robert Breen, *Literature As Experience* (New York: McGraw-Hill Book Company, Inc., 1959), p. 215.

In the above examples, onomatopoeia occurs when the sound of the words suggests the meaning. The recurring *s* sound imitates the skates on ice, and the *m*'s suggest the murmuring sound of the doves and bees. doves and bees.

The repetition of words and phrases can delight the ear as well as make the meaning clear. Repetition of certain phrases or words can give cumulative power, as in this passage from Shakespeare's *The Merchant of Venice* (Act V, Scene i, lines 192-198):

> *Sweet Portia,*
> *If you did know to whom I gave the ring,*
> *If you did know for whom I gave the ring*
> *And would conceive for what I gave the ring*
> *And how unwillingly I left the ring,*
> *When nought would be accepted but the ring,*
> *You would abate the strength of your displeasure.*

Such repetition establishes rhythm which, in turn, stimulates emotion and reinforces the meaning of the language. Children's poetry, nursery rhymes, and children's stories make discerning use of this appeal to the ear, as in the Dr. Seuss stories.

Enriched language extends the meaning by evoking comparisons and contrasts. Literature rich in sense imagery, as Ray Bradbury's *Dandelion Wine*, is especially effective for Readers Theatre. By re-creating the sense images in the material, the reader can fully experience the sights, sounds, smells, and other sensory details and thus respond more completely to the situation. Kinesthetic imagery also greatly enriches the experience for the reader and for the audience. In *The Order of Poetry*, kinesthesia is defined as

> the perception or feeling of movement. . . . [T]his term is usually reserved for that kind of imagery which appeals, not to our senses of smell, hearing, etc., . . . but to our residual memory or imagination derived from the nerves and muscles which govern bodily movement and physical attitudes. Through kinesthesia we get "the feel" of an action, whether perceived directly or described in language; on the basis of having moved or arranged our own bodies in the past, we can imaginatively identify ourselves with, or project ourselves into, the motions or postures of others. The use of "body-English" in games like pool or golf acts out our kinesthetic identifications, which work more inwardly in our response to such poetic images as Keats's "limping and trembling hare."[2]

Kinesthesia is, of course, closely related to empathy, the imaginative projection of one's own consciousness into another being. In other words,

---

[2]Edward A. Bloom, Charles H. Philbrick, and Elmer M. Blistein, *The Order of Poetry* (New York: The Odyssey Press, Inc., 1961), p. 154.

we imaginatively identify ourselves with the motions of the characters in the literature. We can also empathize with, or "put ourselves into," a physical response to the emotions felt by others. Because this identification and empathy make the literature more real as well as more enjoyable to the reader and the audience, it is advisable to choose materials rich in imagery. Curtis Canfield, in *The Craft of Play Directing,* avers:

> The imaginative use of language . . . has but one object: to increase the listener's enjoyment of what he hears. The verbal effects . . . are means to that end. They add one more dimension to a form of communication that can also appeal by means of interesting plots, significant themes, and characters human and engaging enough to enlist our attention and entangle us emotionally in what they feel and do.[3]

Wholeness

Another factor to consider in choosing material for Readers Theatre is the length of the selection; whether a scene or passage from a longer work or the total composition is used, the finished script must possess a wholeness, a sense of completeness; that is, it must have a beginning, a middle, and an end. It must furnish a complete experience for the audience. It is also important to select material that can be cut and adapted to fit into a reasonable time limit. In Readers Theatre, as in a play, there must be condensation and a telescoping of events and characters. The material needs to be structured so that the story moves along and comes to a focal high point. The maximum duration of Readers Theatre performances is usually sixty to seventy minutes, and many directors feel that it is difficult to hold an audience longer than an hour and a half. However, the recent trend to adapt full-length novels and plays is tending to change this, and longer programs with intermissions are being given.

SELECTIVE CRITERIA FOR PLAYS

The selection of stage plays for Readers Theatre involves a number of special factors. As with all types of literature, of course, evocative power, compelling characters, provocative conflict, sustained action, vivid language, and wholeness are very important considerations. In addition, however, certain other elements should be taken into account. The plays selected ought to have an unusually lively interchange of ideas *(Major Barbara);* dialogue that reveals each character's motivation, personality, and depth *(The Cherry Orchard);* and strong emotional climaxes *(The Little Foxes).* Plays that are dependent upon a great amount of visual action, particularly farcical action *(Charley's Aunt),* lose much of their vitality when this activity must be either verbalized by a narrator or omitted. For example, murder mysteries dependent upon such special effects as bodies falling from closets or emerging from window seats,

---

[3]Curtis Canfield, *The Craft of Play Directing* (New York: Holt, Rinehart & Winston, Inc., 1963), p. 106.

detailed movements of a mysterious or menacing nature, or a great deal of broad physical action do not readily lend themselves to Readers Theatre adaptation. For effective Readers Theatre, words are still a most important ingredient—words interpreted by sensitive, expressive readers.

These, then, are the essential criteria for selecting materials appropriate for Readers Theatre: The literature should, above all, provide provocative ideas and interesting characters in intriguing action; it should contain rich language with evocative overtones; and it should be capable of being cut to a reasonable time limit and still preserve its essential entity, a wholeness of experience. Ideally, literature chosen for this medium will provide the audience with an enduring experience.

ADAPTING THE MATERIAL

Once appropriate material has been selected, the next step is the actual adaptation for Readers Theatre. Basically, as we shall see, the form this takes depends upon the material. However, such external influences as the time limit of the performance, the available talent, the nature of the occasion and the audience, the physical characteristics of the theatre, and the overall mood to be established must also be considered.

Although there are certain precepts and general procedures for adapting nearly all types of literature, their specific application will vary somewhat, depending upon the form and nature of the original material. For example, the problems encountered in adapting a humorous short story for Readers Theatre may differ appreciably from those involved in reshaping a serious one-act play; an approach that might be desirable in handling a lengthy narrative poem may not be particularly useful to the adapter who is trying to arrange and link a series of newspaper editorials around a central premise. In the discussion which follows, therefore, an attempt will be made to explore the techniques ànd problems of adapting each literary form, specifically the dramatic literature of the stage and radio play, the prose fiction of the short story and the novel, and the compilation of scripts derived from such materials as poems, essays, letters, diaries, and newspaper items. Brief çomment will also be made concerning the creation of an original script.

Adapting dramatic literature: the stage and radio play

Often the play is the easiest form to adapt because it is written expressly for oral presentation. The main problems are to cut it to an acceptable time limit and to translate the visual elements into words. In its original form, the typical play can be performed in approximately two hours or slightly less. For Readers Theatre, as previously explained, this running time must be reduced to about an hour or an hour and a half, although occasionally a longer time is acceptable. The intense concentration demanded by this oral art form makes it difficult to hold an audience much longer, even with an intermission.

In adapting a play for Readers Theatre, the adapter usually assigns but one role to each reader. However, if there are a number of minor roles, a reader may interpret more than one character satisfactorily by making each one quite distinctive. This requires skill in characterization; there must be no doubt in the minds of the audience as to the identity of any character at any given moment.

In preparing the script, the adapter need not retain the act and scene divisions of the original play. The narrator can provide a bridge from one segment to another and describe the action that is not inherent in the lines. If an intermission is needed, the adapter or director should select a suspenseful or climactic point at which to break in upon the progression.

At the beginning of the script, the scene must be set and the characters introduced. This is usually accomplished by a narrator. Although not all the author's descriptions need be included, this narration must be vivid. Sometimes, instead of providing an "outside" narrator (one not included in the original play), this narrative function may be assigned to a minor character. If a major character reads the narration in addition to his own lines, the size of his role may be enlarged out of proportion; and it is preferable to keep the lines fairly well distributed among the cast. Having a large number of readers on stage with very little to say can be distracting.

To demonstrate how the problems of narration may be handled in an actual script, let us examine in some detail an adaptation of the Spanish play *The Women's Town* (or *The Women Have Their Way*) by Serafín and Joaquín Álvarez Quintero. The character of Dieguilla served as the narrator; and since, in this instance, the original playscript had been cut to thirty minutes, this minx-like servant girl not only introduced herself and the other characters and set the scene but also narrated the preliminary action. She provided this introduction in a storytelling manner and in character.

DIEGUILLA. *(To audience.)* Buenas noches. Good evening. My name is
Dieguilla, and tonight we *(indicating herself and the others)* want to tell
you the story of *The Women's Town,* or *Pueblo de las Mujeres.* It takes
place in the Spanish house of my good friend, Don Julián Figueredo, the
parish priest of the Women's Town. The action occurs in the combination
patio and reception hall. *(With descriptive gestures.)* Here the ceiling is
vaulted, and the floor is of red tile. It is a plain room with little furniture,
but a large glass door leads into a beautiful garden with whitewashed walls,
red brick walks, trees, and lovely blooming plants in pots all painted blue.
The patio is a cozy enclosure, cool and very pleasant. It is night and in the
month of June. The time, the present. *(Her manner and tone become
confidential.)*

I work as a servant here. As I mentioned before, Don Julián is my very
good friend. But his deaf sister, Santita—who lives here with her two daughters, Ángela and Pilar—is not such a buena amiga. She thinks me a little
flirt and a little disobedient. *(Shrugs.)* And she is not a little wrong.

(Briskly; changing her tone.) Now let us meet some of the people in *The*

Women's Town, and then we'll be on to our story about how the women have their way. *(She approaches the various characters as she introduces each in turn.)* First, Don Julián and his sister, Santita. They are both more than sixty and less than sixty-five years of age. Don Julián hears all there is to be heard, since he confesses most of the women in the town; and Santita hears absolutely nothing, for she is deaf. But she understands gestures and lip movements perfectly. Just the same, her manner is one of constant observation and suspicion. Here we have Adolfo Adalid, a handsome young lawyer from Madrid and the hero of our story. Bueno, no? Concha Puerto, a very pretty lady but very meddlesome—in other words, the town gossip. Ángela and Pilar, the young, teen-age daughters of Santita. And Pepe Lora, a dark, suspicious youth, is the rejected suitor—rejected by *(indicating)* Juanita la Rosa, the rosebud of the town. Accompanying Juanita is her patronizing aunt, Doña Belén. *(In disgust.)* Ay, caramba! *(Shrugs, smiles at audience.)* Now, you have met the people who play a part in *The Women's Town.* And so, as I promised you before, our story. *(She moves to a new position and resumes in a narrational manner.)* Earlier this evening our hero, Adolfo, came to visit the good Don Julián and request a favor. It seems that Adolfo's uncle had recently died, and when he passed away, left all his papers badly mixed up. So Adolfo, being a lawyer, was summoned from Madrid to put his uncle's business in order. To begin this task, he had to have a letter of introduction, and this was the favor he asked of Don Julián. Although they had never met, Don Julián was very glad to be of service. However, as Adolfo was about to depart on an important errand, Don Julián pointedly mentioned a rumor he had heard in the town—a rumor that the handsome young lawyer had lost no time in finding some *(insinuatingly)* feminine diversion. Adolfo, all injured innocence, protested that he did not know of what or of whom Don Julián was talking. Don Julián replied that it was already apparent to many people that a certain girl who lives on the other side of the street—and who was accustomed to coming to Don Julián's casa evenings—had turned Adolfo's head with her pretty eyes. Adolfo, of course, denied this rumor, too. *(With a sly, amused chuckle.)* Little good it did him, though; for once the feminine population of the Women's Town make up their minds about something, that's the way it is. *(Suddenly peering off.)* Ay . . . but Concha Puerto, the town gossip, is coming now to visit Don Julián.[4]

Even easier to adapt than the conventional playscript is the radio play because, as in Shakespeare's plays, all the action and environment have been included in the dialogue. Notice, for example, how Shakespeare skillfully and swiftly sets the scene for Lorenzo's speech to Jessica in Act V, Scene i, lines 54-59, of *The Merchant of Venice:*

> *How sweet the moonlight sleeps upon this bank!*
> *Here will we sit and let the sounds of music*
> *Creep in our ears: soft stillness and the night*
> *Become the touches of sweet harmony.*

---

[4]Serafín and Joaquín Álvarez Quintero, *Pueblo de las Mujeres* or *The Women's Town, Four Plays in English Version,* trans. Helen and Harley Granville-Barker (New York: Little, Brown & Company, 1928).

> *Sit, Jessica. Look how the floor of heaven*
> *Is thick inlaid with patines of bright gold.*

A radio script might reveal time and place in this manner:

NARRATOR. On Washington's Birthday, February 22, 1842, in Springfield, Illinois, Lincoln spoke to the people of that city.

In the radio play, environmental information might be provided as in the following passage:

NARRATOR. Yes, I remember the day very well. It was a bleak afternoon in November—one of those melancholy days when the sun and clouds intermingle reluctantly in a drab autumn sky.

Among the radio plays most frequently used for Readers Theatre are those of Norman Corwin, such as *Mary and the Fairy* and *My Client Curly,* and Archibald MacLeish's "The Fall of the City." Stephen Vincent Benét's delightful Christmas play, *A Child Is Born,* also makes an excellent script for presentation in this medium.

Adapting prose fiction

The first step in adapting prose fiction is to read the material appreciatively and carefully, noting its impact—the type of response it draws forth. Next, it should be examined or analyzed to ascertain what the author has said, what story he has told. Then it should be read again with the idea of "cutting in" or marking those scenes and those lines that must be included if the selection is to retain its full significance. Once these steps have been taken, the director may start "cutting out"—that is, omitting those scenes unsuited to his basic theme or purpose. He must, however, remember that a number of fully developed, close-up scenes should be retained. The term *close-up* is familiar to any moviegoer. In this context, it refers to a scene which is supposedly of special significance to the story and for which the camera is zoomed in very close to the actors' faces in order that the lens may not only capture minute details —the twitching muscle, the eyes widening in fear, the worried crease of the brow, the defiant thrust of the chin, or the lips inviting a kiss—but may also *magnify* these meaningful manifestations. In Readers Theatre the term *close-up* is used to describe a scene which is not only especially crucial or climactic but which is sufficiently infused with significant details to generate a strong empathic response from the audience and thereby assure its deep emotional involvement.

The adapter should not, however, select only strongly dramatic scenes; a balance of tense and relaxing, quiet and climactic scenes is needed to give light and shade to the performance. It is better to select fewer scenes and develop them well than to skeletonize the text. Occasionally, long portions of the material must be cut and a bridge written to make a smooth transition from segment to segment. And, to reiterate, enough narration and description must be retained to preserve the style of the author and to make the scene vivid, but it is advisable to avoid extremely long speeches.

The point of view—the angle from which the story is told—is extremely important in adapting prose fiction. It tells us on whose authority we learn what the characters think and do in the story. For this reason, point of view will largely determine the allocation of lines to the various readers or interpreters. The narrator, through whose eyes we view the story, may stand in different vantage points, physically and emotionally. He may "know all" and be *an omniscient observer,* seeing into the minds and hearts of all the characters and commenting philosophically about them but being detached from them. The omniscient narrator is restricted by neither time, place, nor character. Or the narrator may be *an observer outside the action,* seeing and hearing the events but not able to get within the character. A minor character may, for example, tell the story not as a participant but as an observer. Still another viewpoint the narrator might take is that of a *participant.* As one who participates in the action, either as a primary character or as a secondary character, he will have an emotional as well as a physical involvement. These diverse viewpoints naturally affect the telling of the story and help the adapter decide which scenes and actions to include. As previously mentioned, they also guide him in determining who is to speak not only the dialogue but portions of the narration. A character may, from his point of view, vocalize his inner thoughts and may narrate the action that is related to him. Some authors shift points of view within the story, now observing from one vantage point and now from another, now slipping into this character's mind and now into another's. All of these factors must be taken into consideration in adapting prose fiction for Readers Theatre. James Thurber's short story "A Unicorn in the Garden," which is discussed in the next section, exemplifies one way in which the various characters might describe the action at the moment of its happening, instead of having a single narrator provide the commentary.

Much of the value and fun—and it is fun—of adapting material for Readers Theatre results from the infinite variety of ways adaptations may be evolved. But to repeat a note of caution: sufficient description must be retained to set the scene and to permit the audience to see the characters in their minds; and, of course, the necessary action must be retained in the narration so that the audience can visualize the chain of events as they occur in the story.

The short story.   The short story is probably the most popular type of prose fiction to be adapted for Readers Theatre presentation. As in the case of all prose fiction, a narrator often provides the narrative and descriptive portions, with other readers supplying the dialogue. Obviously, the identity of the person speaking must be kept very clear at all times in order to ensure audience comprehension. To accomplish this, the "story" names of the persons involved in the interpretation should be said clearly and with some frequency, not only by the narrator but also by the various characters in the story. Another procedure in allocating lines is to have each character read both his dialogue and portions of the narration, as well as certain nondialogue sequences that are written from his point of view. For example, in Thurber's "A Unicorn in the Garden" the husband may speak the opening lines:

> Once upon a sunny morning a man who sat in a breakfast nook looked up from his scrambled eggs to see a white unicorn with a gold horn quietly cropping the roses in the garden. The man went up to the bedroom where his wife was still asleep and woke her. "There's a unicorn in the garden," he said. "Eating roses."

The wife responds by reading:

> She opened one unfriendly eye and looked at him. "The unicorn is a mythical beast," she said, and turned her back on him.

The husband then reads:

> The man walked slowly downstairs and out into the garden.[5]

In the same manner, the policemen and the psychiatrist in this story could read not only their own dialogue but also any narration told from their point of view. In a long script, *two* narrators are sometimes employed, as in the professional Readers Theatre script, *Under Milk Wood* by Dylan Thomas.

The novel. The problems of cutting and adapting a novel are fundamentally the same as those for a short story, but the process is complicated somewhat by the greater length of the material, the larger number of characters involved, and the more complicated plots and subplots usually found in this form of literature.

Ray Bradbury's *Dandelion Wine,* which was presented at the 1960 convention of the Speech Association of America, can serve as a useful model to illustrate some of the principles and procedures which may be followed in adapting a novel. Bradbury's book is made up of a series of incidents that occur during one summer in a small town, and many of these incidents involve characters that are seen only in one episode. The main characters—those seen in successive scenes—are two young boys, Tom and Doug, who are enjoying summer and helping their grandmother make dandelion wine to brighten winter days.

Although this novel is too long to use in its entirety, there are several threads in the story which can be followed to make a unified script of the proper length. For instance, a number of episodes deal with machines: the time machine, the happiness machine, the fortune-telling machine, the trolley car, the Green Machine (as this forerunner of the automobile

---

[5]*The Unicorn in the Garden*. From *Fables For Our Time*. Copyright © 1940 James Thurber. Published by Harper and Row. Originally printed in *The New Yorker*.

was called), and the machine for making dandelion wine. Another thread running throughout the story concerns time: the past which still lives in Colonel Freeleigh's head and the past that never was for old Mrs. Bentley, who the children said could never have been a little girl; there is the time for rug cleaning, for dandelion wine making, for the first mowing, for saying good-bye, for dying. Another theme is that of rites and rituals. For Tom and Doug, the two young boys, all of living seems to be made up of rites and rituals. In the first of these symbolic rites, on the day after school is out, we see Doug standing in the third-story cupola bedroom of his grandmother's house, commanding summer to begin. This is followed by the ritual of making the first batch of dandelion wine which is, in turn, followed by other rituals, including lawn mowing, rug beating, putting up the front-porch swing, lemonade making, and buying tennis shoes. Still another theme is that of discoveries and revelations. Doug discovers one day that he is alive. After the death of Colonel Freeleigh and Great-Grandma, he also discovers the saddening thought that someday he, too, must die.

Although any one of these threads could have been used as a unifying device in the adapted script, the one that seemed to enfold most of the others—and the one finally chosen—was the theme of discovering the joy in being alive and the saddening thought that we must eventually die. Accordingly, scenes were selected to develop Doug's declaration: "I am alive." Other scenes were chosen to bring out the antithetical thought: "I must someday die." These scenes were used as close-ups. The idea of rites and rituals, particularly of dandelion wine making, was used as a secondary unifying device. As each episode in the story was concluded, another bottle of wine was placed on the shelf, lovingly labeled so that on some wintry day this bottle would recall this particular day of summer.

The script opened, as does the book, with Doug's ritual of awakening the town to summer and closed eventually with his sending the townspeople off to sleep on the last day of summer. Many of the book's scenes could not be worked into the adaptation, of course; but a few lines from excluded segments were selected and inserted at appropriate places in the final script. An example was Tom's delightful response to Doug's worrying about the way God runs the world. Tom, after thinking a moment, replied, "He's all right, Doug. He *tries.*" In its final form, the cast included: (1) the characters who handled scenes in dialogue; (2) a narrator who commented upon the story and the action and vocally set and changed the scenes; and (3) a group of voices that evoked moods, made comments, and narrated events somewhat in the manner of a Greek chorus.

An example of a bridge that was created to link two close-up scenes was the one leading from the death of Great-Grandmother to Doug's fever dream. This passage illustrates how the adapter may employ a variety of voices to present narrative material rather than assign long passages to a single reader. In this particular bridge, composed of dialogue between Doug and his thoughts, the thoughts were vocalized by the chorus, each member speaking alone, rather than in unison as in choral speaking.

DOUG. Here it is, all written down in my nickel tablet: "You can't depend on things because . . .

VOICE ONE. Like machines . . . they fall apart or rust or run down.

VOICE TWO. Like tennis shoes, you can run so far, so fast, and then the earth's got you again.

VOICE FIVE. Like wine presses. Presses, big as they are, always run out of dandelions, and squeeze, and squeeze to a halt."

DOUG. "You can't depend on people, because . . .

VOICE FOUR. They go away . . .

VOICE FIVE. People you know die . . .

VOICE FOUR. Friends die . . .

VOICE SIX. Your own folks can die."

DOUG. So . . . *(with a big breath)* so . . .

VOICE ONE. So if wine presses and friends and near-friends can go away for awhile or go away forever,

VOICE TWO. Or rust,

VOICE SIX. Or fall apart,

VOICE FIVE. Or die,

DOUG. And if . . . someone like Great-Gran'ma . . .

VOICE FOUR. Who was going to live forever . . . can die . . .

DOUG. Then . . .

VOICE ONE. Then, you, Douglas Spaulding, someday must . . .

DOUG. Then I, Douglas Spaulding, someday must . . . no!

VOICE ONE. Colonel Freeleigh . . .

VOICE FIVE. Dead!

VOICE ONE. Great-Gran'ma . . .

VOICE SIX. Dead!

DOUG. Me! No, they can't kill me!

VOICE FOUR. Yes.

VOICE TWO. Yes.

VOICE SIX. Yes!

VOICE FIVE. Yes, anytime they want to . . .

VOICE ONE. No matter how you kick or scream . . .

VOICE TWO. They just put a big hand over you,

VOICE FIVE. And you're still.

DOUG. I don't want to die!

VOICE SIX. You'll have to, anyway.

VOICE ONE. You'll have to, anyway.

VOICE SIX. Write it in your notebook, Douglas.

VOICE FOUR. "I, Douglas Spaulding, someday must . . . "

DOUG. "I, Douglas Spaulding . . . someday . . . must . . . must . . . *(very small)* die."[6]

---

[6]Ray Bradbury, *Dandelion Wine* (New York: Bantam Books, Inc., 1959), pp. 142-143. For the complete script, see pp. 127-155.

Placing all of the narration in the present tense heightened the immediacy of this particular story. Using many voices rather than a lone narrator in descriptive passages, as well as in part of the narration, made the production more vivid, allowed for greater variety, and assured better balancing of the lines for the readers. Speeches ranged in length from one word to a page or more, although both of these extremes occurred infrequently.

Many vocalized sound devices were used in this production of *Dandelion Wine*. When Doug lay ill and the day seemed interminable, one voice ticked off the time while other voices told of the scenes going through Doug's fevered brain. The sound of this relentless ticking counterpointed the rising excitement in the other voices as the fever caused wilder and wilder ideas to surge through Doug's mind. The scene was climaxed by voices singing "Shall We Gather at the River?" in harmony at first, then in the discordant sounds that the feverish Doug was presumably hearing. Singing was also introduced when Colonel Freeleigh was recalling Civil War songs. As each song came to Colonel Freeleigh's mind, a voice sang a portion of it, as though far away.

This Readers Theatre script of *Dandelion Wine* was arranged for six readers, each reading two or more specific characters as well as being a voice in the chorus. The printed program, the contents of which are reprinted on page 128, listed the characters involved in each scene and named the respective interpreters reading those roles. Each scene had a title, as did the two major divisions of the script. Because it showed the basic structure of the adaptation and supplemented this with information about the author of the novel, the program was a useful guide to the audience.

Adapting poetry, essays, letters, and diaries

Poetry, too, may be adapted for Readers Theatre. Long poems can furnish provocative and stimulating materials for a full-length program, and shorter selections may be interspersed with other literary materials or combined for an evening's entertainment built around the life and work of one author. An example of the latter is *An Evening's Frost,* presented off-Broadway in 1965. A very moving, effective, and fully rounded script can be developed from Peter Bowman's *Beach Red,* a story of war which describes the attitudes and feelings of soldiers with such intensity and vividness that both readers and audience become excited participants in this concentrated adventure. Milton's *Samson Agonistes* has been adapted to a fifty-minute script that, when presented, is vital theatre. Dante's *Inferno* also makes a stirring script, as does W. H. Auden's *Age of Anxiety.* Many short poems likewise lend themselves admirably to group readings, among them Amy Lowell's "The Day That Was That Day" (see pp. 215-221), Robert Frost's "Home Burial," Roy Helton's "Old Christmas Morning," and Christina Rossetti's "Goblin Market"—

all of which tell a story through dialogue. Although there is no dialogue in Federico Garcia Lorca's "Lament for a Matador," it provides the basis for a powerful script; in fact, a whole program of Lorca's poetry is effective. For a program on Lincoln, Millard Lampell's *The Lonesome Train* is especially suitable. On the whole, poetry that tells a story with dialogue is easier to adapt to Readers Theatre, but nondialogue poems have also been read successfully in this medium.

Letters, essays, and similar materials require special handling if they are to be used successfully. To convert an essay into appropriate material for Readers Theatre, it is usually necessary to add characterization to the lines. In order to have some action or conflict or at least a degree of contrast, more than one point of view needs to be represented. This opposing attitude or outlook is also required when a script is read by more than one person. For example, the Corey Ford essay "How to Guess Your Age," although originally written as if it were spoken by one man, can be presented as though two men were standing in a bar, exchanging comments on how the world is changing. "The Ten Worst Things About a Man" from Jean Kerr's *The Snake Has All the Lines,* can in similar fashion be divided between the husband and the wife. (See pp. 210-214.) In adapting Addison and Steele's *The Spectator Papers,* a secretary can be added so that conversation can occur between her and Sir Roger de Coverley. Letters should be arranged to tell a story, to reveal a change in awareness between the recipients, or to allow the audience to perceive a progression from one state of awareness to another. One way in which an exchange of letters has been arranged to tell an entertaining story can be seen in *Eneas Africanus,* by Harry Stillwell Edwards. (See p. 93.) Diaries also should contain a story line, reveal character progression or regression, or unfold successive new perceptions. Mark Twain's *Adam's Diary* and *Eve's Diary* have been combined to reveal the thoughts of the first man and the first woman on a series of identical topics, to manifest their growing awareness of each other, and to tell the story of their expulsion from the Garden of Eden.

COMPILING A SCRIPT

In the preceding discussion we have examined ways in which a Readers Theatre script may be built from a single source of prose or poetry. However, a script may also be prepared with components selected from miscellaneous sources. Usually these are tied together with a single theme. The professionally produced *In White America* is a full-length script composed entirely of nonfictional materials—essays, letters, diaries, and news items—that tell the story of the Negro in America from the time he was brought here in slave ships to present-day agitations.

Using these kinds of miscellaneous materials, students at Southwest Missouri State College have compiled similar scripts; and the following examples, with notes on their presentation, suggest ways of building effective Readers Theatre programs around timely themes.

Ebony Ghetto, presented by Southwest Missouri State College at the "Imagination '62" Festival sponsored by the University of Kansas, was a script compiled from an autobiographical account of Frederick Ramsey, interspersed with poems by Langston Hughes and Fenton Johnson and Negro folk songs. Setting forth a saga of the despairs, the blues, the longings of the Negro and his hopes for a brighter future, the elements of the script were arranged in climactic order and tied together by the words of an old Negro telling his story. His emotions were exemplified and made universal through the poems of Hughes and Johnson, which, in turn, were echoed by the songs. The cast was composed of three readers and a folk singer. The interpreter of the old Negro's words sat on a stool in the Right Center area of the stage, his script on a nearby lectern. At the Center of the stage, the two readers of the poetry, a girl and a boy, employed some movement; at times they sat on a short bench, sometimes the boy sat at the girl's feet, and sometimes both stood, depending upon the mood and the relationship expressed in the material being read. Both carried their scripts in small black notebooks which were unobtrusive and easily handled. When they read, they were bathed in a pool of light. The folk singer stood at the left of the group, with one foot occasionally placed on a short stool and his script on a lectern close by. The auditorium remained in darkness throughout.

Another example of a script composed of miscellaneous materials was entitled *Good Evening, Mr. Brecht,* which was prepared by two students as a class assignment. It was patterned closely to the concept of the off-Broadway production of *Brecht on Brecht,* but its compilers had not seen the New York production. In their search for materials, they found it necessary to use the interlibrary loan service to procure copies of Brecht's poems and other writings. In all, they spent almost two months gathering materials, studying poetry, listening to the songs of *The Three-Penny Opera,* and examining plays, essays, letters, and pithy sayings.

The next step in their preparation of the script was deciding how to incorporate, blend, and unify the miscellaneous components into a satisfying whole. These were eventually arranged under the unit headings: "Communism," "War," and "Theatre." A guitar player sat at one side of the stage near a stand bearing placards, which he changed to show the progression from one unit to the next. The stage was arranged in levels, with a short runway into the auditorium; and a reader, when presenting some materials, walked out almost into the midst of the audience. Another reader sat on the edge of this runway and read the intimate ballad entitled "The Children's Crusade, 1939." The other readers stayed on the stage at all times, but changes in lighting helped focus attention on the ones involved in a particular segment of the script.

When the arranged script was first read aloud, it was discovered that this version had too many short passages; it did not hold together. Some of the short bits were then eliminated and replaced by longer selections. The concluding section consisted of a cutting from Brecht's play *The Jewish Wife*. One of the songs from *The Three-Penny Opera* was sung in German; "The Pirate Jenny" was sung in English. The readers sang these two songs, and the guitar player contributed other songs that commented upon the ideas being presented.

For a Readers Theatre Workshop held on the campus of Southern Illinois University, a group of Southwest Missouri State students took the title *Is There a Doctor in the House?* and constructed a humorous script inspired by the late President Kennedy's emphasis on physical fitness. The first step originating the script was a brainstorming session. Ideas were batted about; plays, stories, and poems were suggested. One student had just purchased Richard Armour's *The Medical Muse* containing the poem "Is There a Doctor in the House?" Another student remembered the Thurber selection describing the humorist's physical examination on entering college. Still another spoke of Irvin S. Cobb's hilarious account of an operation. Someone else remembered the comic essay by Patricia Collinge called "The Rest Cure." In searching for more materials, the students talked to their English instructors, to librarians, and to their friends. Wherever the planners gathered together, they shared ideas. One found a humorous poem called "Appendectomy, Square Dance Style." A number of current humorous sayings were taken from newspapers and magazines. Each student brought to class the possible selections he had found and read short excerpts aloud; then the material was made available for all to read. The student coordinator of the group provided especially pertinent introductory and concluding poems which she had written. After the selections to be included were finally chosen, these were arranged in a climactic order; transitions were written to make a smooth flow from one segment to another, and the resulting scripts were placed in identical black notebooks.

The next step was determining an effective physical arrangement of the readers. After some experimenting, it was decided to keep all readers on stage throughout, some on stools and others in chairs. At times, all the readers stood; and in "Appendectomy, Square Dance Style," a suggestion of the rhythm of the square dance was caught in the reading and in the physical stance of the readers, although there was no actual movement from place to place. At times, when only two readers were involved in the reading at a given moment, these two would step forward and away from the group. (A more detailed discussion of the techniques of staging Readers Theatre productions will be found in the next chapter.)

CREATING THE ORIGINAL SCRIPT

In the early years of experimentation in Readers Theatre and up to the present time, most performances have been adaptations or compilations.

However, thanks to the rapidly increasing interest in this art form, writers are beginning to create new materials especially for this medium. A case in point is the original work *The Locomotive,* written by Frank Galati, a student at Northwestern University, and presented at the 1966 Conference of the Central States Speech Association and elsewhere. Another example of an original script was created by a group of students who wished to share with an audience their experiences while touring Europe with the musical comedy *Finian's Rainbow* for the American Educational Theatre Association in 1961. This is an excerpt from the script:

VOICE THREE. Then quite unannounced and unexpectedly we were in Munich. Munich—that exciting, bustling city!

VOICE FOUR. Munich, where Hitler began his rise to power. I stood quietly a moment on the vast Nazi parade ground. I went to see the huge World War I Monument in the heart of the city, and the infamous Nazi Brown House that once held Hitler's elite storm troopers.

VOICE FIVE. Munich had everything we expected from an old German city: the royal palace of Ludwig I, with its spacious gardens and huge canals . . .

VOICE ONE. The Glockenspiel in the tower of the Rathaus or city hall . . .

VOICE TWO. The famous Hofbrauhaus and the new gigantic Mathausen Beer Garden . . .

VOICE THREE. The pulsating open market place in Marianplatz . . .

VOICE FOUR. . . . And Dachau . . .

VOICE ONE. Dachau! As I stood alone on the grounds of the former concentration camp and heard the wind whispering through the stunted pines, I had thoughts of the thousands of Jewish people who had taken their last breath there. I sniffed at the air, and it was fetid and oppressive; I gazed at the open furnace pits, at the experimental hospital, and at the towering mounds of mass graves left just as they had been, undisturbed through the years. Atop one of the large mounds a tiny yellow flower blossomed. It may have been my imagination or the twisting shadows of the approaching night, but for a moment it resembled the Star of David.

Instruction in the technical intricacies of scriptwriting is not the province or intent of this book. Suffice it to say, it is no more simple to write an original Readers Theatre script than it is to write a new stage play. Each requires creative imagination, literary skill, the insight to draw convincing characters, and the ability to write believable and purposeful dialogue—all imbued with that intangible something called "dramatic sense." But it is a challenging field of endeavor and one well worth the interest of enterprising writers.

From the foregoing discussion it should be evident that the preparation of a Readers Theatre script can take many directions and forms, the choice being guided primarily by the nature of the material to be adapted, the time limit of the program, and the skill of the readers. The conventional play and the radio play, originally written in dialogue form for oral presentation, are comparatively easy to adapt, for they usually demand only a condensation in time and a verbalization of the action and setting.

Prose fiction—both novels and short stories—provides one of the largest sources of Readers Theatre material. Key passages must be selected carefully and connecting material or bridges must often be written to link the scenes together. Care must be exercised to retain the proper proportion of the original description and narration in order to reflect accurately the author's style of writing. Moreover, the scenes must be selected and arranged to ensure a rhythmical flow and alternation of tense and relaxed moments. Point of view is a very useful guide in determining the division of the script material among the characters; frequently a character will be assigned the narrative portion that is told from his point of view instead of having an "outside" narrator relate the events. Sometimes, for the sake of variety, certain narrative and descriptive passages may be given by a group of readers, somewhat in the manner of a Greek chorus.

Poetry, especially poetry containing dialogue, may be used with good effect. Essays may be adapted, but this kind of literary material ordinarily requires the addition of characterization and more than one point of view. An exchange of letters, being similar to dialogue, can readily be arranged into a successful script; those letters having a strong personal element and a revealing story line tend to work best. Finally, regardless of the nature of the original material, the adapted script should reveal insight into the characters and their reactions to the situations within the story; it should maintain an urgent or suspenseful progression from one point of awareness to another; it should stimulate an empathic response from the listeners; and it should have a beginning, a middle, and an end: a sense of wholeness for the audience.

CHAPTER FOUR

The Director Prepares

"This production was really vital—*alive!* Some reading programs I've seen have been so dull and uninspired. What makes the difference?" To no small extent, the answer to this question lies in the director: his knowledge, perception, and skill. A vital, unified, effectively paced presentation is essential to any Readers Theatre venture; and the responsibility for this achievement rests primarily in the hands of the director. It is just as necessary to have a creative director at the helm of a Readers Theatre production as it is in any other form of play production. It is the director who must activate and guide all the elements of the program into a cohesive whole, accurately analyzing the script and infusing it with the interpretive spark, the pacing, and the "builds" to insure causal progression from its opening line to its final words. And it is the director who must mold the interpretive group into an ensemble that will bring the literature to life in the minds of the audience.

Framed in rather broad categories, the director's tasks may be considered as (1) his analysis of the script; (2) his selection and handling of the physical elements involved in its staging; and (3) his directing of the rehearsals. Each is heavily dependent upon the other; all are part of an ongoing process. In this chapter, we will concentrate upon script analysis and the physical elements.

ANALYZING THE SCRIPT

It cannot be said too often that there is *no one way* of presenting a script. Once the director has identified his objectives—and this he *must* do first of all—he is free to experiment with many different approaches and techniques to help achieve them. As William Archer, commenting on new drama trends in his *Playmaking,* said, "Any movement is good which helps to free art from the tyranny of a code of rules and definitions."[1] Half the fun, satisfaction, and value in working with Readers Theatre is that the experimentation with different approaches often results in very exciting productions. Of course, common sense, taste, and discrimination must always be guiding factors in the creative direction of the Readers Theatre script. And the fact that there are no rigid formulations for this medium does not mean that there are no basic principles and guidelines. There are. In his analysis of the script, the director may take a number of logical steps which will lead him to knowledge and insights helpful to both himself and his readers as they jointly strive to chart for their audience a fresh, meaningful, and memorable journey into the wide, enthralling galaxy of literature.

Determining the meaning

To achieve a successful production in this medium, the director may use many of the techniques of conventional play directing. His method of studying the script, for instance, will be much the same. Of course, if he has made his own adaptation, he has already analyzed the structure and meaning of the literary work. Even so, he should think it through again. In private, before meeting the cast, he must master the script, comprehend its many facets.

At first it is well for him to read it appreciatively, giving himself to the aesthetic experience. In the second reading, he should be analytical as he searches for the central or dominating idea, the theme of the work, the principal premise which the author is trying to illustrate through the behavior of the characters in their environment. He finds, for example, that in *Macbeth*, Shakespeare is saying, among other things, that excessive ambition leads to a man's downfall; Maxwell Anderson, in *Winterset*, declares that love has a redeeming power; Ibsen, in *A Doll's House*, observes that a successful marriage rests on mutual respect; Sophocles, in *Oedipus Rex*, asserts that man cannot escape his predestined fate; Keats, in "Ode to a Nightingale," avers that man does not have immortality as does the beauty found in the song of a bird.

Often the author does not stop with illustrating a theme but may take a psychological, anthropological, sociological, or ideological position with reference to it. In *A Doll's House*, Ibsen was not only concerned with the need for conjugal respect; he was also seeking a reform in the then prevailing attitude toward marriage—an attitude which insisted that the woman was but the plaything of the man. The director must decide what the writer's subject is and what he is saying about it. A complex work or compilation may have many themes. The director needs to be aware of all of them and of their relative importance. Only with this

---

[1] William Archer, *Playmaking: A Manual of Craftsmanship* (New York: Dover Publications, Inc., 1960), p. 32.

awareness can he hope to aid his cast in discovering these meanings for themselves.

Ascertaining the author's attitude

One of the most important parts of the director's analysis is ascertaining the author's or speaker's attitude as expressed in the material, his attitude toward his subject and toward his audience. This attitude, sometimes called *tone,* is revealed in the author's choice of words—in the affective qualities of those words.

It might be well to pause at this point and define *tone* more fully. Some writers and practitioners use *tone* and *mood* interchangeably or employ a reverse usage. For our purposes here we make this distinction: tone equates with *attitude;* mood equates with *atmosphere* or *emotional aura* (which we will discuss later). Recent writing and experimentation tend to reinforce this distinction. In *Understanding Poetry,* Brooks and Warren say:

> The *tone* of a poem indicates the speaker's attitude toward his subject and toward his audience, and sometimes toward himself. The word is, strictly speaking, a metaphor, a metaphor drawn from the tone of voice in speech or song. In conversation we may imply our attitude—and hence our true meaning —by the tone in which we say something. . . . Tone, in a poem, expresses attitudes.[2]

Armstrong and Brandes, in *The Oral Interpretation of Literature,* define tone

> . . . as the attitude of the writer toward his material and his audience. Therefore, an analysis of the tone of a selection will lead the student to the emotions that the poet has used to surround his ideas. There is no limit to the shadings of tone that an author may choose from. . . . Tone may also be spoken of in the terminology used to classify emotions, for the poet may be angry, sad, joyful, hateful, proud, and the like.
>
> We are continually taking attitudes toward what we say in our daily conversation, thereby imparting shades of meaning to what we say by our *tone* of voice.[3]

Before the director can hope to bring out the particular attitudes in a given work, he must first study the material to ascertain the author's attitude or tone and then decide how this may best be expressed. The author's attitude is usually revealed in his choice of words. For example, in *Hamlet,* Shakespeare establishes a tone of gloom by using metaphors referring to decay and corruption, both physical and moral. When the

---

[2]Cleanth Brooks and Robert Penn Warren, *Understanding Poetry* (New York: Holt, Rinehart & Winston, Inc., 1960), p. 181.
[3]Chloe Armstrong and Paul Brandes, *The Oral Interpretation of Literature* (New York: McGraw-Hill Book Company, Inc., 1963), p. 255.

director starts rehearsing, he will make certain that his interpreters, through their use of the expressive human voice, through proper intonation and inflection, are able to "read out" or elicit the changing attitudes within the piece. Similarly, in reading Edwin Markham's "The Man with the Hoe," the interpreter must express the speaker's indignation, his outrage at those who have caused this unfortunate man to become the abject thing he is. In reading the poem "Departmental," the interpreter must manifest Robert Frost's satirical attitude. In Donne's "The Canonization," he will want to reveal the alternating tones of exasperation, irritation, ironic banter, and defiant tenderness.[4]

Although the voice is the main vehicle for communicating the author's attitude, it alone cannot always effectively convey this attitude. The director must help his readers to become totally involved—both in mind and body. The mind must comprehend the particularities of the experience, and the reader must so enter into the experience that his face and body manifest his inner feelings. For instance, the reader of William Rose Benét's "The Skater of Ghost Lake" might respond to the mysterious aura of the setting and events of the poem in the following ways: The reader leans forward as Jeremy skates with long, lean strides across the ebony ice; he tenses as Jeremy hears the faint, mysterious, whirring sound; he relaxes for a moment as Jeremy recognizes his sweetheart; he tenses again in response to Jeremy's vague, impinging fear; he hears the roar of water in his ears as Jeremy sinks down and down in the deep, cold lake. By thus empathically entering into the particularities of the poem, the reader has experienced it, has responded to it mentally, emotionally, and physically.

In analyzing prose fiction, the director must orient himself and his subsequent emphasis to the point of view from which the story is told and the relationship of the narrator to the events, as well as his attitude toward them. As we explained in the preceding chapter, this narrator may be an omniscient or all-knowing commentator outside the story, such as the author; or he may be a subjective narrator, possibly the main character; or he might be an objective observer, a secondary character in the story. Whatever kind of narrator is used, the degree of all the participants' involvement in the reading will be determined by the relationship of the narrator to the other characters and the events. Moreover, the narrator's use of the past or present tense will dictate the degree of immediacy of the emotions in the literary piece. Not only must the director be alert to any shift in point of view and the emotional urgency prompted by it, he must also guide his readers in making the necessary interpretive adjustments.

---

[4]Cleanth Brooks, *The Well Wrought Urn* (New York: Harcourt, Brace & Company, 1947), p. 174. For a valuable discussion of attitudes, also see Don Geiger, *The Sound, Sense, and Performance of Literature* (Glenview, Ill.: Scott, Foresman and Company, 1963), Chapter 2 and pp. 83-84, 93.

Identifying the mood

The director should also take careful note of the predominant mood, the prevailing atmosphere, of the literary work. Although this atmosphere is determined in part by the setting or locale, it is more than that: it is the emotional aura which the work possesses and which guides the reader's expectations and attitudes. Ibsen's *Ghosts* opens in an atmosphere of gloom, which is intensified by the darkness and the cold rain. Poe's "The Raven" has a pervading mood of gloom and despair. The dominant mood of Stephen Crane's "War Is Kind" is bitterness; of "High Flight" by John Gillespie Magee, Jr., exultation. Although one mood will prevail, it may vary throughout the poem. Or the mood may change entirely. In Thomas Hardy's poem "When I Set Out for Lyonnesse," the speaker is at first lonesome and unhappy; gradually, however, this dissatisfaction changes to radiant joy. In other words, the emotional aura of the first stanza fades away and gives place to a new feeling in the third stanza. The director of the Readers Theatre script must first become aware of these emotional variations and then must induce the readers to ring out the varying moods through changes in muscle tone and vocal elements—tempo, pitch, intensity, volume, and quality. This variety maintains the attention of the audience and evokes from them an empathic response to the mood of the literary selection.

Analyzing the characters

One of the most important tasks facing the director is that of analyzing the characters through whom the author presents his theme. Not only must the director know what the characters are, what their personalities and potentialities are, but he must also be aware of what *makes* them what they are.

The first determinant in analyzing a character is his relationship to the situation and his emotional involvement in it. Is the character the protagonist or the antagonist? If he is neither, with which of these is he aligned? What has he to gain or lose by a change in the situation?[5] A knowledge of the character's place in the action will elucidate many useful facts about him.

The second major determinant in analyzing a character is his motives. *Why* the character says and does what he does reveals more about the type of person he is than his actual words and actions. This *why* evolves from the major desire or desires of the character. Not only must the director know what this basic drive or major desire is, but he must also be aware of any obstacles in the character's path to achieving this desire, and he must understand how far the character will go to attain the goal. For example, Medea was so intent on taking revenge upon Jason that she killed her children; although this caused her pain, it was the surest

---

[5]Canfield, op. cit., p. 48.

way of hurting Jason. The character's potentiality for action and his basic desire determine the response he seeks from the other characters and provide important clues as to how his lines should be read.

Both the character's place in the action and his motives will, of course, shed light on his personality. In seeking further for the sources of these motivations, the director will want to study the character's educational and social background, his profession and nationality, age and sex. The director should be aware of the character's intellectual acumen, his emotional depth and stability, and his degree of maturity. He should ask what the character laughs at and what he is moved by. Answers to these and similar questions guide the director and the reader in interpreting the lines, in providing the degree of casualness or intensity needed to project the character's emotional responses to the situations in the script. Finally, having determined the character's place in the action, his motivations, and his personality traits, the director must, in turn, see to it that his readers clearly understand the characters and their interrelationships and convey them with maximum effectiveness to the audience.

Studying the structure and author's style

The director should study the structure of the writing and become thoroughly familiar with the elements of the author's style. He needs to know each step in the plot development, the specific function of each component and its relationship to the entire script, the prevailing emotion of each portion and the emotional response it should engender in the audience. He needs to know where the high point of interest is, the factors that build suspense, the clues or forewarnings of the outcome that have been written into the material. Moreover, he will need to make a careful study of word choice, word order, and sentence structure. He must note how the author uses parallel sentences, periodic sentences, antithesis, figurative speech, sense imagery, and rhythm. Often the meaning and atmosphere of the piece are inherent in the recurring use of images and connected metaphors. The imagery can clarify and illuminate the work.

The director will need to be especially alert to the sound or auditory values in the script: the author's employment of onomatopoeia, alliteration, assonance, consonance, and other repetitive devices. He must be sensitive to the music made by words, the tunes and cadences within the language. Being aware of the images and the aural values of the author's special use of language, the director will encourage the readers to underscore them, to make these devices count with the audience. He will point out to them that rich verbal texture demands stylistic verve in the reading, that both the cognitive and connotative impact of the words must be projected. For instance, in Vachel Lindsay's "The Congo," the director must elicit from the readers strong rhythms, response to the images, a vocal montage. To achieve these goals, he must first recognize these elements in the writing. In this respect the director's task is not unlike that of the symphony conductor or concertmaster. A significant part of the delight in Readers Theatre comes from this symphony of sound.

STAGING THE PERFORMANCE

Among the other problems facing the director of Readers Theatre is the staging of the performance: what type of focus to use; how to handle the entrances and exits of characters; what the physical arrangement of the stage is to be; what kind and degree of movement is to be accommodated within this arrangement; how to effect transitions; what type of lighting, costuming, or music (if any) is to be integrated with the presentation. And he must see that the working script is properly edited and prepared for the readers.

Focus

It is the director's responsibility to determine the type of interpretational relationship and contact the readers are to have with one another during the performance. This is a realm of Readers Theatre in which imagination and experimentation are particularly valuable. A key factor in this contact, of course, is the eyes of the readers, for the eyes are what establish focus. The three possibilities from which the director can choose are onstage focus, offstage focus, and a combination of the two.

Onstage focus means that the readers relate to each other on the stage, sensing each other's presence, sometimes even turning to the person being addressed and actually establishing eye contact. (See Figure 1.) It should be apparent, of course, that the larger the number of readers in a given scene, the more difficult it is to use onstage focus, because each

FIGURE 1. Onstage focus

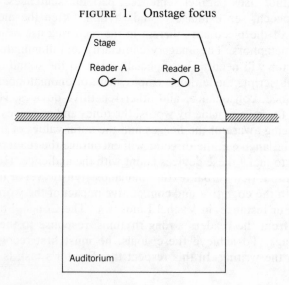

reader has to be able to see and relate directly to all the others. Some directors believe that under these circumstances a semicircular arrangement of the readers provides the most workable solution, but they realize that the audience will have more difficulty in seeing all of the readers if they are placed in this fashion. Other directors feel that the use of various *levels* in the playing space affords a more satisfactory arrangement. Basically, the techniques employed by the director of a Readers Theatre production involving a large number of readers with onstage focus are quite similar to those used by the director of a conventional stage play.

Offstage focus, by contrast, refers to the technique of having the readers envision the scene out in the audience, of figuratively placing the scene of action in the midst of those witnessing the performance. Wallace Bacon, in *The Art of Interpretation,* refers to this imaginary location as *locus.*[6] Offstage focus requires that the character, in conversation, direct his words to the other characters as though they were out in the audience. The other characters, in turn, speak to him as though he, too, were similarly situated. When the readers are participating in a scene with offstage focus, their lines of vision intersect a hypothetical area about midway out in the center of the auditorium and slightly above the heads of the audience. (See Figures 2 and 3.) This midway point works better than the back wall because it focuses the scene closer to all segments of the audience. Also, it holds the narration (given directly to the audience) closer to the scene which all of the interpreters are envisioning. The offstage focus has the additional value of putting the readers in a full-front stance or posture in relation to the audience—the strongest stage position for all readers—and this closer focal point also aids in maintaining the illusion that the readers on the stage are talking to each other.

The director must emphasize to his readers the necessity for keeping in mind that they are not seeing a specific point or spot somewhere in the audience; they are seeing characters doing something in a definite locality—a scene. The readers can help themselves establish this imaginary scene or picture if they will but fill in the details; that is, in their mind's eye they should be seeing how the imagined characters are dressed, how they are standing or sitting, what they are doing, how they are reacting—what the scene is. For instance, in Roald Dahl's delightful children's story, *James and the Giant Peach,* when James first sees the Centipede, the latter is lolling on his back with his legs crossed above his knees, a straw hat tilted rakishly to one side of his head. At one point in the script, these characters see tall, wispy men angrily throwing huge hailstones at them, stones that go "ping, ping, ping" as they sink into the flesh of the huge peach. The readers should experience this so vividly that their bodies react to the falling hailstones.[7] In this method of focusing,

---

[6]Bacon, op. cit.
[7]For a discussion of kinetic and kinesthetic imagery, see Chapter 5, p. 64.

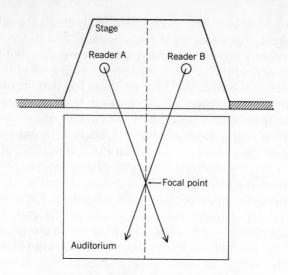

FIGURE 2.   Offstage focus; two readers

both the readers and the audience are creating the characters and the scene with their imaginations. In both onstage and offstage focus, the narration is given directly to the audience. However, if the focus is off-stage, it is imperative that the director make sure—from an outfront vantage point—that at a given moment all readers involved in a given scene are placing that scene in the same locality, that their eyes are consistently directed toward this area, that their focal gaze converges properly upon it. The reader cannot determine this for himself because he is not seeing the person sitting or standing beside him onstage but is reacting to the character role that person is portraying in the imaginary scene which is taking place out in the realm of the audience.

As a third possibility, the director may elect *to combine* onstage and offstage focus. Marion and Marvin Kleinau of Southern Illinois University, in discussing scene location through focus, speak of productions that utilize the combination. Their contention is that the imaginary field in which the audience places the scene is a constantly shifting one that is determined by the nature of the literature being read. In descriptive material the audience is more likely to see the scene close to themselves in their imaginations; but in dialogue, with the two readers physically present, the audience probably places the scenes onstage with the readers. This, Marion and Marvin Kleinau say, is hypothetical, as is any theory of audience reaction, but they cite several examples in support of their point of view:

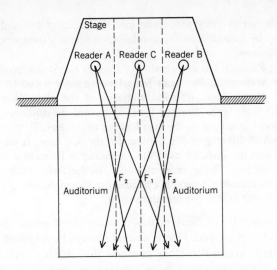

FIGURE 3.   Offstage focus; three readers. The focal point when A
and B look at each other is F_1; for A and C, F_2; and for C and B, F_3.

Dr. Elbert Bowen of Central Michigan University, in a production of John
Cheever's novel, *The Wapshot Chronicle,* used change of focus to achieve
variety in staging, to heighten humor, and to reinforce the author's use of
point of view. Throughout the major part of the production, the readers placed
the scene visually in the realm of the audience. But in a specific scene, a parody
on industrial psychology which consisted of an interview between a doctor
and a job applicant, the two characters seated themselves facing each other,
and the scene was suddenly on stage. Dialogue at this point became more
direct, with less intrusion by the author; the directness of contact between
the two readers heightened the farcical elements in the scene.

Another example may be cited from a Readers Theatre production of
Othello, directed by Dr. Wallace Bacon of Northwestern University. Some
of the scenes were deliberately set on stage and some were set off stage. In
the fight between Cassio and Roderigo, Act V, Scene 1, the readers focused
toward the audience; but when Iago wounded Cassio *from behind,* without
explanation of the stage business in the lines of the text, Iago actually ran up
behind Cassio to deliver the thrust. *What happened* was the point here—not
what was heard, not what the characters felt at the moment, but what actually
happened. The eye was the significant witness at the moment; thus the scene
was presented to the eye. Later, in the murder of Desdemona, the director
felt that the significant action was the effect, on Othello, of his own action—
not the deed itself, but what the deed did to the Moor. The actions were
performed—the strangling, Desdemona's struggle—but the scene was focused
toward the audience so that the major emphasis was placed upon Othello's face
and thus on his personal suffering. Here an interesting tension was set up between *physical cues,* which tended to draw the scene on stage, and the readers'

focus, which acted to draw the scene into the realm of the audience. This tension, it may be assumed, acted to reinforce Othello's own struggle within the audience member.

Finally, in a Readers Theatre version of *Dark of the Moon,* produced at the University of Wisconsin, Dr. Jean Scharfenberg used focus to isolate and reinforce one of the main dramatic climaxes of the play. Throughout the production, the lines were directed forward toward the audience, but at the climactic moment in question, the two leading characters, Barbara and John, turned and looked directly at one another for the first time. It was a moment of awareness, and the director used the technique of focus in a way to make that moment unique. These productions . . . deliberately made use of the dynamic interrelationship between eye and ear to emphasize certain values and meanings found within the literature itself.[8]

In the final analysis, of course, the director must make the decision on the focus to be employed. Focus should always be handled with great care and subtlety; some directors contend that mixing styles of focus is distracting. If the switching from offstage to onstage focus jars the audience and calls its attention to what the readers are doing rather than keeping its mind on the literary experience being shared, the director is not accomplishing his goal of making the literature the foremost element in Readers Theatre. Through experimentation, the director should find the means that best illuminate the literature being presented.

Perhaps the most important factors in guiding the audience to visualize and experience the scene are the concentration with which the readers themselves visualize the scene and the way they listen to one another. If the interpreters are truly seeing the characters in action in their minds, the audience is likely to do the same. It is this ability to be *in* the scene imaginatively that enables the readers to project that scene to the audience. No action or shifts in focus should break this concentration.

Entrances and exits

In the performance of a Readers Theatre script, the readers do not ordinarily move into and out of the physical setting in the same realistic manner used by actors in a conventional stage play. The entrances and exits of the readers must necessarily be more symbolic, more abstract, and—in a physical sense—more restricted. Therefore, the problem of letting the audience know which characters are in the scene and which ones are out of it calls for considerable attention, imagination, and judgment on the part of the director.

In Readers Theatre, some directors prefer to have on the stage or platform only those interpreters who are involved in a given scene or segment of the script; when they are finished, they leave, and other readers come on as new characters enter the picture. This can, of course,

[8]Marion L. and Marvin D. Kleinau, "Scene Location in Readers Theatre: Static or Dynamic?" *The Speech Teacher,* XIV (September, 1965), 198. For a detailed discussion of this topic, see Part IV of this handbook, pp. 225-251.

be distracting, if the readers have to enter and exit many times during the performance. Another approach to the problem is to have the readers either turn their backs to the audience or lower their heads when they are not involved in the scene being read. A turned back tends to draw attention to itself more than does a lowered head. Still another solution is to have those readers who are immediately involved in a particular scene stand while the nonparticipating readers remain seated. The "freeze"—having readers hold a position without moving—may be employed to take characters out of the scene until they are needed again. This is useful if there are a series of short scenes being played in such a way that the action shifts back and forth rather quickly from one group to another. Finally, singling out a set of readers by means of spotlighting or other special illumination can designate who is in the scene. Whatever method is used to convey this highly important information to the audience, it is imperative that the reader "enter" the scene at exactly the right moment.

Physical arrangement and movement

In addition to making the basic decisions about focus and entrances and exits, the director must also determine what physical facilities and arrangements he will use in placing the readers onstage. Some directors use stools and lecterns for this purpose; others use only the stools; still others prefer chairs. Stools with back rests are, of course, more comfortable for the readers. By utilizing stools of varying heights, the director can create better pictorial compositions, or he may experiment with levels for the same reason. The use of raised platforms makes it easier to arrange a group of readers so that all their faces may be seen by the audience. Ladders also have been used successfully for this purpose. They were, for instance, employed with especially good effect in a Readers Theatre version *(Maria)* of Irving Shulman's novel taken from the musical drama, *West Side Story.* (See picture on page 52.) A pyramidal arrangement of the readers, employing platforms of various heights, is good because it will keep the faces of all the readers within the eye span of the audience—a highly desirable objective but a difficult one to accomplish if a large number of readers are extended across the stage on the same level. (See picture on page 53.)

Whatever arrangement is used, the sightlines of the audience must be checked to ensure that the faces of all the interpreters can be seen from all points in the auditorium.

In Readers Theatre, scenery is usually kept to a minimum; but some background, such as draperies or a dimly lighted scrim (curtain with an open weave), may serve a useful function. A lighted scrim behind the readers helps give a three-dimensional picture and is less distracting than a conventional curtain or drapery, especially if the fabric is dark. The lighting on this scrim can change to help establish mood, to mark transi-

In Maria, *an adaptation based on* West Side Story, *ladders, although used primarily for scenes played on the fire escape, also provided variety in scenes involving many readers. Additional elements of the setting: two platforms of different heights, short stools, and one chair. Offstage focus was used throughout.*

tions, and to give variety. In a presentation of the children's script *Charlotte's Web* by E. B. White, a huge spider web constructed of white rope was suspended behind the readers. It stood out clearly before the black drapes and was quite appropriate to this story about a spider.

It should be emphasized that the arrangement of the readers does not have to remain static. A purposeful rearrangement or realignment from time to time is desirable for reasons of variety, emphasis, pictorial effectiveness, and revelation of changing character relationships. For instance, a character who has been seated might stand for a climactic passage in his speech. As an illustration, Aunt Rachel, in Stephen Vincent Benét's "Freedom's a Hard-Bought Thing," stands when she makes the decision to put "freedom in the heart of Cue." She says:

> "I do to you what I never even do for my own. Because you are fit to follow after your Grandaddy Shango, I put freedom in your heart, son Cue. You'll be sold and sold again. You'll know the chains and the whips. You'll suffer for your people and with your people. But while one man's got freedom in his heart, his children bound to know the tale. Now, I come to the end of my road, but the tale don't stop there. The tale go backward to Africa and it go forward, like clouds and fire. It go laughing and grieving forever, through the earth and the air and the waters, my people's tale."[9]

---

[9]Stephen Vincent Benét, *The Selected Works of Stephen Benét* (New York: Rinehart & Company, 1940) p. 55.

52   *Origins, Concepts, and Precepts*

The interpreters may also move as their relationship with other characters changes. If a scene requires conversation between two characters, both might step out from the rest of the group. In *Dandelion Wine,* when the two boys, Doug and Tom, are the only ones in the scene, they may rise and step forward while the other four readers remain seated on their stools. At the end of the scene, on the line "Come on, Tom, I'll race you home," the boys may return to their seated positions.

Some of the readers may exchange places from time to time to establish the best psychological relationships, such as closeness or separation in ideas and emotions. To illustrate the operation of this principle, let us examine Edna St. Vincent Millay's *The Murder of Lidice,* as it was staged at Southwest Missouri State College. In this production, which was played

In James Clavell's The Children's Story, *a series of step units and a platform (a pyramid arrangement) enable the new teacher to sit at the top with the children grouped around and below her. The old teacher remains slightly back and to one side—an arrangement which makes it possible for the audience to see all phases of the presentation at one time.*

The atmosphere for this scene from The Murder of Lidice, *based on a poem by Edna St. Vincent Millay, was suggested by the hammer and sickle projected onto the scrim in the background.*

on three platform levels with steps connecting them, Byeta, the young girl, sat on the floor of the top-level platform as she talked with her sweetheart Karel. Later, Byeta rose, left Karel, came down the steps to the second platform where her mother and father were located, and told them of her engagement. Thus the shifts in psychological relationships were reinforced; and, although there was variety in the physical placement of the readers on the platforms, the scene remained in the audience's imagination because the *focus* of the characters was in the imaginary scene out front.

In Readers Theatre, the movement of readers from place to place must be clearly motivated and carefully handled or it will break the concentration both of the interpreters and of the audience. To be effective, physical adjustments must be unobtrusive; literal movement can and does become obtrusive. This was demonstrated in the presentation of a children's script, *Homer Price* by Robert McCloskey, in which one reader said, "Here, take this coin," and held his arm out full length, with his fingers clenched on the imaginary object. Another reader then extended her arm full length, pantomimed taking the coin, and said "Thank you." However, subsequent experimentation proved that a *suggestion* of the movement was more effective than the more complete, literal one. The less elaborate, symbolic gesture stimulated the imagination of the audience and allowed the listeners to complete the action in their own minds. Movement, whether it be through space or merely a shifting of weight or a tightening or relaxing of the muscles, helps hold attention. It is a cogent way of externalizing a change in thought.

To sum up, whatever physical arrangements or staging devices are used, they should be pictorially effective. It is better to present Readers Theatre in a space small enough that the farthest viewer can see the subtle play of facial expressions. Readers Theatre demands interplay and co-operation between readers and audience, and close physical proximity encourages this interplay.

Transitions

Fluidity of scene progression is, as we have seen, an essential aspect of good Readers Theatre, and that is why the director must make clear where one segment of the story ends and where the next begins. He must also make sure that in both an oral and visual sense the scenes and segments are clearly and appropriately *linked,* that there are no distracting or unexplained gaps. The necessary bridges or transitions may be accomplished in a variety of ways. One common device is to have all the readers relax and slightly change their sitting or standing positions before starting a new scene. And, since the introduction of a new plot element almost invariably brings a change in the physical and psychological relationship between the characters, the director may have a set of readers stand or move to a different position on the stage as they lead into a new phase of the story. Sometimes a musical bridge is used. At other times a change in lighting will mark the beginning of a new segment.

Lighting

Productions may sometimes be enhanced with special illumination. The one essential in lighting is that the faces of the readers be seen clearly. The eyes can help the ears to hear, and audiences can hear better when they can see the readers' faces. Not only must the face of the one who is reading be illuminated, but the faces of all interpreters who are "in the scene" and reacting to the speaker must also be lighted.

Pinpoint lighting is sometimes used to designate readers in a scene. In Irwin Shaw's *Bury the Dead,* a spotlight singled out successive characters as they spoke. The attention of the audience was shifted by having a light come up slowly on a new set of speakers and fade out on the preceding group. In another program, one made up of several stories, lighting was used as a linking device. Standing at the right front of the stage, was a narrator wearing a railway conductor's cap. At the left front, a group of readers were seated, two by two, as though on a train. The narrator-conductor, similar to the Stage Manager in Wilder's *Our Town* or the conductor in Wilder's *Pullman Car Hiawatha,* was singled out by a spotlight as he told how he had learned the stories of his passengers' lives by studying their faces. Then, as he proceeded to introduce the life story of one individual, a pinpoint of light picked up that passenger's face; the passenger rose and walked into a place in the center of the stage, and his story was told. At the end of this segment, the light faded out on him; in the darkness, he and the other readers involved in his story moved off, and the spotlight again picked up the conductor at the right front of the stage. As he began to relate the story of the second passenger, the pinpoint of light came up on the face of that character as he walked into place for his story—a pattern that was repeated for each successive passenger involved in the progression. (See page 94 for additional details.)

In certain productions the use of projected light and images can serve a valuable function. To emphasize the timeliness of Edna St. Vincent Millay's *The Murder of Lidice,* the readers stood for a moment in silhouette at the beginning while a swastika was thrown on the scrim behind them; then, at the end, the silhouette was repeated, but this time the sickle and hammer emblem was projected onto the scrim. In James Clavell's "The Children's Story" a similar device was used; but in this production, the American eagle was replaced by a projection of the sickle and hammer as the young Communist teacher won the children to her ideology.

Costuming

The readers' apparel must, of course, be given careful consideration, for it can be very useful in reinforcing characterization. Few programs call for special costuming; as a rule, the readers choose appropriate suits and dresses from their own wardrobes and avoid light-reflecting or jangling jewelry. This unobtrusive clothing is essential if one reader is interpreting many roles, as is sometimes the case. Attention should, however, be given to choosing appropriate colors: dark, sombre colors for very serious or heavily dramatic presentations; bright, cheerful material for light or humorous programs. Often the clothing worn by the readers is selected for its character-suggesting possibilities. For example, the group that presented *Spoon River Anthology* on Broadway used basic costumes which were changed by the simple addition of scarves, shawls, and hats; by wearing blouses and dresses with adaptable necklines that could be low for one character and high for another; by quickly altering hemlines by tucking up the skirts; and by using shawls either as a head-covering or as something to be thrown lightly across the shoulders. In a class production of the children's script adapted from Ian Fleming's *Chitty-Chitty-Bang-Bang,* the twins both wore red sweaters, the father a darker coat sweater, and the mother a plain dress. The interpreter who read the role of the green sports car, Chitty-Chitty-Bang-Bang, wore a green sweater. This made a colorful picture for this humorous tale and, at the same time, helped suggest the relationship of the characters to the story and to each other.

Music and sound effects

Music and sound effects are often used in the production of Readers Theatre scripts. Vocal sounds, such as humming or the sounds of the crowd muttering or exclaiming, often add a dimension to the scene. However, these auditory elements should not dominate a performance; the author's material is primary. When they are used, the director must exercise great care and judgment in selecting just the right ones and then proceed to integrate them skillfully and subtly into the presentation as a whole. If any kind of auditory effect is to be used as background for the narration and dialogue, its loudness-level must be tested to make sure that the words of the reader can be heard above it. Well-known music is likely to attract too much attention to itself; but a musical interlude, if used with discernment, can often add a humorous note or underscore scenes of romance or tragedy. Elbert Bowen's production of *The Battle of the Sexes,* presented at the National Convention of the Speech Association of America in 1962, used drums to punctuate and highlight segments of this compiled script. In Robert McCloskey's *Homer Price,* an intriguing original tune was introduced to mark transitions. For *The Reluctant Dragon,* lute music helped establish the ancient time in which the story unfolded.

Use of scripts

It has been pointed out that some directors require readers to memorize their lines and others require the readers to use scripts which they carry in their hands during the rehearsals and performance. The script, it should be noted, is a symbol of the Readers Theatre medium; and even though the material is memorized, the script is usually present. Each member of the professional group presenting *In White America* would pick up his bound manuscript from a table in the center of the stage area, glance at it a moment, put it down, and then speak from memory. All of these readers were clearly using the manuscript as a symbol. Their material was factual; the presence of these manuscripts established the authenticity of the words.

If a script is used—and it usually is—some uniformity in size and color is desirable; and if it is to be held in the hand, a small notebook is less obtrusive and easier to handle than a large one. Moreover, a small notebook does not hide as much of the reader's body. Of course, if the script is to remain on a lectern, the size does not matter; but if not, it should be firmly backed and bound in such a way that the reader can hold it open in one hand, leaving the other hand free for gesturing. The script should be held out slightly, away from the reader's body and angled so that the light which falls upon it does not reflect from the white page and distract the audience.

Not all of the readers should turn the pages at exactly the same time; for this, too, may prove distracting. If a character is out of the scene for a long interval, the reader can clip together the pages of the script for those episodes or segments in which he does not participate. However, it would be well for him to insert a warning signal at least half a page before he is to resume reading so that he will be ready for his cue to re-enter.

In typing a Readers Theatre script, it is important that the reader's or character's name stand out clearly from the dialogue. To ensure this, the character's name is customarily positioned on the left side of the page, and the dialogue extends from it toward the right. Usually the character name is typed in capital letters; brief interpretive notes or suggestions are enclosed in parentheses *within* the passages of dialogue, and longer directorial notes are set off in separate parenthetical paragraphs *between* successive sections of dialogue or narration. Important technical cues are similarly denoted. Double spacing is used throughout the manuscript, and the margins should be ample.

These, then, are the physical elements of a Readers Theatre production: focus, entrances and exits, physical arrangement and movement, transitions, lighting, costumes, music, sound effects, and the script. When the director has carefully and discerningly combined them and has stimulated and guided his readers to an effective reading of the lines, the readers have a better chance of bringing out the best that is in the literature of the script and evoking the desired audience response. A presentation of *Iphigenia in Aulis* illustrates how certain of these physical elements can be synthesized. In presenting this Greek classic, a chorus of three readers wore robes of three different colors that made a pleasing, harmonious picture. Iphigenia was a striking figure in rich red. There were platforms at two levels, with two columns—one on either side—positioned on the upper level to provide a suggestion of the scene. A scrim curtain, serving as a background behind the pillars and platforms, was indirectly lighted. The three readers in the chorus stood on the upper level and read from attractively bound manuscripts which were identical in size and color, and Iphigenia read from the lower level. In this way, the suggested costuming, setting, lighting, and other physical elements generated a visual stimulus that appreciably enhanced the aural stimulus of Euripides' words.

Whatever is done in the way of using and combining costuming, music, lighting, and set pieces on the stage, everything should be suggestive rather than explicit, nonrealistic rather than realistic. The strength of Readers Theatre is that it is, indeed, the theatre of the mind. The goal is to stir the audience's imagination, to create in their minds all that the words imply. The very nature of this art form—often with a few characters taking many roles and with scenes shifting as facilely as the written word—precludes rigid realism.

CHAPTER FIVE

Casting, Rehearsing, and Performing

Once the director has analyzed the script for meanings, attitudes, style, and characterization and has determined how to handle the various physical elements in staging the production, he is prepared to cast the show and start rehearsals.

CASTING THE CHARACTERS

In selecting the readers, the director's prime concern is not their specific physical appearance. Physical type-casting is sometimes helpful to the audience in that it aids them to "see" the characters they hear; but of greater importance than physical appearance are sensitivity, a flexible voice and body, and an expressive face. Mobility of facial expression and responsive body tone are essential factors in the reader's ability to project the emotional and intellectual elements of the literary material to the audience. The personal tonality of the reader is another factor. Some readers almost invariably provoke laughter in fellow readers and in the audience and are unable to read a serious role effectively. A story is told that the late Zazu Pitts, an actress whose trademark was her fluttery hands, was once cast in a serious role in the motion picture, *All Quiet on the Western Front.* Unfortunately, the film had to be remade with a different actress because the audience automatically laughed whenever Miss Pitts appeared on the screen. The ideal interpreter for Readers Theatre is one who can adapt to the needs and nature of the material, whether it is serious or comic. The reader especially needs a wide vocal and emotional range when he is to play many roles in one script, as is sometimes the case in this medium. The director should, therefore, choose readers who can project variety in vocal quality, thus assuring contrast between successive characters. And, as in casting for any artistic and interpretive endeavor, the reliability of the reader and his enthusiasm for the script are two elements essential for effective rehearsals and performances.

INITIAL AND EXPLORATORY REHEARSALS

When the director is satisfied that he has a capable cast, he calls the first rehearsal. In introducing the script, he may read it to the group, or he may ask that the cast read it aloud. A good reading by the director does much to reveal the possibilities within the script and to arouse enthusiasm for it. However, there is a danger in this procedure, for the readers may think this is the way each role is to be read and try to imitate the director's interpretation. On the other hand, an "at sight" reading may leave the group unimpressed with the beauty and strength of the writing. Perhaps a combination of telling the story or plot and reading excerpts from the script is the best approach; this seems to preserve the excitement of discovery while at the same time decreasing the dangers of imitation.

It is extremely important that all readers be thoroughly familiar with the whole script and its original sources. If the script is a cutting of a longer work, the readers should familiarize themselves with that work in its entirety. In the selective process, passages may have been cut that will guide the readers in their interpretation of lines that have been retained; and their study of these excised passages will give them a deeper insight into the characters whose lines they will be reading.

On the first reading and for several readings thereafter, the cast should read in an exploring manner. In other words, they should read with a minimum of expression until they discover the most desirable and effective expression. Otherwise they may form erroneous vocal and interpretive patterns that can be difficult to eradicate later. For instance, at first reading a given character may seem quite gay and merry, and the interpreter will read the lines with a corresponding emotion. Later, he may discover that the character actually is heartbroken but is attempting to put up a brave appearance. Thus, the light-hearted reading would be misleading. This is why it is better to read exploringly, with little expression, until the meaning and emotion back of the words are correctly determined. The director can do much to insure a unified performance if he and his readers explore the script together in this way, with the cast remaining free to express ideas and to ask questions.

In trying to determine how best to express the meaning, the readers should thoroughly explore the author's choice of words—their meanings and connotations—and the allusions in the script. A rewarding and oft-repeated question is "What does the author gain by using this word rather than some other?" Note, for example, the varying positive or negative feelings associated with these words: *fastidious, finicky, delicate, scrupulous, hypercritical*. Although there is similarity in their literal meanings, each word carries a different degree of approval or disapproval.

These first readings are tremendously important, and with each additional reading, the interpreter should develop a more sensitive perception of the material he is reading and a deeper insight into the character he is developing.

REHEARSALS FOR GROWTH

The growth period will require many rehearsals. During these developmental sessions, the readers should continue to evolve their characters, to ascertain motivations, to discover the basic ideas and conflicts, to respond to the imagery and emotions, and to experiment with different ways of expressing them. As the work proceeds, the director will, of course, encourage an interplay among the characters, a verbal hitting back and forth. In a figurative sense, this interplay is somewhat like a tennis game in which the ball is knocked back and forth between the players. The emphasis is upon returning the ball or—in Readers Theatre —answering the idea, or registering the character's response to the words he has heard. This interaction is one of the most important elements in bringing a script to life on the platform. As the growth rehearsals continue, the director stimulates, encourages, asks leading questions, and suggests new approaches for the creative activities of the readers.

During these rehearsals for growth, the director and the readers should concentrate on *segments* of the material rather than working on the total script over and over. Working in depth on a unit that can be read more than once in the rehearsal period allows more time for ferreting out the meaning. In aiding the interpreters to find symbolic meanings, the director may ask questions or make suggestions that will evoke new insights into the lines, making it possible for the reader to express the meaning and emotion inherent in the words. Once the segment has been analyzed and worked on for details in this manner, it should be read through again without interruption to develop the rhythmic flow, to re-emphasize the cause and effect, to allow a build-up in emotion, to create a give-and-take among characters, and to enable the readers to sense progression in the scene.

Usually the script will have sentences and passages which build to a climax, and often these will be divided among several readers. In rehearsing materials of this type, the interpreters should read the total passage *together* until they sense the flow, the movement, and the "build." Then each individual reader should speak his assigned portion of the passage, meanwhile making sure that he retains the special qualities of flow and movement necessary to sustain the ascendancy of the work as a whole. Admittedly, this is difficult to do and requires patient drill.

As an illustration of this principle of reading first with "togetherness" and then with individuality, notice how the following lines from James Thurber's "The Last Clock" were divided among the townspeople:

VOICE ONE. Factories and schools remained closed.

VOICE TWO. Church bells no longer rang,

VOICE THREE. Because the bell ringers no longer knew when to ring them.

VOICE ONE. Dates and engagements were no longer made,

VOICE THREE. Because nobody knew when to keep them.

VOICE TWO. Trains no longer ran,

VOICE THREE. So nobody left town.

VOICE ONE. And no strangers arrived in town to tell people what time it was.

VOICE TWO. Eventually, the sands of a nearby desert moved slowly

VOICE THREE. And inexorably

VOICE TWO. Toward the timeless town,

VOICE THREE. And in the end it was buried.[1]

In rehearsing passages like this, the director will wish to experiment, asking various readers to express the lines until the best "symphony of sound," the best vocal montage, has been gained. Thus the director works with the interpreters so that their voices bring out the full aural values of the material.

The director may frequently have to remind the cast to keep the imaginary scene consistently in the same area of the auditorium. If offstage focus is being used—that is, if the imaginary scene is placed in the midst of the audience—it is helpful to divide the cast into two groups, placing one in the middle of the auditorium and the other onstage. The readers onstage will note that the readers in the auditorium are not concentrated in one tiny spot; that is to say, they are not merely a theoretical dot or pinpoint in space but physically occupy a visual area of several square feet. Therefore, the readers on the stage will find that they must aim their gaze directly at one of the auditorium characters and then *re-aim* it slightly in order to look at another character in the same group. (See Figures 2 and 3, pp. 48 and 49.) This adds a very necessary sense of *dimension* to the offstage focus. After seeing actual characters grouped in the auditorium and rehearsing with them in that location, the readers will often find it easier to imagine or visualize them there in later rehearsals and in performance.

The reader should know that his eyes are his most expressive feature and that he must use them to help convey the intellectual and emotional meanings of the writing. The eyes are the main determinant of facial expression, and facial expression is needed in projecting characterization and attitudes. Furthermore, the eyes are used in revealing the reaction of one character to the words of another. Thus, to sustain the desired concentration and visualization by the audience, the readers should not direct their eyes constantly at the script. Moreover, if the eyes are kept continuously on the page, the reader tends to turn his whole face down-

---

[1] *The Last Clock.* From *Lanterns and Lances.* Copr. © 1961 James Thurber. Published by Harper and Row. Originally printed in *The New Yorker.*

In Readers Theatre the interpreter takes advantage of his entire physical aspect to convey feelings and ideas appropriate to the story. In this scene from the compiled script, Mother to Son, *note particularly how these two readers employ flexible facial expression to reveal characterization and attitude.*

ward, and as a result, the sound waves are directed toward the floor and are difficult to hear. The reader should, therefore, keep his eyes as free of the script as possible. This does not mean that he is to ignore the script; rather, he must train himself to grasp the words in a quick glance so that he may use his eyes for expressive purposes.

During these rehearsals, the readers must learn to enter the scene at exactly the right moment. To do this, they must follow the progression of the action and events closely at all times. Each reader must know *why* he is entering, what his mood is, how he feels toward others in the scene, and how he will adapt to them and to "what is going on." Like the actor, the reader must not allow the tempo and volume of the scene to drop on his entrance. To mark a new scene—and the entrance of a character does begin a new scene in that it changes the existing character relationships —the reader scrupulously avoids picking up and imitating the tempo, volume, and pitch of the interpreter who has been speaking immediately prior to his entrance.

Vivifying the reading
Reading that is alive—vivid—must be the mutual goal of the director and the readers. If the cast is inexperienced, it may be necessary during the rehearsal period for the director to assist them in improving their inter-

pretive skills. In order to bring the script to life, the readers must bring out each nuance in the writing, each significant shade of meaning.

Responding to the image. One way to accomplish this is for the readers to make the descriptive passages come alive so vividly in their own minds that through their concentration on the mental images of the scene, they will cause the audience to experience very similar images. The audience will tend to think with the reader, being guided by the manner in which he interprets the lines. This responding to the image or "thinking with the senses," the term used by Lowrey and Johnson in their book *Interpretative Reading*,[2] aids the reader to gain an empathic response to the literature which, in turn, stimulates the audience to a similar response.

In "thinking with the senses," the reader imagines, at the moment of speaking, that he is experiencing with his own senses the sights, smells, sounds, tastes, tactile sensations, and movements described in the text. He smells the roast pig, the honeysuckle, the ether. He tastes the sauerkraut, the lemon juice, the fudge. He springs through the air on his Para Litefoot tennis shoes. He strains to release the ropes binding his wrists, and he plunges through the line, carrying the football. The readers, responding to the images within the material, express the words with intonational and inflectional patterns that are believable and capable of drawing the audience empathically into the situation so that they, too, experience the literature in this way. "Thinking with the senses" helps the reader to concentrate, for it gives him something definite upon which to center his attention. Since in Readers Theatre the characters move within a setting created in the minds of the audience, it is of paramount importance that the reader first create this scene in his own mind, that he see the characters in action within this mentally visualized setting. In so doing, he can appreciably aid the audience to re-create in *their* minds the scene, the characters, and the event.

While the reader, as we have noted, thinks in terms of the traditional five senses—sight, sound, smell, touch, and taste—the senses of greatest importance to him as an interpreter are the kinetic and kinesthetic. The kinetic sense is an *overt* muscular response to the action inherent in the words. It is the muscular response to leaping into the air and plunging downward as one says "He leaped into the air, arched his body, and then glided down, sliding into the water with scarcely a sound." Kinesthetic imagery calls for a *covert* muscular response to the emotion within the lines. To demonstrate this to yourself, read the following line aloud, responding to the images as you do so: "As she stood at the window, watching the children play, she wished desperately that she had not left home." If you were aware of a tensing of your muscles, you were responding kinesthetically. Similarly, a pleasant kinesthetic image would cause a relaxing of the muscles, as in this line: "Just seeing him move toward

---

[2]Sara Lowrey and Gertrude E. Johnson, *Interpretative Reading* (New York: Appleton-Century-Crofts, 1953), p. 30.

her across the lawn made her ecstatically happy." Not only must the interpreter respond with his total body to the imagery of the writing, but he must also hold the images in his mind until an emotional response is evoked and externalized—made audible and visible to the audience.

Warming-up exercises.   Warming-up sessions at the beginning of each rehearsal are a useful way of increasing the reader's power to respond to the images. Some directors use them during the run of a show as a means of warming up before the performance. In a sense, this corresponds to a

From Chitty-Chitty-Bang-Bang, *a children's story by Ian Fleming, these two pictures demonstrate the concept of suggested movement and readers' concentration on and participation in the imaginary offstage scene. In the upper photo, the two characters' sitting with their backs to the audience indicates that they have not yet "entered" the scene. In the lower picture, having entered, they now face front—a movement facilitated by the use of swivel stools.*

singer's vocalizing. Taking from literature some words and passages that demand an emotional, sensory response, the director asks the readers to express them, giving full vocal and bodily response. Here are examples of words and phrases that might be employed:

miserable	happy	gay
tired	hot	cold
dejected	elated	delicate
hard	soft	swashbuckling

He slid into third base.
Leaping from rock up to rock.
Crouching miserably in fear.
Released from all cares, I swing into action.
I held still, not moving a muscle.

This warming-up phase should also include vocal-projection exercises. Vocalizing words with open vowels, such as *home, hold, hark, tone,* and *dawn,* the reader may figuratively take the word in his hand and bounce it high on the back wall, "following through" on the throw with his whole body. In exercising with words having an initial *h* sound, the reader should try to project the words forward through the mouth. Just as the voice needs warming up, so, too, do the muscles of the body. The football coach has his men flex their muscles and do other body-conditioning exercises before a game; the director instructs his readers to tone their muscles before rehearsing or performing. The right kind of physical activity helps tone up the muscles, and good muscle tone is important in producing full vocal tones. Stretching, leaping, and alternately expanding and contracting the body will result in the good muscle tone needed for an energetic, "alive" rehearsal or performance.

Responding to the verbs. If the reader will re-examine the warming-up sentences described above, he will notice that *verbs* or action words were given considerable emphasis. The verb supplies the action in Readers Theatre. In the oral interpretation of literary material, the verbs must be as definite and specific in their suggestion of movement as the actual physical movements which characterize the conventional stage play. Through his empathic response to the inherent movement in these verbs, the reader vivifies for his audience the action in the script. For example, if he is responsive to the following phrases, he should note a slight muscular involvement as he reads them:

Striding and striding
Leaning into the wind
Slinking quietly to the door
Pouncing upon the unsuspecting victim
Turning around and around giddily, dizzily, happily
Jerking the handkerchief from off her face
Sweeping into the room in full sail
Sitting quietly, miserably, unable to help in any way

In narration the forward movement of the action is carried from verb to verb. A crisp handling of these verbs by the reader will endow the production with a strong sense of progression, a sharp and well-defined impression of action that is going somewhere exciting.

Vivifying through acting.   Another way of securing vivid reading of the lines is similar to the one above in that it, too, calls for an empathic response to the words, particularly to the verbs. In this method, however, the readers first completely enact the scene, giving full movement as called for by the script. After sensing the movement in the muscles of the body through acting out the scene, the readers then retain the muscle tone demanded in the full action, without performing the action. In other words, the interpreter reads the words without the action but with the same inner bodily response that he had when he acted it out. Although this is an *internal* response, there will be some vestigial movement. For example, while working on *James and the Giant Peach,* the interpreter reading the role of James literally crawled through a small opening made with chairs, bumped his head, and then saw the Centipede, Earthworm, Spider, and the other characters sitting together as the book suggests. In this way, the readers achieved a sense of physical action and real interplay which carried over to the next reading when it was placed in the imagination. The same group actually rehearsed the ocean scene in the Atlantic Ocean at Vero Beach; they huddled realistically together as called for in the script and reacted to the expanse of water, the clouds floating by, and the moonlight. Later, as they read their lines and recalled their earlier muscular response, they seemed actually to be experiencing the situation at that moment. Once the elements of the scene had been truly experienced, the muscle memory—as well as the emotional memory— enabled the readers to re-create the scene fully.

Vivifying by interpolated comments.   Still another device for developing vividness in the reading is the use of interpolated comments in rehearsal. Stanislavski calls this *inner monologue.*[3] It may also be termed *interior dialogue.* The reader is asked to speak aloud the thoughts that form the basis of the text, to say aloud the subtext. For example, read the poem "Warren's Address to the American Soldiers" by James Pierpont:

> *Stand! The ground's your own, my braves!*
> *Will ye give it up to slaves?*
> *Will ye look for greener graves?*
> *Hope ye mercy still?*
> *What's the mercy despots feel?*

---

[3]Stanislavski is quoted as having given this advice to his actors: ". . . speak not only your text but also all the thoughts that come into your mind during the scene. . . . Don't mutter because I must hear you. I must see that your thoughts about Grace—or, as we call it, your inner monologue—is correct." From Nikoloi M. Gorchakov, *Stanislavski Directs,* trans. Miriam Goldina (New York: Funk & Wagnalls Company Inc., 1954), p. 51.

In this scene from Jules Feiffer's story, Passionella, *note the use of syncopated motion suggested by the three characters constituting the chorus. In this pose,* Passionella *is the glamorous movie star. As the chimney sweep, she slumped over; her knees were not crossed; there was a dull look in her eyes; and her mouth hung slightly open. The narrator is observing the scene which is supposedly occurring offstage.*

> *Hear it in that battle peal!*
> *Read it on yon bristling steel!*
> *Ask it—ye who will.*[4]

With interior dialogue, the passage could read:

Stand! *(Don't give way!)* The ground's your own, my braves! *(This is your property!)*

Will ye give it up to slaves? *(Are you going to let a bunch of hired soldiers take it from you?)*

Will ye look for greener graves? *(Is there a better place to die?)*

Hope ye mercy still? What's the mercy despots feel? *(What kind of mercy are tyrants aware of?)*

Hear it in that battle peal! *(The roar of battle tells you the kind of mercy you will receive from them.)*

Read it on yon bristling steel! *(Those bayonets coming at you tell you what to expect.)*

Ask it—ye who will. *(All right. Go ahead. Ask for mercy if you dare.)*

Interpolations of this kind will aid the reader in bringing out the desired emotion and the central idea of the lines while, at the same time, revealing any misunderstanding of their meaning. With patient and careful rehearsing of this kind, the reader is likely to retain the intonations thus achieved when he reads the lines in their original form.

---

[4]Edmund Clarence Stedman, ed., *An American Anthology* (New York: Houghton Mifflin Company, 1900), p. 34.

Correcting faulty line-reading

In correcting faulty line-reading, the reader may use two approaches: one is to develop a fuller understanding of the line, and the other is to use specific techniques that will lead to a more sensitive reading. Checking grammatical structure and paraphrasing are frequently helpful in achieving total comprehension of especially difficult or complex lines.

Checking grammatical structure. When the reader finds the subject and the verb, he should identify the object, if any, and the qualifying phrases and clauses. He should then analyze the relationship of these phrases and clauses to the main idea. For instance, in this sentence, "Irks care the crop-full bird?" the student will discover that the subject is *care* and the verb is *irk*, with the object *bird* modified by the adjective *crop-full*. Rearranged, it reads "Does care irk the crop-full bird?" Having ascertained the correct meaning in this way, the reader can then convey it to the audience through his intonation pattern.

Paraphrasing. Another method for determining meaning is to paraphrase the passage. Choosing words that have not been used over and over will demand a fresh appraisal of the thought. The sample sentence in the above paragraph could be paraphrased in this manner: "Can anxiety bother the bird that is satiated with food?" or "What does the well-fed bird have to be unhappy about?" Having discovered the meaning by restating the thought, the interpreter will vocally lift or emphasize the words *care* and *irk* in such a manner that the listener will comprehend the meaning the instant he hears it.

Counting: a mechanical device. An understanding of the line is the best way to ensure an appropriate reading. At times, however, the reader may have developed such a firm pattern of wrong reading that he is unable to change it. In such cases, he may try a number of specific techniques. Although counting is a mechanical device, it frequently works well in breaking a stubborn, habitual pattern. In this procedure, the reader counts the number of syllables in the line, noting which syllables should be emphasized in order to convey the thought accurately; he then says the line, substituting numbers for syllables and emphasizing the correct numbers. For example, in the question, "Do you want Mary to go?" there are seven syllables. If the meaning is to be "Do you want Mary to go or to stay?" the stress would be on *7*.

Do you want Ma ry to go?
1   2   3   4   5 6 <u>7</u>

If the meaning is to be "Do you want Mary or John to go?" the emphasis is upon *4*.

Do you want <u>Ma</u> ry to go?
1   2   3   <u>4</u>   5 6 7

By this means, the reader hears the correct intonational pattern; and since he is using new words rather than the ones with which he has been practicing, he should be able to reproduce this more meaningful pattern.[5]

This counting device also works well with another type of faulty line-reading, that in which the reader fails to read complete thought-groups or fails to carry through to the end of the thought. This problem occurs quite frequently with a run-on line of poetry, because the reader tends to pause arbitrarily at the end of the printed line rather than at the end of the thought-group. The director, after thoroughly exploring the meaning with the reader, may use the counting procedure. If in this or some other way he can guide the interpreter to voice whole thoughts, he will find that a number of other persistent faults in reading may have been eliminated more or less automatically. Skill in phrasing complete thought-units is a "must" for natural, meaningful reading whether it be in Readers Theatre, in solo reading, or in acting.

Packaging ideas.   Quite often in a script, a long series of sentences must be vocally combined or "packaged" together as a unit, with a "build" to the important idea and a proper subordination of the qualifying elements. Packaging means revealing the relationship of a series of ideas that, together, express one thought. It binds together the phrases, clauses, and sentences that amplify an idea.

In the following passage (Act I, Scene vii, lines 12-28), for example, Macbeth is enumerating to his wife the reasons for not killing Duncan. He gives two reasons: first, he is a blood relation and Duncan's subject; second, he is Duncan's host. But, as another argument, he adds that Duncan has been so humble and blameless as king that his virtues will cause people to decry his murder, and pity will cause all the people to weep for him. The relation of these ideas must be brought out in the reading.

> He's here in double trust;
> First, as I am his kinsman and his subject,
> Strong both against the deed; then, as his host,
> Who should against his murderer shut the door,
> Not bear the knife myself. Besides, this Duncan
> Hath borne his faculties so meek, hath been
> So clear in his great office, that his virtues
> Will plead like angels, trumpet-tongued, against
> The deep damnation of his taking-off;
> And pity, like a naked new-born babe,
> Striding the blast, or heaven's cherubim horsed
> Upon the sightless couriers of the air,
> Shall blow the horrid deed in every eye,

---

[5]Instead of numbers, Stanislavski used *ta* and *ti* for the syllables. See Leslie Irene Coger, "Stanislavski Changes His Mind," *Tulane Drama Review,* IX, No. 1 (1964), 63-68.

That tears shall drown the wind. I have no spur
To prick the sides of my intent, but only
Vaulting ambition, which o'erleaps itself
And falls on the other.

The first fourteen lines must be given as a package because, as a *whole,* they tell why Macbeth feels he should not murder his king. To communicate these reasons clearly and effectively to an audience, the reader must show their relationship to each other and tie them all together. To accomplish this in a sustained and vocal context is no casual task.

Projecting lines and meanings. Not infrequently, faulty reading results because the reader mumbles his lines. To overcome this, the interpreter needs to become more aware of the importance of the words. He must comprehend the idea and project, both mentally and physically, the key words which express that idea. To project words, to make them more easily audible, the interpreter vocally "arches them up and out" into the auditorium. He intensifies the sound; with an ample, well-controlled supply of breath, he sustains the vowels—the heart of words— to allow time for the sound to travel. The reader needs to be aware that thinking must always precede and accompany his speaking the words, and that the thought-carrying words stand out from words of lesser importance. This, of course, implies a change, a change in relationships.

Pointing, as it is sometimes called, focuses audience attention upon a thought or an emotion. It may be accomplished in a variety of ways. The main way to effect vocal pointing is to provide *contrast.* To make a word stand out from other words, the reader may give it longer duration on a higher or lower pitch, or he may give it greater stress or force. Thus the word or the idea is "pointed" or made to stand out.

Physical pointing may accompany vocal pointing or be employed by itself. Again, the basis for pointing is change: a turn of the head or body or a change in the facial expression. For example, when a character makes a difficult decision, often he will lift his head, straighten his shoulders, and take a deep breath. He has physically pointed his decision. Sometimes the pointing is accomplished by the reaction of the person who hears the line. As a rule this will involve facial expression, although larger bodily responses may be used. The response may—and frequently does—take the form of words or a vocal noise of some kind. This reinforcement or pointing of an idea from reader to reader and between reader and audience is a powerful means for implanting and vivifying it.

Marking transitions. Failure to mark the beginning of a new thought or a change in emotion will make the performance seem either unnecessarily slow or pointlessly rushed. Here again variety is basic. Quite often the problem is not in the pace itself but in the monotony of the reading. If the readers will establish and sustain the forward-moving pattern of the plot by emphasizing the shifts in thought and emotion, they will inject the necessary variety and avoid the monotonous pace which characterizes the "dragged out" production. Every change of idea and feeling demands a difference in pitch, intensity, tempo, and sometimes in tone. The readers must mark the beginning of a *new* incident, idea, or phase with a different tempo, a new pitch level, a change in atmosphere, or by a physical relaxing of their muscles and a slight shift in their positions with reference to each other and to the audience. This variety, so necessary for the line-reading, is also of great importance in providing proper balance for the series of scenes in the script. If the climax is not the highest point in the production, in all likelihood the preceding scenes are being read at too high a pitch, with too much intensity, or at too fast a pace. It is as important to conserve mental and physical energy in minor scenes as it is to unleash it at peak moments. Temper the reading of these secondary or transitional scenes, and the climax will take on added excitement.

Using the tape recorder. Perhaps the most effective means of improving line-reading—and certainly one of the quickest and most efficient —is for the reader to hear himself on a tape recorder. Despite all the director may have said about the line and its interpretation, many times the reader does not really understand what is wrong with his reading of it until he actually hears himself. While listening to the recording of his own voice the reader becomes readily and acutely aware of false emphasis, monotony in pitch and in pacing, lack of emotional coloring and vitality in the reading. Once the reader is aware of these deficiencies, most of the difficulties can be eradicated promptly, and a vastly improved interpretation will be the result.

To improve or correct faulty line-reading, then, two major approaches are possible: one is to develop a full understanding of the line, and the second is to use specific techniques that can help the student achieve an acceptable, even a sensitive, reading of the line. In the first approach the reader should analyze the line by studying its syntax and by paraphrasing it. In the second, the reader may employ a variety of useful procedures: the counting device for correcting stubbornly set, erroneous patterns; "packaging" the series of related ideas; proper vocal and physical projection; marking transitions for shifts in meaning and emotion; and the "feedback" from tape-recording sessions.

EVALUATIVE REHEARSALS

As the time for performance approaches, the director should conduct a rehearsal in which he evaluates what has been accomplished by the readers thus far in order to determine what remains to be done for an effective production. First, he should ask himself if the meaning of the script as a whole is clear, if the author's attitude has been clearly represented. If not, is the trouble in the reading, or is the adaptation inadequate? Another question he should ask concerns the movement of the story. Does it progress? Does it move along at the proper pace to its high point of interest? This matter of pacing is, as we have stressed, tremendously important to an absorbing production. Cues must be picked up promptly. The tempo must be varied as demanded by the script. Climaxes must be reached and clinched. The performance must have a definite ending; it must culminate, leaving no doubt in the minds of the audience that this is, indeed, the end.

Many productions fail to achieve their full impact upon the audience because this sense of finality is lacking, because the ending is inconclusive. The listeners do not know whether they should applaud or not. The director can avoid this by making sure that the readers give concluding passages a special definiteness, a tone of finality. Also, the final physical positions or bodily attitudes of the readers must be given careful consideration. In a Readers Theatre production of Fielding's *The Tragedy of Tragedies: Or the Life and Death of Tom Thumb, the Great,* directed by Charlotte Lee of Northwestern University, the interpreters, representing dead bodies, leaned far forward over their lecterns. There could be no doubt that this was the ending. In an adaptation of Wilbur Daniel Steele's short story "So Beautiful with Shoes," the production opened and closed with music as the characters stood in silent silhouette for a moment. This visual framework added definiteness to the ending. In some scripts, especially appropriate endings may be drawn from the original literary source. This is exemplified in the ending of Ray Bradbury's *Dandelion Wine.*

As the evaluative rehearsal proceeds, the director will want to ask other useful questions. Has the proper mood been established? Are the emotional elements of the material projected? Do the scenes reach emotional climaxes as intended? The director should also examine the characterizations: Are the characters interesting and believable? Do the readers reveal these characters through their body tone, as well as through their voices and their facial expressions? Do the readers *listen* "in character" and *react* to what the others are saying? This staying "in character" is of great importance in keeping the total scene alive and unified. The readers must respond to all that is happening. They must not look directly out at the audience or consistently down at their books while they are supposed to be participating in the scene. Is it clear who is "in" the scene? Do the readers combine energy with ease; that is, do they project vitality without strain? Are they alive? The director should recheck the reading of the individual lines, especially those which have proved troublesome. Is the meaning clear? Are the thoughts properly phrased? Are the key words and thoughts unmistakable? Do the voices carry easily? Do the voices provide sufficient variety and contrast? Is the quality pure, unless it is intended to be otherwise for a special effect? Is the diction uniform and consistent with the characters being presented?

POLISHING REHEARSALS

If the director, after evaluating what he has accomplished, is satisfied with the results and is confident that all elements are contributing to an organic and dynamic whole, then he can continue with the "setting" or polishing rehearsals. These final rehearsals should be a series of run-throughs with no interruptions, stressing a well-sustained pace, an ebb and flow of intensity, and unbroken concentration. No new elements should be added at this time. The performance should be allowed to take form, to solidify.

If possible, these final rehearsals should be held under the same circumstances as the performance, even to the clothes the readers will wear. The exact lighting should be used in order that the director can make certain that readers' faces are easily discernible. If there are music and sound effects, these too must be checked for proper cueing and for optimum volume. The presence of a small audience during these culminating rehearsals will help the readers get the feel of an audience, to note reactions, and to learn to hold for laughs. As part of the polishing procedure, the cast should practice its initial entrance and final exit; it is imperative for them to know the exact order in which they are to enter and leave the stage, and the cues for so doing. At the end of the performance, the readers should not drift aimlessly off or collapse into the nearest chair. The act of walking on and walking off the stage should be done with definiteness, as if it were a part of the performance, which of course it is.

PERFORMANCE

In these last rehearsals and before each performance, the director prepares his cast psychologically. For the "aliveness" essential to an infectious, audience-stirring performance, the director will need to evoke fresh enthusiasm in his readers. He may hold warming-up sessions before each performance in which the readers run through stretching and relaxing exercises to achieve the physical tone necessary for mental alertness; he may have them improvise scenes from the script in order to instill ebullience and immediacy in the reading of the lines. Above all, the director desires for his readers the joy of achievement, the stimulation of knowing an audience is completely engaged in the performance. He must convince them, through his own positive attitude, that they will entertain those who have come to hear them. Confidence in their ability to present a successful performance will encourage the readers to maintain the proper alternation of heightened tone and relaxation which they will need to do their best work while, at the same time, experiencing a sense of ease and enjoyment.

In the well-directed Readers Theatre production an aura of contagious enthusiasm prevails. The performance has freshness and spontaneity—

"the illusion of the first time." It has cumulative power with strong characterizations, vivid descriptions, forward-moving narration, and indissoluble unity. And in its final form, it creates a memorable event for the audience, an event in which they are a creative participant.

The director's function does not end with the final dress rehearsal, of course. He may say to his readers, "I have done all I can. What happens in performance is up to you. It is in your hands." In truth, however, if Readers Theatre is to be a genuine, enduring experience, one which will contribute to the readers' intellectual and emotional growth and will sharpen their interpretive perception and skill, the director's task does not end when the audience is seated, the hush falls over the house, and the first reader begins. His most important responsibility is a continuing evaluation of what is happening during the performance in order to improve subsequent presentations. Serving as an impartial observer insofar as it is humanly possible, the director will witness the event in its uninterrupted totality and endeavor to determine where he has succeeded and where he has failed. He will try to judge as fairly and honestly as he can the many facets and elements of the production, addressing his attention primarily to the performance *per se,* to the validity and usefulness of the staging, and to the effectiveness of the script as literary-presentational material intended to evoke from the audience the intellectual and emotional responses necessary to their experiencing the literature in that most exciting of all places—the theatre of their minds. The director may find the following check list useful in making these assessments and in conveying his findings to the readers after the performance.

Evaluation of Readers Theatre Script and Production

A. Performance

1. Does the performance have an overall unity?
2. Is the meaning of the script projected?
3. Does the performance have flow and effective pacing? Does it move from segment to segment with a sense of progression? Does it build to a high peak of interest?
4. Does the performance have a spontaneous "first-time" quality?
5. Is the narration delivered in a manner making it an integral part of the script and the performance (or does the action stop for the narration)? Is the narration vivid? Does it reveal the speaker's attitude? Is the point of view clear? Does the narration seem to create images of scenes and action in the minds of the audience?
6. Does the narrator use a storytelling manner, relating directly to the audience? Does the narrator seem to visualize the imaginary scene when he is not speaking?
7. Do the readers project distinct and believable characters?
8. Do the characters change as dictated by the literary experience?
9. Are the readers "thinking with the senses" and creating mental images as they speak the words?
10. Do the readers possess an aliveness? Do they have projective energy—a reaching out to the audience—in their reading and action?
11. Do they *listen* when they are in the scene? Do they *react* through facial expression and muscle tone?
12. If an interpreter reads lines for more than one character, does he use voice and body tone to make a clear distinction among the various characters?
13. Is it clear at all times which readers are in the scene? Are the readers who are not in the scene sufficiently unobtrusive?
14. Do the interpreters handle their scripts efficiently and unobtrusively?
15. Is there consistency in the focus of the readers? Do all the readers locate a given scene in the same area?

B. Staging

1. Are the readers arranged so that all faces can be seen clearly?
2. Are readers arranged for best psychological effect?
3. Is the arrangement of the readers pictorially effective?
4. If levels are used, do they seem appropriate?

5. Are the readers sufficiently close together for the audience to see the reaction of other characters to the speaker?
6. If movement is used, is it unobtrusive? Does it serve a definite purpose for showing psychological relationships? For marking a transition of time or place?
7. Is the lighting effective? Can the faces of the readers be clearly distinguished? If lighting is used to pick out scenes and to mark transitions, is it handled smoothly and unobtrusively?
8. If music or other sounds are used, do they add to the total impact of the performance? Does the music interfere with audience-comprehension of the words?
9. Does the clothing of the readers aid in unifying the production? Does it contribute to pictorial effectiveness? Does it aid in suggesting who the characters are?

C. Script Evaluation

1. Does the material evoke a definite response from the audience? Is it likely to give the audience a "memorable experience"?
2. Does it have "wholeness"? Does it leave the audience with a sense of having participated in a complete experience?
3. Are the story line and characters clear?
4. Is the division of lines logical? Do the characters have lines that would have been more effective if given by the narrator? If a character speaks narration or description, is the material clearly from his point of view? Does the narrator have lines that would have been more effective if given by characters?
5. Does the script have "close-up" scenes—scenes that reveal details of emotion, of motivations, of environment, of characterization?

D. Evaluation of Script in Performance

1. How would you rate the script? Very interesting_____ Interesting_____Moderately interesting_____Dull_____ Very dull_____
2. What degree of empathic response did it evoke from you? Very strong_____Strong_____Medium strong _____Weak_____None_____
3. What degree of intellectual response did it evoke from you? Very strong_____Strong_____Medium strong_____Weak_____None_____
4. To what extent did the readers cause you to experience the situation, to see and to hear it? Excitingly so_____ Experienced it_____Moderately experienced_____ Didn't experience it_____

CHAPTER SIX

Readers Theatre
Is for Children Too

Readers Theatre has proved a delightful way to enrich the cultural life of a child. Wherever it has been tried, the results have been very gratifying. At Brooklyn College, a curtain-raiser presentation of Dr. Seuss' "Thidwick: The Big-Hearted Moose" proved more intriguing than the main feature, a puppet-show presentation of *Cinderella*. Carrie Rasmussen, well-known author of *Speech in the Elementary Classroom* and *Poetry for Children,* said in a recent letter to the authors, "I find storytelling does not seem to be used as much now as previously. This [Readers Theatre] is another way of bringing good literature, both old and new, to children. I saw this activity a year ago in Springfield, Missouri, tried it out with children in Madison, Wisconsin, and found it very successful."

The event to which she referred was a Readers Theatre performance for children given in the Tent Theatre on the campus of Southwest Missouri State College. Reacting to comments that almost nothing was presented in Springfield for the young and the very young, a group of college students prepared a forty-five minute program for children. Using the theme "Animals Are Only Human," these readers interpreted materials that varied from Joel Chandler Harris' *The Tar Baby* (which proved to be the children's favorite) to passages from Kenneth Grahame's *Wind in the Willows,* the portion concerning Mr. Toad. Encouraged by the success of this program, the interpreters presented a second one, entitled "Adventure, Fun, and Escapades," and were forced to add an extra performance to accommodate the enthusiastic overflow of children.

VALUES AND ADVANTAGES

Readers Theatre for children has many of the same values as storytelling to the young. Probably of foremost importance is its worth as sheer pleasure—as fun for fun's sake. For adults, as we have noted, this form brings dramatic joy and has the power to charm the mind. For children, these satisfactions are multiplied to an even greater degree. As an interpretive and participatory art, Readers Theatre quickens children's imaginations. It helps them appreciate language, affording models of desirable standards of usage and expression. Furthermore, since stories and poems, as well as plays, may be read and interpreted, it is one of the very best ways to introduce young people to the world's wealth of literary materials. With an introduction to literature through this medium, the child can be motivated to read and explore on his own initiative.

Those who perform for children are also enriched by the experience. One of the greatest satisfactions in Readers Theatre for children is that the interpreters have the opportunity of adapting to an audience whose response is given freely, frankly, and audibly. This feedback proves a potent stimulant to the readers; rapport develops between them and the audience. Because youthful audiences are among the most attentive, appreciative, and spontaneous, reading for them is a highly gratifying experience.

Clearly, Readers Theatre affords significant advantages both to the youthful audiences whose emotional and intellectual lives are enriched by the experience and to the interpreter who finds challenging opportunities to deepen his perception of audiences and to sharpen further his own skills and techniques. And there are still other advantages in using this particular medium with young people: Productions can be physically accommodated in classrooms and areas where standard stage plays could not be presented; and an interpretive program of this kind is, in several ways, less costly than a conventional children's theatre production that often demands elaborate costumes and settings.

SELECTING SUITABLE SCRIPTS

In Chapter 3, we discussed what literature is suitable for group reading and what criteria to use in selecting it. These same considerations are, to a great extent, applicable to the literary materials to be chosen for a young audience. The stories selected should create wonder and laughter, offer action and dramatic excitement, appeal to the imagination, and inspire a love of beauty both through the noble quality of the characters and through the beauty of the language. As we can probably recall from our own childhood, three favorite children's stories are "The Three Bears," "The Three Little Pigs," and "Little Red Riding Hood." In each of these, something is constantly happening; the events are familiar but still a bit strange, and the stories are full of repetition. These special qualities can serve as useful guides for seeking and selecting materials for Readers Theatre scripts to be presented to young audiences. Another helpful consideration is that sound effects have an exceptionally strong appeal for youthful listeners.

Poetry may also be used successfully in programs for children. Ruth Strickland, in her book *The Language Arts in the Elementary School*, says: "Being required to read poetry tends to decrease interest and build bad reading habits, while *listening* to poetry is, for most children, a pleasant and satisfying experience."[1] (The italics are ours.) May Hill Arbuthnot is another well-known writer who attests to the value of poetry in a child's life. Poetry, because it heightens, deepens, and enriches experience, "becomes a shining armor against vulgarity and brutality—taking as it does the experiences of the child's everyday world and giving them a new importance, a kind of glory that they did not have when they were just experiences."[2] Children enjoy the singing quality of poetry, the rhyme, the rhythm, the repetition of sounds, words, and phrases, the "playing with words." They also enjoy a good story element, and the stimulation supplied by colorful and evocative words. They receive great satisfaction from humorous poems such as A. A. Milne's "The King's Breakfast" and Eleanor Farjeon's "Hannibal Crossed the Alps." Old ballads like "Get Up and Bar the Door" also delight them.

DIRECTING THE SHOW FOR CHILDREN

The director approaches a Readers Theatre production for children in the same way he does material for adult audiences: he allows the text to guide him. Literature for young people usually depicts strongly drawn characters; the plots are highly imaginative and filled with strong action; the language has pronounced rhythmical patterns, abounding in concrete imagery and rich in sound devices, such as assonance, alliteration, and onomatopoeia. The interpreters should bring out and emphasize these qualities in their reading of the lines. The characters may be broadly drawn, even exaggerated, both in their personality traits and in their reactions to the events of the story. The readers may mimic the voices of the characters and utilize broad facial responses and strongly suggested movement. For example, the insect characters in *James and the Giant Peach* can slump their shoulders, draw in their heads, and try to make themselves small as they attempt to escape being hit by the hailstones hurled at them by the Snow Men. When the peach in which they are riding falls on top of the Empire State Building and is spiked upon its slender needle with a "squelch," all the readers may jolt backward and forward again as though they had suddenly stopped. When the huge peach tilts, causing these same characters to slide across the room, the readers may lean to one side and then draw themselves sharply upright as the insects supposedly collide with the opposite wall.

Drawing the audience in on the act

As children witness the performance, not only are they drawn into the action of the piece through empathic responses, but they may literally be

---

[1]Ruth Strickland, *The Language Arts in the Elementary School* (Boston: D. C. Heath & Company, 1951), p. 301.
[2]May Hill Arbuthnot, *Time for Poetry* (Glenview, Ill.: Scott, Foresman and Company, 1961), p. xxiii.

invited to participate in the action itself. For instance, during a reading of Bernard Waber's delightful "How to Lay an Egg," the children were asked to stand up to see if they had laid an egg. This delighted the youngsters and allowed them to rise and stretch. This "squirming" pause—a moment to wiggle a bit and relax—is necessary for young audiences; children can sit still only so long before they need to move. The knowing adapter will write passages into the script that will allow, even demand, this relaxing moment for his audience.

The young audience may not only participate in the movements but sometimes may also participate in the sounds of the script. In a performance of "Toad the Terror," taken from Kenneth Grahame's *Wind in the Willows,* the adapter of the script had added many "Peep, Peep's" for the horn of Mr. Toad's car. Each time Mr. Toad blew his horn, the children delightedly repeated these sounds with the reader. Brought joyously and excitingly to life, children's literature invites self-identification with the characters in their interesting adventures.

By their bodily response to this offstage scene from James and the Giant Peach, *a children's story by Roald Dahl, the readers epitomize the sense of "aliveness" so essential to good performance. Note, too, the ease and naturalness with which they handle the scripts.*

Readers Theatre Is for Children Too 81

Requisite skills for the reader

If youthful listeners are to be successfully involved in this heightened participation, the interpreters must first empathize with the text; they must embody the characters so vividly that the youngsters will be utterly convinced that these characters are indeed breathing, thinking, feeling, and moving with their bodies as genuine people do. If the readers themselves can activate and respond to the literature in this manner, if they can re-create the imagery, identifying with the flesh-and-blood characters and embodying their respective emotions and thoughts, they cannot fail to endow the literary material with pulsating life, to make of it a truly rewarding and unforgettable experience both for themselves and their young audience.

As in any Readers Theatre performance, the voice must be animated, alive, and expressive; and the interpreter should make effective use of pauses to "dig a hole" for an important idea or event before he "plants" it. Readers for children will find it useful to cultivate a "once upon a time" vocal quality which is characterized by tones of wonder, enthusiasm, and suspense. A sense of sharing which comes from direct eye contact is highly essential, but there must be no talking down to the audience. Excitement and a suggestion of something important about to be revealed must be reflected in the voice, the face, and the body; but the reader must not be overly dramatic.

The reading of each part of a story demands the same consideration as any Readers Theatre interpretation. Dialogue must create a believable character, and the reading of description must evoke mental pictures in the listener's mind, some close-up, some panoramic. The reading of narration must be very direct, warmly personal, and have a sense of progression— a quality of being "headed somewhere." For children especially, the narration ought to be touched with a hint of suspense, a suggestion of something marvelous about to occur.

Proximity—that is, a feeling of being physically close to people and events—will increase the degree of participation for the child audience. Just as children enjoy a play more if they can be close enough to see all the facial expressions, so they enjoy a Readers Theatre performance more if they are close to the interpreters. For this reason, it is often advisable that one or more of the readers make their initial appearance by approaching the stage through the audience. In this way they psychologically take the children onto the stage with them.

Even from the brief overview provided in this chapter, it should be apparent that Readers Theatre can be a highly dynamic and enjoyable way of broadening the lives of young people by allowing them a keener understanding of the world about them, of their fellow human beings, and of themselves. It introduces them to the wealth of literary materials that have been written especially for them. When vividly interpreted, this living canvas of literature creates for them an aesthetic adventure—a brush with beauty. Only now are educational, religious, and recreational leaders beginning to discover the vast potential in Readers Theatre for children. In the years immediately ahead, we believe it will find an ever widening use in schools, libraries, churches, youth camps, and recreational centers.

PART TWO

This Is the Way
It Was Done

Probably the most effective way to learn how to work in Readers Theatre would be to see many different programs directed by many different directors. Ideally, this observation-analysis procedure would involve the same material, adapted and directed by various directors; for Readers Theatre is, above all, creative. As we have emphasized, what is done with the selected material depends, of course, on many factors: the imagination of the director and his readers, the material they are interpreting, the room or auditorium where it is to be performed, and the point on the continuum between interpretation *per se* and theatre *per se* from which the director wishes to operate.

Unfortunately, opportunities to observe the work of others are often limited. Hence, we have provided here a number of descriptions, some brief and some detailed, of "how it was done." These descriptions are not intended to imply that this is *the* way in which a given presentation must be handled; rather, they are intended to show *one* way, *one* method chosen by *one* director because of the nature of the material. In some instances, the particular mode of staging was determined by arbitrary limitations, such as the available room, stage, or auditorium, the number of readers to be included in the cast, the required length of the program, the desired simplicity or elaborateness of presentation, and related considerations. In a few instances, different productions of the same material are discussed to demonstrate further the wide range of possibilities offered by this highly flexible medium.

As you have doubtless noted, many Readers Theatre presentations have already been referred to in Part I in order to enlarge a concept, illustrate a principle, or explain a particular method. For instance, as an illustration of the way in which introductory material may be given by a reader "in character," see again the account of the reading of *The Women's Town,* or *Pueblo de las Mujeres,* page 27. For suggestions on cutting a novel, restudy the notes on Ray Bradbury's *Dandelion Wine,* page 31. *Ebony Ghetto,* a script arranged from an autobiographical account of Frederick Ramsey, with poems of Langston Hughes and Negro folk songs, and, *Good Evening, Mr. Brecht,* a script composed of miscellaneous poems and other writings of Bertolt Brecht are described on page 36. Possible presentational procedures for "Is There a Doctor in the House?" can be found on page 37, and for *Iphigenia in Aulis* on page 58. Shorter summaries of various Readers Theatre productions have also been cited in Part I.

In the descriptions to follow, certain terms introduced in previous chapters are employed. For instance, *offstage focus* means that the readers placed the action in the midst of the audience; *onstage focus* means that the readers kept the scene on the playing area or stage, turning to the actual person being addressed and making direct eye contact with him. If both onstage and offstage focus were used in the same presentation, this is noted. Unless otherwise specified, all readers stayed within view of the audience at all times and made their exits and entrances by such suggestive or symbolic devices as rising from chairs and stools and returning to them, lowering their heads in order to disappear from a scene, or reversing the process by raising their heads, standing, or turning front —as the nature of the material and the style of the production required.

To clarify and simplify these descriptive summaries, certain established stage directions or "geographical" terms are employed. The chart below will help in visualizing the physical elements of the various productions. *Downstage* refers to the front of the stage or the playing area nearest the audience; *upstage,* to that part of the stage farthest away from the audience, toward the back wall. The chart indicates nine conventional divisions of the stage, with C meaning *Center;* DC, *Down Center;* UC, *Up Center;* R, *Right;* UR, *Up Right;* DR, *Down Right;* L, *Left;* UL, *Up Left;* and DL, *Down Left.*

FIGURE 4.   The geography of the playing space

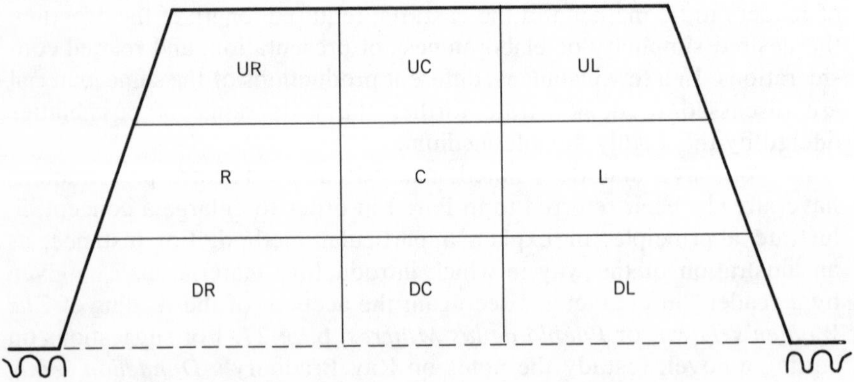

In Abraham Lincoln, *a play by John Drinkwater, simple sets, lights and shadows subtly blended, and suggested costuming were all sensitively combined. The reader groupings provided a strong sense of forward action and inventive variety.*

The selections included here were chosen because they represent various types of literature, because they illustrate different methods of adapting material, because they show a wide variety of approaches in presentation—for example, in staging and in lighting and costuming—and because each has proved successful in actual performance.

For the convenience of the reader, the following summary-descriptions are arranged alphabetically by title.

Abraham Lincoln   by John Drinkwater

A stage play in seven scenes, adapted and directed by Preston Magruder for presentation at the University of Arkansas.

This was a full-length Readers Theatre performance of Drinkwater's play on the life and death of Abraham Lincoln. The acting version called for thirty-four actors: thirty men and four women, plus "clerks, a messenger, an orderly, guards, ladies and gentlemen, officers, and a doctor." By assigning several roles to most of the readers, the director reduced the cast to six men and four women. The men wore black suits, white shirts, and black ties; the women wore floor-length black skirts and white blouses. The setting, also black, consisted of a platform across the back of the stage with a screen behind it at UC. By means of rear-view projection, a succession of dates, period pictures, and historical documents were flashed on this screen. The props included several black boxes and boxlike benches on which readers could sit. Entrances and exits were made from and to the backstage area. Stark white area-lighting picked up the playing locations. In short, this was a highly formal, stylized presentation.

The readers placed the focus offstage and did not relate to one another on the stage. However, a shift was made from offstage to onstage focus in the closing scene, enacted in "The small lounge of a theatre, April 14, 1865." Here, the formal concept was broken, and the director brought the action onstage. Briefly, this is what happened in the climactic scene: The audience at Ford's Theatre was relaxing in the lobby between the acts of *Our American Cousin,* the play they had been witnessing. They talked about the comedy and also about President and Mrs. Lincoln. Lincoln appeared and gave a brief speech. A boy passed through the crowd, calling out, "Last act, ladies and gentlemen." The President left to return to his box; and then, just as the rest of the audience started to return to their seats, a shot was heard backstage. In a horror-stricken voice, the maidservant Susan cried out, "Master, master! No, no, not my master!" Those theatre-goers remaining in the lobby were stunned, but slowly began to react. Others who had left the stage returned. Edwin M. Stanton, Secretary of War, came out from backstage and said, "Now he belongs to the ages"; and the curtain fell on the stunned onstage audience—a highly theatrical, effective climax.

The Barretts of Wimpole Street   by Rudolf Besier

A comedy-drama in three acts, adapted for Readers Theatre by Melvin R. White and presented at the University of Hawaii, as well as on the islands of Maui, Kauai, and Hawaii.

The stage play of this poignant love story called for a cast of seventeen characters and one dog. For Readers Theatre it was cut and condensed to run without intermission for one hour and fifteen minutes and to be read by four readers—a so-called "drama quartet." This was accomplished by emphasizing the main plot line, the love story of Elizabeth Barrett and Robert Browning and the opposition of her father, Edward Moulton-Barrett, to their romance. Most of the atmosphere scenes, such as the visits paid Elizabeth by her younger brothers and sisters, were left out. For example, in Act I of the play, both of the sisters, Henrietta and Arabel, talked at some length with Elizabeth. For the drama quartet, all necessary dialogue was given to Henrietta, and Arabel was excluded. When Octavius and five of Elizabeth's other brothers entered, all lines necessary to the story were given to Octavius, because, as the excitable stutterer, he definitely contrasted with the other characters who had been retained. The entire opening scene between Doctor Chambers and Elizabeth was eliminated, its content being revealed in later dialogue.

The four readers were assigned these roles:

MAN #1: Narrator and Edward Moulton-Barrett.
MAN #2: Octavius, Robert Browning, and Captain Surtees Cook.
WOMAN #1: Henrietta, Wilson, Bella Hadley, and Arabel.
WOMAN #2: Elizabeth Moulton-Barrett.

The adaptation was arranged so that no reader "talked with himself" in another role. Since Elizabeth was on the stage throughout, she was assigned only the one role.

The physical arrangement for successive presentations was changed in accordance with the room or auditorium in which the play was being read. When there was a front curtain and an apron stage in front of that, the curtain was opened several feet to serve as a door. A piano bench was placed in front of this opening, and it served as Elizabeth's "bed like a sofa." Since she is in bed throughout much of the play, it seemed best for her to arrange herself on the bench in a semireclining position. The other three readers entered and departed through the curtain opening. When a curtain was not available, four chairs were placed upstage of the bench and facing the audience, with the role-readers rising from and returning to these as the action required. However, since three of the readers had to read several roles, actual entrances and exits proved more effective.

Period costuming was not attempted, but the father wore a black suit and severe tie; Woman #1, who read many roles, a dress with some color; Robert Browning, a handsomely stylish suit; and Elizabeth, a colorful but not frivolous dress. In short, attire was chosen for its character-suggesting possibilities.

The Battle of the Sexes

A compiled script, arranged and directed by Elbert R. Bowen for presentation at Central Michigan University and, subsequently, for the National Convention of the Speech Association of America in Cleveland, Ohio.

The Battle of the Sexes was composed of widely diverse materials on a theme popular with everyone. Its elements ranged all the way from farce to tragedy, and it was intended primarily for entertainment. Although inspired by *A Thurber Carnival,* the format of this show encompassed a far greater variety of material and mode of performance.

Employing four women and five men, one of whom was a drummer, the program opened with salvos of short, pithy sayings, punctuated by drum rolls. This was followed by a section entitled "How It Really Began," taken from Elizabeth Goldsmith's "Ancient Pagan Symbols." The third section, "Resumption of Hostilities," continued the battle with lines from Dorothy Parker, Arthur Schopenhauer, Phyllis McGinley, and George Jean Nathan. The women had their say in the fourth section, "Feminine Artillery," with some lines from Edna St. Vincent Millay's poems and "Mehitabel Tries Companionate Marriage" from the pen of Don Marquis. In the fifth part, "In the Days of Chivalry," the antiquity of the battle was underscored by Alfred, Lord Tennyson's "Merlin and Vivien." The last part, "A Temporary Cessation (a la Victoria)," included a "Toast to Woman" by Chauncey Depew and "The Woman Who Understands" by E. J. Appleton.

The more serious aspects of the battle were detailed in the segment, "A New Campaign," through Susan B. Anthony's "Speech to Outstanding Legal Minds, 1873" and scenes from August Strindberg's *The Father.* George Bernard Shaw's idea of the Life Force as expressed in *Man and Superman* comprised the unit entitled "Mother Nature, the Peacemaker." In "The Battle Continues," taken from James Thurber's "A Couple of Hamburgers," the group shifted to a different style in staging. Turning from formal interpretation techniques, the performers gave this in the manner employed by Thornton Wilder in his one-act play, *The Happy Journey to Trenton and Camden;* that is, the readers, although seated in chairs which faced the audience, interacted directly with one another on the stage. And in the portion, "One Who Never Loses Hope," the reader of "The Song of Mehitabel," by Don Marquis, ran excitingly wild in a modern "Twist" rendition of her "life in the old dame yet." The program came to a well-wrought end with "Closing Salvos" from James Thurber. Throughout the production, the drummer used his drums in a very lively manner to emphasize, to punctuate, and to comment upon the proceedings. Combining a wide spectrum of materials with a stimulating variety of styles, *The Battle of the Sexes* was a highly entertaining program.

A Christmas Carol   by Charles Dickens

A Yuletide story, adapted for Readers Theatre by Melvin R. White and presented for the Progress Club of St. Andrew's Episcopal Church, College Park, Maryland.

Dickens' immortal Christmas story made an effective program, approximately forty-five minutes in length. Students from the University of

Maryland vividly brought to life the well-known characters: Scrooge, Bob Cratchit, the Ghost of Marley, the Ghost of Christmas Past, Sister Fan, Fezziwig, the Ghost of Christmas Present, Mrs. Cratchit, Tiny Tim, the Ghost of the Future, Fred, and five minor characters. The cast of sixteen characters, twelve men and four women, were portrayed by eight readers; the lead readers took but one role; the rest interpreted many characters. To keep the cast visually close together, the presentation was staged in pyramid style on a series of platforms and steps with several stools. The Narrator and Scrooge were in the front line of the pyramid; the various apparitions were placed at or near the top. The focus was consistently offstage; and each character stayed "alive" throughout the presentation, listening and reacting to the story, but becoming physically animated only when actually "in" a scene. The readers were attired in unobtrusive, modern clothing, and no special lighting effects were employed.

Eneas Africanus   by Harry Stillwell Edwards

A short story in letter-and-journalistic form, adapted for Readers Theatre by Melvin R. White for presentation at the University of Hawaii and at Brooklyn College.

This script is an example of the way in which letters and newspaper items can be adapted for Readers Theatre. However, it must be remembered that in *Eneas Africanus* these missives and reports are fictional. The setting consisted of a row of chairs, arranged in front of a large and prominently displayed wall map, which included an outline of the states of Tennessee, North Carolina, South Carolina, Mississippi, Alabama, Georgia, and Florida. Boldly marked on this map was the trail of Eneas' journey, spanning eight years and covering 3350 miles through these seven states, starting near Rome, Georgia, in 1864, and ending near Louisville, Georgia, in 1872. From time to time, as the story unfolded, the narrator pointed out on the map the various stops that Eneas made.

At the University of Hawaii, *Eneas Africanus* was read by eight readers, two men and six women, but this was a far from ideal casting since the script calls for fourteen men and four women. One lectern was placed DR and one DL, and the readers sat on chairs in between the two. The interpreters, generally using offstage focus, alternated between the two lecterns. The final scene, however, was played with the focus onstage, the readers relating to each other. Because this section of the story departs from the letters and news items and becomes a play with regular dialogue, the onstage focus emphasized this difference in form.

> *A compiled script, arranged and presented by Leslie Irene Coger and her Readers Theatre class at Southwest Missouri State College.*

Essentially a framework to show how miscellaneous selections may be incorporated into a unified program, the final script contained a comic essay, a poem, three short stories, and a passage from a novel. A train conductor unified the materials by commenting on the faces of the people riding in a railroad coach car. One reader from each "story" sat in the train, which was represented by two parallel rows of chairs at L. As the program began, the readers for the first selection, "Mrs. Bentley's Story," were seated on stools at C (except Mrs. Bentley). A spotlight came up on the area at R to single out a man in a conductor's hat. He looked at his watch, listened for the whistle of a train, nodded, and began to speak.

CONDUCTOR. Hello! Yep, she's right on schedule. I'm the conductor on that train over there, have been for thirty-five years. I was once asked why I like my job, and the first thing that popped into my head was—faces. As I take tickets, I like to look into the faces of the passengers, and sometimes I feel that each face wants to tell me why it is happy or sad. A person can fool his heart and his head, but he can never conceal his true feelings from his face. Every face has its story! Sometimes I pick out an interesting face and just let my imagination go. *(Train whistle is heard.)* Well, it's time to get aboard. This way, please. All aboard! *(Music comes up under his words.)* Take this little old lady, for example—that faraway, dreamy look. Do you suppose she's thinking of a new recipe for Thanksgiving, or is she remembering . . . remembering a yesteryear more important to her than today?

(The lights come up on MRS. BENTLEY *as she rises, walks from L to C, and joins the other* READERS *involved in her story. The music fades out.)*

READING: "Mrs. Bentley," from *Dandelion Wine* by Ray Bradbury.

(As the story ends, the lights go off; in the darkness, MRS. BENTLEY *and her* READERS *return to L; the stools they have been using are removed; a table and two chairs are brought in and arranged at C;* TWO LADIES *rise from their seats at L, cross to C, and seat themselves in the chairs. Meanwhile, the spotlight comes up again on the* CONDUCTOR *at R.)*

CONDUCTOR. Those two ladies ride this train at least once a week, but they usually ride in the club car. Wonder why they're riding in my car today? *(The lights come up on the* TWO LADIES *at table C.)*

READING: "How to Guess Your Age" by Corey Ford.

(At the conclusion, the lights go down on the TWO LADIES; *they return to their seats at L; the table and chairs are removed; a* MAN *enters to C, and the spotlight comes up on the* CONDUCTOR.)*

CONDUCTOR. Once this woman's face was happy, but it hasn't been the same since she lost her child.

(The lights brighten on the WOMAN *as she rises from her chair in the "train" at L, and crosses to the* MAN *at C.)*

READING: "Home Burial" by Robert Frost.

(The lights go down on the WOMAN *and the* MAN, *who remain at C. Three stools are brought in and positioned at C. Meanwhile, the spotlight comes up on the* CONDUCTOR.*)*

CONDUCTOR. Here's an interesting face. This old boy looks as if he's just put something over on somebody. There's age in that face, and I'll bet he's enjoying every minute of his life.

(The lights pick up an OLD MAN *as he rises from his seat in the "train" at L, walks to C, and joins the* MAN *and the* WOMAN. *The three seat themselves on the stools.)*

READING: "Heyday of the Blood" by Dorothy Canfield Fisher.

(When the reading is concluded, the light dims on the OLD MAN, *the* WOMAN, *and the* MAN. *In the darkness, the* MAN *disappears; the* WOMAN *and the* OLD MAN *cross to L and resume their former seats on the "train." A* BOY *and a* GIRL *enter and take positions at C. Meanwhile, the spotlight comes up on the* CONDUCTOR.*)*

CONDUCTOR. Now here's a young man who doesn't look too happy. My guess is there's a girl in this boy's story somewhere. And from the looks of him, I'd say his plans didn't exactly work out.

(The spotlight comes up on ANOTHER BOY *as he rises from his seat at L, walks to C, and joins the* BOY *and the* GIRL.*)*

READING: "Love Is a Fallacy" by Max Shulman.

(The lights fade out on the group at C. In the darkness, the BOY *and the* GIRL *disappear;* ANOTHER BOY *returns to L and resumes his seat; and* FIVE MEN *and the* SECOND WOMAN *enter and take positions at C. Meanwhile, the spotlight comes up again on the* CONDUCTOR.*)*

CONDUCTOR. Here's a face that epitomizes drudgery, toil of the earth; yet, there's something in this plain face that shows that the girl has been touched by beauty.

(The light comes up on the SECOND GIRL *as she rises from her seat on the "train" at L, walks to C, and joins the* FIVE MEN *and the* SECOND WOMAN.*)*

READING: "So Beautiful with Shoes" by Wilbur Daniel Steele.

(At the end, the lights fade out on the SECOND GIRL, *the* FIVE MEN, *and the* SECOND WOMAN; *and the spotlight comes up on the* CONDUCTOR. *There is a long, mournful sound of a train whistle. The* CONDUCTOR *glances at his watch with an air of finality.)*

CONDUCTOR. Yep . . . right on schedule. *(The train whistles again.)*

Every Face Tells a Story 95

Feiffer Sketches

> *A compiled script, arranged by Jerry Darnell and Leslie Irene Coger and presented at Southwest Missouri State College and at Joplin High School.*

This full-length program was composed of the captions for Feiffer's cartoon strips combined with his short stories: "Passionella," "Munro," "George's Moon," and "Boom." The college production was simply staged with stools and lecterns; the high school production added four large screens placed at the rear of the stage as background. On one side of each screen was the title of the short story; on the reverse side was a cartoon sketch of the major character involved in that particular segment. As a given story was presented, two girls—in the cast of ten—changed the title side to the cartoon side. Thus, at the end of the program, the four large cartoons comprised the back "wall" of the stage.

The characters in each story were appropriately costumed. In "George's Moon," for instance, the four readers were dressed as people from outer space and wore wigs to match their gaily colored costumes. These readers sat in spaceships with the letters *U F O* on the sides. In the short cartoon numbers which had no words, "The Dance to Spring" and "The Dance to Autumn," a girl performed a dance interpretation of the cartoon as popcorn "snow" fell in the former, and one large leaf floated from above in the latter. The readers used varied groupings, depending upon the material being interpreted; and sometimes two people walked forward to deliver short witticisms. Munro, the little boy, sat on a low stool surrounded by the army officers, with the narrator sitting slightly to one side; Passionella and Prince Charming stood during their sequences.

The Food of Love

> *A compiled script, arranged and directed by Norman DeMarco and Earl McCarroll at the University of Arkansas.*

Under the title *The Food of Love*, taken from a line in *Twelfth Night*, a series of scenes concerning love from Shakespeare's plays were combined to produce an effective presentation. Transitions from one episode or scene to another were achieved by quotations from Shakespearian sonnets and by electronic sound effects created by Mr. DeMarco. The set was eye-pleasing, with a low platform at R and a high one at L. During the blackouts between scenes, various "period" benches and stools were brought to the stage area at C and moved about as needed. Falstaff's scene was played at C; Romeo and Juliet's balcony scene was performed at L, using the high platform; solo speeches were read almost everywhere on the stage; and in each instance, spotlights singled out the playing area. Tights and simple slip-on jackets of various colors provided each man with attire suggestive of the period, and the women's floor-length skirts with blouses also suggested Elizabethan times. Lear was in black; Juliet, in white. This stylized clothing added appreciably to the visual aspects of the production.

The Grass Harp by Truman Capote

A novel, adapted and directed by William D. Bonham for presentation at Southern Illinois University. Marion Kleinau provided the following information on the adaptation.

In this production the director attempted to give a visual presentation of memory, to have the audience recollect with the central character, Colin. Colin was seated DR, script in hand; and his focus was always offstage, toward the audience. He began his journey into memory, and the other characters appeared as he mentioned them, entering from UC with scripts in hand and moving to chairs placed on a mid-stage plane, slightly toward L. Thus, from the audience's viewpoint, the other characters were behind Colin and to his left. As the characters entered, some of them began to speak and soon "took over" in the remembered scene. When Colin was part of the scene, he spoke his lines directly front, never turning to look at the others. They, however, looked directly at the person they spoke to, whether this be Colin or one another. As Colin remembered, he did not go back into the past, but let the remembered scenes materialize in the present. In other words, Colin always remained in the present, even when he spoke lines from the past. There was no movement among the readers except entrances, exits, and one major shift of positions.

Happily Sedated

A compiled script, arranged by Leslie Irene Coger and presented at Southwest Missouri State College.

The idea for this script came from the phrase *happily sedated*, found in an editorial by Norman Cousins in *Saturday Review*. Taking the theme that we human beings are sitting on powder kegs without being aware of it, the compiler used four selections: "Boom," by Jules Feiffer, emphasized the problem of the Bomb, as did Philip Wylie's "The Answer"; the threat of communism was treated in James Clavell's "The Children's Story"; the Negro situation in *They Call It Freedom;* and original

sketches and songs bridged the four. The compiler tied the program together with Carl Sandburg's poem "Four Preludes on Playthings of the
Wind." The first two sections of the poem were used for the opening; the
remainder served as framework for the closing portion of the show,
thereby bringing the script full circle. The readers acted as a chorus in the
opening and the closing number and took various roles in the presentation of the stories.

The stage was arranged with platforms, ramps, and stools, but no
lecterns. As visual background, projections were thrown onto a scrim:
rat footprints (for Sandburg's poem), a bomb explosion, and the American eagle, which was eventually replaced by the hammer and sickle
emblem for "The Children's Story." The color on the scrim changed to
fit the mood of the selections. In "Boom," placards carried by two girls—
such as "Big Black Specks Are Good for You!"—reinforced the TV
Commentator's remarks. For the opening and closing segments of the
program, the whole stage was used; for the stories, only specific areas.
In "The Children's Story," a pyramidal arrangement of the readers
placed the teacher at the top, with the children below her. (See p. 53.)

In this scene from the compiled script, Happily Sedated, *the faces and
physical attitudes of the characters suggest action filled with verve
and vitality, as they project their varying responses to the speaker in
the imagined scene offstage.*

The Importance of Being Earnest by Oscar Wilde

A play, adapted for Readers Theatre by Melvin R. White and presented at Brooklyn College.

Much as one may enjoy the period costumes and settings of this comedy of manners, the characters and their dialogue are the most important ingredients. Thus, *The Importance of Being Earnest* readily lends itself to Readers Theatre presentation. By cutting out the subplot involving Miss Prism and Dr. Chasuble, the presentational time was shortened to approximately one hour. The cast, comprised of faculty members, included three men, four women, and a narrator who could be played by either a man or a woman. After moving readers about from chair to chair in early rehearsals, the director finally chose a permanent seating arrangement: from stage R to stage L—Lane, Algernon, Jack, Gwendolyn, Cecily, Lady Bracknell, Miss Prism, and Narrator. The readers were seated in a straight line across an ordinary room without a stage or platform of any kind. In order to be seen, characters stood up when they were in the scene, read to a focus offstage, and sat down when they left the scene. All dialogue involving action and all movements or activity usually designated as stage business, such as the butler preparing the table for tea and serving cucumber sandwiches, were eliminated. The readers' attire was unobtrusive rather than character-suggesting.

An Irish Faustus by Lawrence Durrell

A stage play, adapted and produced for Readers Theatre by Elbert R. Bowen at Central Michigan University. Mr. Bowen provided the following information concerning the production.

Previous Readers Theatre programs at Central Michigan had been performed in a ballroom with audiences of three hundred to four hundred persons. *An Irish Faustus* was scheduled for an auditorium seating fourteen hundred, thus losing intimacy. Upon reading the play, the designer-technician saw it as an ideal vehicle for rear-screen projection. To quote Mr. Bowen directly: "You cannot have readers reading from behind lecterns in front of a big-screen projection in full color and expect a play to come through. Hence, we left the scripts and devised a 'skeletal' degree of portrayal which could hold attention."

The slide projections consisted of scenes, abstractions, and—in one instance—action. In the latter, the readers read, while the slides suggested the activity. For example, as the executioner drove a stake through the heart of the sleeping vampire, a symbolic stake came down through the abstract forest; and when the stake "hit bottom," the screen became a huge blob of red blood. Hellmouth, as used in medieval drama, was projected with a silhouette of Faustus and Mephisto against it. Other than the slide projections, the only physical elements were two chairs, two stools, and a table. Mr. Bowen concluded:

> Durrell's rhetoric came through for those who were interested; the slides fascinated those who did not wish to bother with the play. I was proud of the show but not exactly of the production; I'd like to try the play back in the ballroom with the possible intimacy of the smaller audience. . . . When Readers Theatre attempts the spectacle of big-house production, it runs the risk of losing its own inherent advantages and suffering the pitfalls of another form.

Little Moon of Alban   by James Costigan

A television and stage play, adapted for Readers Theatre by Mr. and Mrs. A. D. Breneman and presented at the University of Hawaii.

Two lecterns, side by side at C, served the one man and one woman who read this touching drama. The cut script was primarily concerned with the love story of Brigid Mary Mangan and Lt. Kenneth Boyd. When narration was needed—whether to reveal the location of the action, to disclose the identity of the characters involved, or to condense the story—one of the readers would supply it. Usually, this was determined by whether a male or female voice was to pick up the story immediately following the narration. If two or more characters were involved, sometimes one reader "talked to himself"; in these instances, the woman reader would interpret all the female roles, and the man would read all male roles. These exchanges, however, were kept to a strict minimum; the major part of this Readers Theatre adaptation was made up of scenes involving only the lovers. Much of the remaining story was developed through narration. The readers, in placing the focus offstage, did not look at each other; but they did react to one another as characters in the *imagined* scenes. Since the two readers handled so many different roles, they used no special make-up, costuming, scenery, sound effects, music, or lighting—just two scripts and two lecterns.

The Little Prince   by Antoine de Saint-Exupéry

A children's story, adapted for Readers Theatre by Marion Kleinau and produced under her direction at Southern Illinois University. Mrs. Kleinau furnished the notes on this production.

The central narrator, the Little Prince, moved between the past and the present—that is, he played himself in the present as well as in the past.

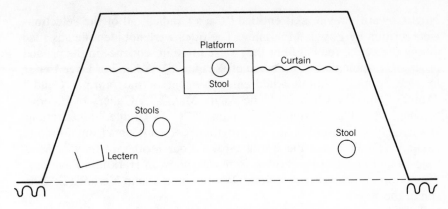

FIGURE 5. *The Little Prince* floor plan

When he was playing in the present, he stationed himself at a reading stand DR and used a script. But as a "remembered" scene began to materialize, he would leave the stand and the script, walk into the scene being enacted on the stage, and become a part of it. All other characters were "off book"; that is, they had memorized their lines and were using some movement of a limited nature. Original music was written for the show. The staging was very simple; three stools, one platform, and a reading stand were arranged as shown in the diagram above. The platform and stool UC were used for the readers who represented the Planets. As the Little Prince traveled from planet to planet, he moved in a circle around the stage. For instance, the reader on the stool UC moved off, and another took his place to become the inhabitant of the next planet, and so on. Mrs. Kleinau observed, "I thought at first this might be a little 'corny,' but the music was good and the characterization so sensitive that it carried quite well." The other three stools served as playing areas on Earth and on the planet of the Little Prince.

Mainly Mirth, Mostly McGinley

A compiled script made up of materials written by Phyllis McGinley, Dorothy Parker, and Noel Coward, arranged and directed by Melvin R. White and presented at the University of Hawaii and at various branches of the Library of Hawaii.

Mainly Mirth, Mostly McGinley consisted of seventeen short selections read by two readers. With the exception of Dorothy Parker's "Men" and

Noel Coward's revue skit entitled "Cat's Cradle," all of the selections were written by Phyllis McGinley. The titles were not identified as such during the actual reading; but they were listed in sequence in the printed program: "Apologia," "A Choice of Weapons," "A Kind of Love Letter to New York," "About Children," "Lament of the Normal Child," "Men," "Nursery Rhyme," "The Angry Man," "A Gallery of Elders," "Epitaphs for Three Prominent Persons," "Cat's Cradle," "Reflections at Dawn," "Lines Scribbled on a Program," "Two Poems from a Private Room," "Don't Shake the Bottle, Shake Your Mother-in-Law," "Message Found in a Bottle Thrown from a Window in Harkness Pavilion," "Speaking of Television," "Notes Written on a Damp Veranda," "Season at the Seashore."

Since both readers were temporarily handicapped, one with a recent eye operation and the other with a sprained ankle necessitating crutches, it seemed advisable to use a living-room setting consisting of two comfortable chairs, one for each reader, with a floor lamp between and slightly behind them. As the program started, the Woman was discovered seated in one of the chairs, reading a magazine. There was a knock at the door, and the program began with this dialogue:

WOMAN. *(Reacting to the knock at the door.)* Come in.

MAN. *(Entering diffidently.)* Miss Bentley? Miss Lucie Bentley?

WOMAN. *(With a note of inquiry.)* Yes?

MAN. *(Coming a bit closer.)* I don't know if you remember me. I'm Mel White.

WOMAN. *(Pleased.)* Oh, yes, Mel. I had heard you were in town. How do you do?

MAN. Just fine, thank you, in spite of these crutches. But, Lucie, I've heard some things about you that made me wonder . . .

WOMAN. *(Indicating other chair.)* Please sit down, Mel, and tell me what this is all about. I've been having a little trouble with this eye, and . . . well, you may not find me in the best of moods these days.

MAN. *(Laughs slightly, seats himself.)* Yes. I've heard recently you've been making rather . . . what shall I say . . . well, caustic comments on various subjects.

WOMAN. *(Also laughing a little.)* Perhaps I have. But . . .

This brief introduction led into the Woman's reading of Phyllis McGinley's "Apologia." Then, with dialogue written to introduce successive selections, the Man and the Woman presented the various literary items. Most of the selections were divided and developed as dialogue between the two readers, who—with one exception—remained seated throughout. For "Cat's Cradle," in spite of their infirmities, the readers left their comfortable chairs and went DC "into the garden," returning to their seats at the end of this skit.

The Marriage of Mr. Mississippi   by Friedrich Duerrenmatt

A play, adapted for Readers Theatre by Elbert R. Bowen and presented at Central Michigan University.

The following notes were provided by the director, Mr. Bowen:

The style of any production should derive chiefly from the material to be communicated. This little known play is a grotesque drama similar in some ways to *Skin of Our Teeth*. The key to "grotesque" is "incongruity," and we adopted "consistent incongruity" as one of the two keynotes of our style of performance. I saw the play as a sort of *romp,* and so I chose the incongruous [just] to be playful: a mixture of reading and acting. Not really acting. I called it "playing at acting," as children do play at acting. The performers sometimes left their lecterns and manuscripts to play at their roles.

Furthermore, because the only female character in the play is described by another character as "not one but three women" we decided to reveal the different sides of this woman by having a different woman play her in each act: Vanessa 1 (a blond in black—to suggest a pure woman ostensibly in mourning), Vanessa 2 (a brunet in very tight white—to suggest the carnal woman who is ostensibly an angel in the script), and Vanessa 3 (a redhead in red—to suggest what the real Vanessa is revealed to be in the third act). The chief comic-tragic character, Count Bodo, says that the author has deliberately made him ridiculous. We made him doubly so by giving him the only costume in the production: a white jacket, stethoscope, head mirror, and old-fashioned smoked glasses. At the end of the play, he spoke to Don Quixote, standing on a table in helmet, white jacket, and spectacles, defying the world and brandishing a broken lance.

Doing "Mississippi" was an intriguing experience for all of us who were involved with it. I felt the production had an artistic unity which—on the surface—appeared to be missing.

Mary and the Fairy   by Norman Corwin

A radio script, adapted for Readers Theatre by Melvin R. White and presented at Brooklyn College.

This funny, frothy, and imaginative radio script has repeatedly proved its audience-pleasing possibilities when presented in Readers Theatre style. The first time it was given at Brooklyn College, a cast of ten readers and a narrator sat on chairs lined up across the front of the room. In addition to the main roles of Mary Pooter, the five-and-ten-cent-store clerk and the at times impatient Fairy, the cast included a handsome but not too bright Hollywood actor, a fake Prince, a Waiter, and such other characters as The Letter and The Ad. Mary and the Fairy were assigned to chairs at C. They stood during their scenes, as did all of the readers when they were participating in the story. This was almost mandatory because

This presentation of Pamela Travers' Mary Poppins employed a number of suggested settings, two of which are shown here. The lower photo illustrates the ingenious handling of the "hanging from the ceiling" scene.

the performance was given in a room without a platform or stage, thus putting the cast on the same level as the audience. By standing, the readers could be seen more easily. However, no movement other than standing and sitting was used.

The second performance of *Mary and the Fairy* at Brooklyn College had the advantage of a stage. In this presentation, the narrator stood DR and had a lectern on which to place his script. Mary and the Fairy used two chairs UC for their scenes together. Other characters entered from backstage on cue. For example, Mary met Ronald and Reggie DRC, and special lights were focused on that area while the rest of the stage remained in darkness. Later, Mary read her scene with the Prince at DLC, again with area lighting. Pinpoint spotlights focused on the narrator, The Ad, and The Letter; and there was area lighting on Mary and the Fairy at UC. This special lighting, the exits and entrances, and the movements to and from various playing areas combined to create a more mobile, theatrical production.

Mary Poppins by P. L. Travers

> *A children's story, adapted by Charles Closser, Jr., and presented at the University of Missouri. Frances McCurdy provided the information about this presentation.*

Except for the roles of Mary Poppins, Michael Banks, and Jane Banks, the readers assumed multiple roles. Suggestive costuming was used: Mrs. Corry's daughters wore aprons over the black skirts and white blouses that formed the basic costume for all the girls, and the policeman wore a coat and policeman's cap in the park scene. On stage throughout the performance was the suggestion of a nursery setting, consisting of an elevated platform with stools and a large cutout of a bureau; but from time to time, other cutouts were dropped from the grid or rolled on from the wings. A merry-go-round, with silhouette horses and a platform that could revolve on wheels, was rolled on for the scene where Mary Poppins leaves and afterwards was rolled out through the back curtains.

In the scene where Mary and the children visit Mr. Turny on the ceiling, the participants hung upside down on four firmly based chairs. In this position, of course, the readers had to exercise special care to make their words understandable to the audience. At the opening of each scene, Mary Poppins crossed to a large "book" at the side of the stage and announced the impending episode as she turned a page and placed a card with the title of the scene in a special slot. The readers did not use scripts but delivered their lines from memory.

The Mikado   by Sir William S. Gilbert and Sir Arthur Sullivan

*An operetta, adapted for Readers Theatre by Melvin R. White
and produced at Brooklyn College and the University of Arkansas.*

Except for the overture, which provided aural atmosphere before the
show started, this reading version did not include any of the music of
The Mikado; instead, it concentrated on the lines, the characters, and
the plot as the important ingredients. Presented first at Brooklyn College
in a one-hour version, it was done very simply. The script called for a
cast of eight leads (four men and four women), a male chorus, and a
female chorus—both small in number. Because the reading was presented
in an auditorium with a narrow stage and no backstage space, only the
leads were provided with chairs on the stage; the choruses had chairs
out front in the auditorium itself but as close to the right and the left sides
of the stage as possible. For this formal and simple reading, all the men
wore business suits; the women, street dresses. No physical action was
used, other than having the interpreters stand when "in the scene" and
sit when not. Consequently, no special lighting was designed; the reading
area had only general illumination; and the houselights remained on
throughout. No scenery changes were involved, and no props were provided.

At the University of Arkansas, *The Mikado* was offered as a modified
stage production which involved the use of scripts, simple sets, colorful

FIGURE 6.   *The Mikado* floor plan

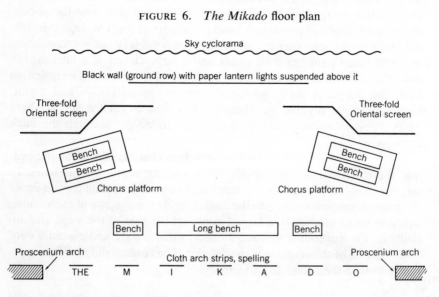

Imaginatively but simply mounted and costumed, this production of the Gilbert and Sullivan operetta, The Mikado, *employed dual platforms and a series of low benches. The swift grouping and regrouping of the performers helped sustain a lively pace throughout.*

attire, and elaborate stage lighting. To enhance the production's effectiveness, oriental "rainbow" colors were chosen for most costumes. The chorus of men wore light summer trousers with knit shirts of many colors; the chorus of women wore bright summer dresses. The Mikado was attired in a green summer suit and a brilliant, red shirt. Katisha was garbed in a dull, unattractive brown dress in order to add to her size and apparent maturity. Ko-Ko wore black trousers with an off-white shirt. Pooh-Bah also wore dark colors. No suggestion of oriental costuming was attempted, merely the overall effect of bright, splashy colors. Oriental costuming can be used, however, to good advantage. For instance, in another performance of this adaptation, given at Southern Illinois University, the entire cast was costumed in kimonos and wore Japanese wigs and make-up.

For the Arkansas production, an oriental, simple and inexpensive, yet very effective set was designed. (See the illustrations on pp. 106-107.) Each of the screens was made from four regular-sized flats, painted in yellow-gold with designs of Japanese trees as decor. The back wall and the two chorus platforms were painted black, as were the seven benches —two on each of the chorus platforms, one long one DC, one short one DR, and another short one DL. However, simple designs in gold and red were painted on the fronts of the three main benches, those at DC, DR, and DL. Above the back wall were three huge paper lanterns, suspended from a bright-colored, pagoda-shaped halter. Hanging in the place of the front curtain were seven separate strips of material, each in a different bright color and each with one of the letters of the title, *THE MIKADO*. During the overture, as the houselights were dimmed out, spotlights singled out the letters; and then, when the cast entered, these title-strips were pulled up out of sight. Dark drapes at the sides of the stage masked off the backstage area and permitted entrances and exits.

Stage lighting was used to focus attention on the most important area or actor at all times and to enhance the rainbow effect. The chorus platform-areas were illuminated when the choruses were reading and were dimmed out when they were not "in the scene" but were sitting quietly with bowed heads. In short, conventional stage lighting was used, adding to the beauty of the reading environment and the visual appeal of the actors. No conventional properties were employed in either the Brooklyn or the Arkansas production. For example, when the death certificate was mentioned, the reader merely held the top page of his manuscript above and away from the rest of his script, thus suggesting rather than using an actual certificate.

In each production, consistency was the important thing. The completeness of the sets, costumes, make-up, lights, and properties depended upon the extent to which the director wished to elaborate his production. In one instance, the reading was a simple one with ordinary chairs, everyday suits and dresses, and no special lights; in the other, it was a rather completely staged affair with many theatrical effects. But in each case, the director decided exactly which style he wanted to follow, and the presentation was consistent with that decision.

Our Town   by Thornton Wilder

> *A three-act stage play, adapted by Melvin R. White for a production at Brooklyn College.*

Adapting *Our Town* for this medium presented no problems initially, since Wilder originally wrote his play without formal sets and properties and used many other Readers Theatre conventions, as we have come to know them. The attempt to simplify it worked well until the final scene, the cemetery episode. After some experimenting, the director concluded that the most effective way to handle this was Wilder's original method: the dead were seated on chairs in the graveyard; and to attend the funeral, the various "living" characters and mourners entered from backstage with umbrellas. Up to this point, all of the readers had been kept on the stage throughout. During the intermission before the

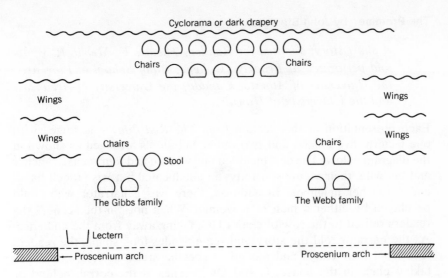

Cyclorama or dark drapery

Chairs

Chairs

Wings

Wings

Wings

Wings

Chairs

Chairs

Stool

The Gibbs family

The Webb family

Lectern

Proscenium arch

Proscenium arch

FIGURE 7. *Our Town* floor plan

last act, however, the chairs were rearranged for the burial episode; and for the remainder of the play, entrances and exits were employed as indicated by the playwright. Memorization seemed somehow more appropriate and advisable in this concluding segment, whereas scripts had been used in the preceding acts.

As indicated in the above diagram, the basic stage arrangement was simple and easily achieved. Two rows of two chairs each at R and DR and at L and DL served as the homes of the Gibbs and Webb families, respectively. Church and wedding scenes were placed UC. Characters also came from this upstage area to meet the Webbs, the Gibbs, or other characters at DR, DL, or DC. Some of the scenes on Main Street were played at UC, others at DC. The moonlight scene between George and his sister Rebecca was read at and on the stool near the Gibbs' home. Occasionally the Stage Manager moved chairs to accommodate the scene. For example, he put two stools together at UC for the ice cream soda episode, adjusted the position of the chairs for the choir rehearsal scene, and rearranged them for the graveyard scene in the last act. Illumination was flexibly designed so that specific lighting could focus attention on the particular area being used in each episode. For instance, while a scene was progressing in the Webb house at L and DL, only the four chairs in that area were lighted. Generally, readers wore their own clothes; but costumes were subtly suggested by choosing colors and styles appropriate to the different characters without striving to achieve full and actual period costuming.

The Promise   by John Steinbeck

> *A short story, adapted for Readers Theatre by Melvin R. White
> and performed at Brooklyn College; Banff School of Fine Arts,
> the University of Alberta, Canada; the University of Arkansas;
> and the University of Hawaii.*

Each presentation of this section from *The Red Pony* was staged with
one lectern, five chairs, and two rather tall stools arranged as shown in
the diagram below. The cast included one woman and four men: a rancher
and his wife, their young son Jody, an uneducated but wise ranch hand,
and a rancher neighbor. In addition, there was a narrator who could
be played by either a man or a woman. When not "in the scene," the
readers retired to the row of chairs UC, facing away from the audience.
As the narrator told the story and the episodes took shape, the readers
rose from their chairs and moved to specific areas, as follows: scenes
taking place in the house, C and DC; scenes at the corral, behind or
slightly to the right of the two tall stools at L and DL, which served as
the corral fence; and to the left of these stools, the barn area where the
colt was born.

The narrator read to the audience but observed the proceedings on the
stage. The readers kept the focus onstage throughout the story and usually performed with their scripts in hand. In one production, however,
only the narrator read from his script; the readers memorized their dialogue. Initially, this adaptation was given as a Readers Theatre demon-
stration at Brooklyn College and was presented in a corner of a lounge
in the Student Center, with the audience sitting informally here and
there about the large room. The cast wore their regular school clothes.

FIGURE 8.   *The Promise* floor plan

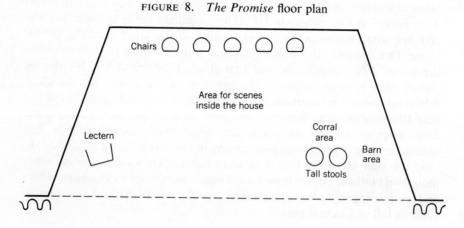

In a later presentation at the Banff School of Fine Arts, in the heart of the Canadian ranch country, a stage was used; and the cast wore their own ranch clothes, including boots and other cowboy paraphernalia. As far as the director could determine, it proved no more effective than earlier productions without special costuming.

Six Times Four

A compiled script, arranged and directed by Vincent C. Brann for presentation at the University of Massachusetts. Mr. Brann provided the following information concerning the production.

This anthology of readings was selected for stage presentation from the first six volumes of *The Massachusetts Review,* a quarterly of literature, the arts, and public affairs, which is published on the campus of the University of Massachusetts as a joint venture of the University and its three neighboring institutions: Amherst College, Mount Holyoke College, and Smith College. The twenty-four issues were searched for materials appropriate for oral reading; and the result was a two-part program with one intermission, Part One being approximately fifty minutes in length, and Part Two slightly shorter. The director's notes suggest the provocative and informative nature of the program and the wide diversity of its materials:

PART ONE
1. "A Few Local Friends." Poems by local poets, plus an opening remark by Emerson and a poem about the most famous local poet, Emily Dickinson.
2. This unit, based on the "Centenary Gathering" for Thoreau, consisted of two poems about him, a letter from Martin Luther King concerning Thoreau's influence on him, and a juxtaposed fictional-journalistic description of a lynching in Mississippi.
3. "The Poets at Random" section included a lecture by W. H. Auden, a poem and a letter by William Carlos Williams, and four "jazz" poems by Keith Gunderson.
4. Offered here was a humorous and slightly sentimental interview with Sean O'Casey a few months before his death. Also included was some of Yeats' poetry and, prior to intermission, a witty conclusion consisting of a poem by Leonard E. Nathan called "A Reading of History."

PART TWO
1. The second half of the program opened with rear-screen projections of John Heartfield's vigorously anti-Fascist "photomontages" from the 1930's which served as a background for Lincoln Kirstein's "Festspielhaus," a bitter poem about returning to Bayreuth after the war.
2. This section offered some humorous poems, including two by E. E. Cummings.

3. To provide contrast, this unit included three short, critical excerpts from essays on the arts in our time, five short "portrait" poems, and—as a finale—a frankly vaudevillian revue entitled "The National Hymn Contest," a parody of the efforts of a handful of "living" poets (living in 1861, that is) as they tried to write a new national anthem to replace Francis Scott Key's "The Star-Spangled Banner."

Eleven readers, six men and five women, were used in this presentation. The stage was set with two separate stacks of six-inch platforms: four levels at R, the top one twenty-four inches above the stage floor; at L, only three levels. A short length of railing was placed around the top platform at L. Ten stools—eighteen, twenty-four, and thirty inches in height —and one Windsor chair were provided. All of these were stained a dark wood shade. The director described the physical arrangement and the action as follows: "I moved the readers about, making different groupings on and off platforms; sometimes they stood, sometimes they sat on stools to read; and sometimes they sat on the platforms. . . . Some of the readers left the stage from time to time; I did not keep all eleven on stage continually."

A rear screen, covered by a gray curtain when not in actual use, served for showing a few photos of Thoreau, a Ben Shahn sketch of William Carlos Williams, and the photomontages. The entire production was played well downstage, on an extended apron, with nothing placed more than ten feet back of the front curtain-line of the stage.

The men wore tuxedos; the women, long dresses especially designed for the presentation. The only jewelry was a simple strand of pearls worn by one of the women. Area lighting was fluidly employed to emphasize the two separate stacks of platforms, the forestage, or the entire stage, as needed. One pinpoint spotlight illuminated the lynching reading, and there were occasional blackouts between units for transition and mood. In addition, a few transitions, possibly a half dozen in all, were accomplished with mood music, but the music never underscored the reading. The program opened with the fanfare from the first movement of Aaron Copeland's "Music for the Theatre," and—to comment on "The National Hymn Contest" parodies—concluded with Charles Ives' witty parody, "Variations on 'America'" for the organ. Each reader carried a complete script in a loose-leaf binder with a soft cover. No reading stands were used at any time during the performance.

Skin of Our Teeth by Thornton Wilder

A three-act stage play, adapted by Melvin R. White for presentation at the University of Hawaii, Brooklyn College, and Banff School of Fine Arts, University of Alberta.

Many of the conventions and devices used by Thornton Wilder in his plays are the same as or similar to those employed in Readers Theatre; for this reason, his plays easily lend themselves to group-reading interpretation. As presented on the conventional stage, *Skin of Our Teeth* is often extremely theatrical, with trick sets, animal characters, and elaborate costumes. This theatricalism has sometimes confused an audience not acquainted with the play, for they tend to watch the fascinating creatures and stage effects rather than concentrate on the dialogue and its meaning. Readers Theatre, by its very nature, tends to trim away the trappings, and perhaps this is one reason why this story of man's ability to escape destruction "by the skin of his teeth" has proved so successful and appealing in its Readers Theatre presentations in the United States and Canada.

In the various productions, the focus (with few exceptions) was onstage, with the characters relating directly to each other. The exceptions were at those places in the original acting edition where Wilder specifically called for performer contact with the audience. Some readers, their lines

This adaptation of Thornton Wilder's Skin of Our Teeth *involved few scenic elements and little costuming. Reality was achieved principally through lighting effects and the imaginative capacities of a participating, rather than a passive, audience.*

and various mob-scene characters—came up onto the stage from the audience.

In the Hawaiian production, no special lighting was possible because of technical limitations; in Canada, no special lighting was used because the presentation was given in a sun-filled music-rehearsal room; in Brooklyn, special lighting was used to establish place and evoke mood. Also in the Brooklyn production, special sound effects of storm and wind were provided for the flood scene, whereas in the other presentations the audience had to use their imagination. Only a suggestion of costuming was ever used: Mrs. Antrobus dressed a bit matronly; Mr. Antrobus, somewhat somberly; the Fortune Teller, with a small shawl; Sabina, in a tight-fitting red dress; and the children, in clothing appropriate for the young. Henry, for example, wore a shirt and trousers in Act I, adding his coat later when he was a man returning from the war.

The cast for this play is large; but even so, it was possible to keep most of the readers onstage in two rows of chairs. There were a few exceptions, of course, including those who made their entrances from the audience and the Fortune Teller, who was not needed until the second act. In Hawaii, the two rows of chairs faced the audience; in Brooklyn, they faced the rear of the stage, an arrangement which is much easier for the readers because they need not sit quite so sedately and motionless for lengthy intervals. In Banff, the platform was very long and narrow, not deep enough to accommodate the two rows of chairs and still have a playing area in front of them. Therefore, the double row of chairs was divided in the middle, and the center of the platform became the playing area for those scenes requiring special movement or enactment. As a result of this space limitation, more readers remained in the audience or returned to their seats in the auditorium once the episode in which they had been participating was completed.

Tenderloin   by Samuel Hopkins Adams

A novel, adapted for Readers Theatre by Melvin R. White and presented at Brooklyn College by an advanced oral interpretation class.

This romantic period novel about sin and society in New York during the Gay Nineties was written with much colorful, dynamic dialogue and involved dozens of interestingly different characters grouped around six leads: Tommy Howard, reporter for the *Police Gazette;* Laurie Crosbie, his lovely fiancée; Dan Adriance, reporter for *The Star;* Kathleen, the ruthless woman Dan loves; Mrs. Steevens Parke, leader of New York Society; and Reverend Brockholst, the pastor known as "Hellfire Farr."

The stage was set with a three-level platform; each level had six chairs, and there were six additional chairs on the stage floor in front of the platform. In all, these provided for a cast of twenty-four readers. Each of the six leading characters, seated in the chairs downstage at the floor level, read but one role; the eighteen other readers assumed multiple roles. The reading lasted two hours with two intermissions. To provide variety, the leads sometimes left their chairs for lengthy scenes in the downstage area; the eighteen on the platforms remained seated unless they read a long scene with one or more of the principals. The narrator and his lectern were DR, and he had a chair in which to relax during long scenes.

Although no special costumes were used, the readers chose the colors in their suits and dresses carefully, with black for the Reverend, red for the temptress, and pastels for the ingénue. The houselights remained on throughout the presentation. The role of Tommy was read by a romantic-looking young man, a singer who composed and sang catchy tunes for several of the songs from the novel. This, of course, added variety to the presentation.

Thidwick: The Big-Hearted Moose by Theodor Seuss Geisel (Dr. Seuss)

A children's story, adapted and directed by Ronnie Moskowitz for presentation at Brooklyn College.

As previously explained, children's stories lend themselves admirably to presentation in this medium; and children's audiences, accustomed to using their imaginations, accept its conventions even more readily than do more sophisticated audiences. The setting for *Thidwick* consisted of nine low stools, four revolving stools, one lectern, and a series of stage steps which became—in the imaginations of the children—Thidwick's antlers. These physical elements were arranged as shown in the diagram on page 116.

The storyteller stood at the lectern. Thidwick and four other moose entered DR from backstage. Thidwick sat down wearily on the bottom step at C, while the other four lumbered and ate their way to the revolving stools at L and DL, eventually turning their backs to the audience and sitting motionless until they were again needed near the end of the presentation. As each subsequent bird and animal entered, he left one of the nine short stools and climbed onto Thidwick's antlers—the steps above Thidwick. Each reader was provided with some suggestion of a costume. For example, the large, heavy students who played the moose were dressed in cumbersome, thick, winter attire: coats, winter caps with earmuffs, and galoshes or heavy boots. The birds had feather boas around their necks and feathers in their hats, and the mouse had big ears—just big enough to tickle the children's imaginations.

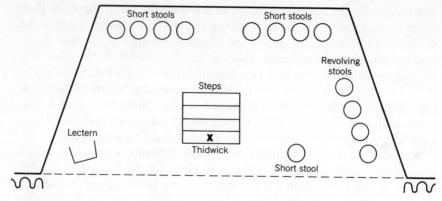

FIGURE 9. *Thidwick, the Big-Hearted Moose* floor plan

The only changes in the dialogue of the story were those about Thidwick running from the hunters. In order to maintain the illusion that the steps were his antlers, Thidwick obviously could not leave his place on the bottom step; instead, struggling valiantly in that position, he pantomimed ducking the bullets. The sound effects of gunshots added to the excitement; and the "inhabitants" of his antlers struggled in unison with him, ducking as he ducked. So the line "took to his heels" became "tried to get up," and the four lines which described Thidwick's running away from the hunters were omitted.

To Kill a Mockingbird   by Harper Lee

A novel, adapted for Readers Theatre and presented by Robert Wilhoit at Drury College.

Mr. Wilhoit's program notes for this production read:

Readers Theatre is our medium . . . it is not new . . . it is not really "theatre" as we have come to expect it. It is a reader who shares with you the first thrill of discovery . . . who brings to you vocally the sounds and sights and emotions of a fine piece of literature. An actor says: "Look at me . . . I am this person." A reader says: "Look . . . here is this person, this experience. Let us share it together." And so, here is *To Kill a Mockingbird.*

This sharing was the guiding principle in the Drury College presentation of Harper Lee's popular novel. According to additional information provided by Mr. Wilhoit, two approaches seemed possible: (1) The script could be presented as if the author were looking back at incidents in her life, or (2) Scout, one of the central characters, could narrate the events as they happened to her, day by day. The latter approach was chosen. The content of the script was restricted to the dialogue scenes already in the novel; these were linked by Scout's narration and commentary. The readers carried their scripts in their hands at all times to impress upon themselves and the audience that this was a reading and not a conventional play.

The adaptation emphasized the mystery of Boo Radley, the death of Mrs. Dubose, and the trial of Tom Robinson. This required a rather large cast of nineteen. The stage space was divided into six playing areas, some of them raised above stage level to facilitate swift and easy transition from one unit of the story line to the next. Each area served only temporarily as a designated place. To aid in the identification of the various readers, a suggestion of costuming and a number of character make-ups were employed.

In adapting *To Kill a Mockingbird* for a summer-session Readers Theatre workshop at the University of Arkansas, the director had one reader serve both as Scout, the grown narrator and as Scout, the little girl. Her "present" location was at a lectern DR, although she did not always return to it when she "returned" to the present. (Sometimes she read narration at another location.) At the lectern she used the script; but as a scene from the past began to unfold, she left the stand to "join her childhood memories" and played the scene in the character of the little girl she once had been. All of these "remembered" scenes were completely memorized by the readers and done on the stage without

Many theatrical enhancements—costuming, make-up, and suggested set pieces placed on multiple levels against black drapes—were employed in this production of Harper Lee's To Kill a Mockingbird. *Scout, as narrator, talked directly to the audience; but in all other scenes, the readers used onstage focus.*

manuscripts. These episodes were given area lighting to fade them in and out as the narrator "remembered" them. The readers in these onstage scenes were dressed in character-suggesting costumes.

. . . To Meet Mr. Eliot

> *A staged reading of some poems by T. S. Eliot, arranged and directed by John W. Gunning for presentation at Ithaca College and, subsequently, at the Convention of the New York State Speech Association in Rochester. Mr. Gunning has contributed the information on the two productions.*

Eliot's theory of the Auditory Imagination and the resultant readability of his work made the choice of selections difficult. Using as determinants the poet's insight into the human condition, the poet's growth in craftsmanship, and his changing emphasis from despair to spiritual vision, the director-arranger settled upon these representative poems: "Preludes," "The Love Song of J. Alfred Prufrock," "The Hollow Men," "Journey of the Magi," and "Ash Wednesday." He was tempted to incorporate excerpts from the plays and thus included "Sweeney Fragments" to illustrate Eliot's idea of the drama as the ideal medium for poetry. "Sweeney Agonistes," to epitomize the poems of desperation, was inserted between the poems of despair and those of increasing spirituality. *The Waste Land* was rejected as too difficult for the undergraduate readers and too obscure for the undergraduate audience. Illustrating Eliot's lighter side were two poems from *Old Possum's Book of Practical Cats:* "Macavity, The Mystery Cat" and "Gus, The Theatre Cat." These were read after "Sweeney Agonistes" and before the two religious poems.

The lines from "Five-Finger Exercises" beginning "How unpleasant to meet Mr. Eliot" suggested the title for the script. Brief biographical and explanatory material served as narration and as introduction to the individual poems. A conclusion which would summarize the body of Eliot's work and serve as a dramatic ending was found in the last section of *The Rock.*

The program was presented with seven voices: four male readers, two female readers, and a female narrator. These gave a harmonious blending of vocal tones. The readers were arranged in two rows, seated in chairs angled from C to DL, the men in the back row, the women in front. The tenors were placed in the center, between the baritones; and the one soprano was flanked by the contralto and the alto. A podium was situated DR for the narrator as well as for solo readers.

The meanings of the poems, the general design of the presentation, and point of view were established in one meeting before oral rehearsals were started. The choral arrangements required for "The Hollow Men,"

"Sweeney Agonistes," "Ash Wednesday," and the final chorus were worked out during the first two rehearsals. Suggestions from the cast proved very helpful. The practice-production schedule required three weeks, totaling some fifteen rehearsals.

Simple lighting was employed for the Ithaca College production: general illumination for the poems involving two or more readers, spotlights for those read by soloists. Since the readings were staged in a lecture theatre, no act curtain was used. As the houselights dimmed, the reading-area lights came up, and the cast entered single file from the rear of the reading area. After the last reading and final bow, they returned to the backstage area. The men wore dark suits and ties; the women, black dresses with no adornment.

The poems were not memorized; the cast held their scripts in hand. During choral passages the scripts remained open on music stands that had been set in front of and angled to the right of each reader. All lines were read directly to the audience. Even where an exchange between individual readers was called for, the cast members did not use direct eye-contact with one another but kept the focus off-stage.

The subsequent performance in Rochester resulted in some last-minute adjustments due to a more limited playing space; neither lighting nor entrances and exits were possible; and except for the narrator and the reader who interpreted "Prufrock," the readers remained at their chairs when reading solo parts.

The Trial of Job   by Douglas Davis

A Biblical script for Readers Theatre, arranged for Readers Theatre by Douglas Davis and presented at the University of Hawaii.

This Master of Arts thesis-project was based primarily on the Book of Job but included additional material drawn from other books of the Bible. The faculty cast of ten included, in addition to the narrator, readers who interpreted the roles of God, Job, Satan, Eliphaz, Bildad, Zophar, and Three Messengers. The physical arrangement was simple. A long, narrow, three-foot high platform with a tall stool at either end occupied most of the upstage playing space. There were three shorter stools at DC, three more arranged at an angle at L and DL, and a short stool and a lectern at DR. The tall stool on the platform at UR was for God; the one at UL, for Satan. Eliphaz, Bildad, and Zophar were seated on the stools DC, the Three Messengers on the three stools at L and DL, and the narrator on a stool at DR. No one stood except the narrator, who rose and took his position at the lectern when he was required to advance the story.

Primarily, the focus was offstage; however, God and Satan—although

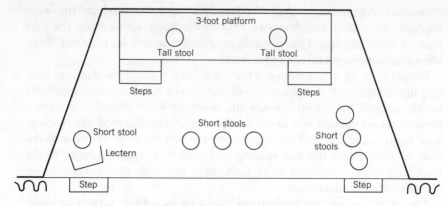

FIGURE 10. *The Trial of Job* floor plan

they did not look at each other—did look down on the human beings, observed them, and listened to them. Because the auditorium was not equipped with a front curtain and had no backstage area, the readers sat in the front row of the auditorium until the presentation was to begin; they then rose, walked sedately up the steps to the stage. and took their seats. All except Satan were dressed somberly in black suits, white shirts, and dark ties; Satan sported a red tie and a red pocket handkerchief.

A Wilde Night

A compiled script, arranged by Sheila Reiter and presented at Southwest Missouri State College and at Rockhurst College.

With *A Wilde Night,* Mrs. Reiter took a novel approach to compiling a script on the life and work of a single author. She read extensively about Oscar Wilde, his reputation as a literary figure, and his personal life as it was viewed during his own era and today. Using this research as a basis for her script, she introduced Wilde through the eyes of four diverse commentators who were familiar with his work and his career. For these four, she composed dialogue to be spoken by a Trinity College classmate, an Oxford classmate, a young American who recalled Wilde's lecture tour in America, and a London society figure. Having presented the central character of the script in this fashion, the adapter switched attention to a narrator who elucidated the contemporary view of this nineteenth-century author and illustrated his remarks with passages from Wilde's writings. These illustrative scenes, adaptations of short stories, were introduced by letters written by Wilde—letters that expressed ideas

120   *This Is the Way It Was Done*

and happenings that could have inspired the writing of the fiction. The specific stories employed for this purpose were "The Canterville Ghost" and "The Nightingale and the Rose." The one-act play, *Salome,* completed the program. A different set of readers was used for each story and for the play.

The production utilized the complete stage. At DL sat the four characters from Wilde's past, with the narrator on a stool to their right. In the center of the stage and slightly back of this first set of characters were the readers for "The Nightingale and the Rose." They sat on two raised platforms, with the mother, the student, and the Nightingale on the higher elevation and the three readers who spoke as voices on the lower. At DR, the seven readers for "The Canterville Ghost" were arranged in a pyramid on platforms, with the ghost at the top. The interpreter who read the part of Wilde's friend, Lord Alfred Douglas, sat on a stool at the far R and moved to DRC when reading the letters he received from Wilde. Lights came up on whatever area was in use at the moment. During the intermission, the stage was rearranged for *Salome,* in which fifteen characters used the entire playing area. This unique script with its varied staging proved exciting entertainment.

Wuthering Heights   by Emily Brontë

A novel adapted for Readers Theatre by Patricia Sheinfeld and presented at the University of Hawaii and Brooklyn College.

Originally, Miss Sheinfeld, a student at the University of Hawaii, selected ten scenes from the Brontë novel of human passion and suffering and used them for a solo, one-woman performance in which she read all of the roles. Later, at Brooklyn College, the adaptation was given by a cast of five, each using a tall stool and a lectern. As the narrator, the servant Nelly Dean told the story of *Wuthering Heights* to Mr. Lockwood, giving a brief introduction and identifying the characters: Catherine Earnshaw, who later married Edgar Linton; and Heathcliff, who loved and was in turn loved by Catherine. The script included:

1. Dialogue between Catherine and Nelly, in which they discuss Catherine's intended marriage to Edgar Linton.
2. Dialogue between Catherine and Edgar after their marriage. Catherine is now quite ill.
3. Heathcliff's comments to Nelly. He has heard of Catherine's illness and wishes to see her.
4. Nelly's description of Catherine and her illness.
5. Nelly's remarks to Catherine beginning, "There's a letter for you, Mrs. Linton."

6. Dialogue between Heathcliff and Catherine, in which Heathcliff realizes she is about to die.
7. Catherine's comments to Nelly: "Oh, you see, Nelly, he would not relent a moment to keep me out of the grave."
8. Dialogue between Heathcliff and Catherine beginning, "You teach me how cruel you've been."
9. Nelly's description of Heathcliff's death.
10. Mr. Lockwood's conclusion to the story.

The readers sat on tall stools in a straight row, each with his script on a lectern before him. In the opening, heads were bowed; subsequently, each reader "came to life" as he participated in a scene, then returned to this bowed-head position when he was not involved in the ensuing episode.

The Zoo Story by Edward Albee

A one-act play, adapted for Readers Theatre by Alex Weaver and John Whalen at the University of Arkansas.

No changes were made in the acting text of the play; it was read in its entirety. The two readers occupied stools placed approximately three feet apart, each singled out by a shaft of white light from a pinpoint spotlight overhead. This dramatically focused the audience's attention on the play's antagonists: Peter, a man in his early forties; and Jerry, a man in his thirties. Jerry, in slacks and a nondescript sports jacket, was carelessly but not poorly dressed; Peter wore a dark business suit. The two conversed, maintaining offstage focus and reacting to each other without leaving his stool and without making eye contact. During the knife incident at the end of the play (which in the stage version called for action), Peter raised his right hand quickly as Jerry started forward from his stool. But just as these movements were made, the pinpoint spotlights were blacked out, and the readers moved quickly out of sight. After a moment of darkness, red pinpoint spotlights singled out the two empty stools for perhaps five seconds before a second and final blackout.

In addition to the Readers Theatre productions described on the preceding pages, several rather complete discussions of other presentations have been published elsewhere. Among these productions, perhaps the most stirring to the imagination are:

AGE OF ANXIETY, by W. H. Auden. See McCoard, William B., "An Interpretation of the Times: A Report on the Oral Interpretation of W. H. Auden's *Age of Anxiety,*" *Quarterly Journal of Speech,* 35, No. 4 (December 1949), 489-495.

THE BEAST IN THE JUNGLE, by Henry James. See Bacon, Wallace A., *The Art of Interpretation* (New York: Holt, Rinehart & Winston, Inc., 1966), pp. 325-337.

HIROSHIMA, by John Hersey. See McCoard, William B., "Report on the Reading of *Hiroshima*," *Quarterly Journal of Speech,* 34, No. 2 (April 1948), 174-176.

JEALOUSY, by Alain Robbe-Grillet. See Breen, Robert S., "A Chamber Theatre Production of 'Jealousy,'" *IIG Newsletter* (March 1966), 4-6.

MORNING IN NAGREBCAN, from *How My Brother Leon Brought Home a Wife,* by Manuel E. Arguilla. See Bacon, Wallace A., *The Art of Interpretation* (New York: Holt, Rinehart & Winston, Inc., 1966), pp. 338-346.

The list of successful Readers Theatre productions could, of course, go on and on. The amount of experimentation and production in classes and elsewhere at all levels—elementary school, secondary school, college and university, as well as presentations in community theatres and by professional groups—is increasing rapidly as interest in Readers Theatre grows. The Production Lists Project of the American Educational Theatre Association makes an annual report on play selection in four-year collegiate institutions which present dramatic productions, and for the past several years it has included statistics on the number of Readers Theatre productions being done. The Interpretation Interest Group (IIG) of the Speech Association of America has a Readers Theatre Bibliography Committee which each year collects pertinent information not only on materials written *about* Readers Theatre but on materials annually *presented* in this art form. Students of this subject are encouraged to familiarize themselves with these sources and materials and to report their own activities in this medium to the current chairman of the Readers Theatre Bibliography Committee. Past bibliographies can be found in the Winter 1961 and February 1966 issues of the *Central States Speech Journal.* (See Selected Bibliography, p. 252.)

PART THREE

Sample Scripts
for Readers Theatre

BY RAY BRADBURY

Dandelion Wine

A novel adapted for Readers Theatre by Leslie Irene Coger and Duane Hunt

Mr. Bradbury's novel abounds in those special qualities which characterize ideal literary material for Readers Theatre: impelling imagery, fluid
phrasing, evocative power, unique characters with whom an audience can
readily empathize, skillfully wrought moods ranging from comedy to deep
sadness, and an overall sense of authentic beauty emerging from the
universal experiences of mankind. The ensuing script provides a definitive
and useful example of one way in which a novel can be cut to a workable
time limit. The approach and procedures used in preparing this adaptation
are discussed in detail in Chapter 3 of Part I, "Selecting and Adapting
Materials for Readers Theatre," pages 21-39.

CAST OF CHARACTERS

*Nine Men, Five Women, and a Narrator, who may be played by
either a Man or a Woman. This adaptation may also be read by Four
Men and Two Women, with lines assigned as follows:* READER #1:
the Narrator, Pawnee Bill, and a Voice; READER #2: *Mom, a Voice,
Lucy Cavins, and the Telephone Operator;* READER #3: *Douglas
and a Voice;* READER #4: *Grandpa, a Voice, John Huff, and Miguel;*
READER #5: *Tom, a Voice, Dad, Mr. Sanderson, and Colonel Freeleigh;* READER #6: *Great-Grandma, a Voice, and the Nurse.*

THE NARRATOR.

DOUGLAS SPAULDING. *A young boy of twelve*

TOM SPAULDING. *His brother; a little older*

Dandelion Wine

by **Ray Bradbury**

Adapted for Readers Theatre
by **Duane Hunt** and **Leslie Irene Coger**

Presented by
Southwest Missouri State College
for
The Speech Association of America
December 29, 1960

Reader One: Dr. Harry J. Siceluff

Reader Two: Gwen Theis

Reader Three: Joe Bowman

Reader Four: Dean Compton

Reader Five: Duane Hunt

Reader Six: Dr. Leslie Irene Coger

THE AWAKENING: The Joys of Summer

The First Ritual
Narrator .... Reader One
Douglas Spaulding .... Reader Three

The First Harvest
Narrator .... Reader One
Douglas Spaulding .... Reader Three
Tom Spaulding .... Reader Five
Grandpa .... Reader Four
Mom .... Reader Two
Voices ..... Readers Two, Three, Four, Five, Six

Wings of Summer
Narrator .... Reader One
Douglas .... Reader Three
John Huff .... Reader Four
Dad .... Reader Five
Mr. Sanderson of
   Sanderson's Shoe Emporium ..... Reader Five

The Time Machine
Tom .... Reader Five
Douglas .... Reader Three
Narrator .... Reader One
Lucy Cavins, a friend of Douglas.... Reader Two
John Huff, a friend of Douglas ..... Reader Four
Colonel Freeleigh .... Reader Five
Pawnee Bill .... Reader One

THE REALIZATION: The Sorrows of Summer

A Game of Statues
Douglas .... Reader Three
John Huff .... Reader Four
Voices .... Readers Two, Five, Six
Narrator .... Reader One

The Closing Window
Voices .... Readers Two, Three, Four, Five, Six
Narrator .... Reader One
Colonel Freeleigh .... Reader Five
Telephone Operator .... Reader Two
Miguel .... Reader Four
Nurse .... Reader Six

A Sum in Arithmetic
Great-Grandma .... Reader Six
Douglas........................... Reader Three
Grandpa .... Reader Four

The Fever Dream
Douglas........................... Reader Three
Tom .... Reader Five
Voices .... Readers One, Two, Four
Mother .... Reader Two

The Last Ritual
Voices .... Readers One, Two, Four, Five, Six
Tom .... Reader Five
Douglas........................... Reader Three
Narrator .... Reader One

GRANDPA. *A lively old man*

MOM. *Doug's mother*

JOHN. *Doug's young friend*

DAD. *Doug's father*

MR. SANDERSON. *Owner of a shoe store*

LUCY CAVINS. *Another one of Doug's friends*

COLONEL FREELEIGH. *An old man with a wonderful memory*

PAWNEE BILL. *A man of the Wild West*

TELEPHONE OPERATOR.

MIGUEL. *Colonel Freeleigh's friend in Mexico City*

NURSE.

GREAT-GRANDMA. *Doug's wise great-grandmother*

CHORUS OF VOICES. *Composed of all the Readers*

THE PHYSICAL ARRANGEMENT OF THE SCENE

Six stools and six lecterns are provided for the readers, all of whom are sitting as the program begins.

I. THE AWAKENING: THE JOYS OF SUMMER

The First Ritual

NARRATOR [R1].[1] It is a quiet morning, the town covered over with darkness and at ease in bed. Summer gathers in the weather; the wind has the proper touch; the breathing of the world is long and warm and slow. To the nostrils of earth comes a sweet scent, the smell of freedom and of living. This, indeed, is the first morning of summer.

Douglas Spaulding, age twelve, freshly awakened, lets summer idle him on its early morning stream. Lying in his third-story cupola bed-

---

[1]The designation [R1] following a character's name and occurring at the beginning of a scene, segment, or episode indicates that this particular role may be read by Reader #1. Later in the script, [R1] may also read the roles of Pawnee Bill and a Voice, [R2] may be assigned the roles of Mom, a Voice, Lucy Cavins, and the Telephone Operator, and so on. These assignments are optional, however, and will vary with the director's preferences and the interpretive abilities of the respective readers.

room, the tall power comes to him, lifts him high in the June wind.

DOUG [R3]. *(Stands.)* A whole summer ahead to cross off the calendar, day by single, wonderful day . . . pluck sour apples, peaches, midnight plums. I will be clothed in trees, in bushes, and in rivers. I will freeze, and gladly, in the hoarfrost of the ice house and each day at dusk sadly cross that number from the page of numbers.

NARRATOR. But now, Douglas Spaulding, a familiar task awaits you. Move slowly, Douglas, through your sorcerer's tower . . . third-story cupola bedroom of Grandma's home . . . dark, secret tower, alive with thunders and visions; move to the portal of glass through which the stars are fading. Lift slowly your finger and perform your ritual magic.

DOUG. *(Steps forward.)* There! Lights on!

VOICE TWO. Lights on!

DOUG. And there! Lights . . . on!

VOICE FOUR. Lights on!

DOUG. Now over here:

VOICE FIVE. Lights on!

DOUG. And now here:

VOICE SIX. Lights on!

DOUG. Windows, up; morning, flow in. Everyone, yawn. Everyone, up! Gran'pa, get your teeth from the water glass. Gran'ma and Mom, fry hot cakes. Street-where-old-people-live, wake up! Cough, get up, move around. Come back, come back to this world of summer. Street-of-children-playing, awake. John Huff, Lucy Cavins, ready? Ready to baseballs lying deep in wet grass. Ready to rope swings hanging unused in gnarled trees. Mom, Dad, Tom, everyone—wake up now!

NARRATOR. Bleak mansions across town open baleful, dragon eyes. Little white cottages lift sleepy blinds to the warm sun. Clock alarms tinkle faintly. Courthouse clock booms. Birds flit from trees, singing sweetly in the morning breeze. Douglas, conduct your orchestra of sight, sound, and smell; point to the east. The sun warms the avenues of wet sidewalks and sleeping dogs and cool milk bottles on back porches.

DOUG. One . . . two . . . three . . . Overture, begin! Everyone, jump. Everyone, run. It's going to be a whale of a fine season. *(Sits.)*

NARRATOR. Give the town a last snap of your fingers, Doug. Doors, slam open; people, step out. Douglas and Tom, out of the house—filled, stuffed, and dressed for the day on Gran'ma's special pancakes—Grandfather ahead of them standing on the wide front porch like a captain surveying the vast, unmotioned calms of a season dead ahead. Summer 1928, begin! *(There is a pause.)*

The First Harvest

TOM [R5]. *(Rises.)* Are the dandelions ready now, Gran'pa?

DOUG [R3]. *(Rises.)* They've got to be ready now, please.

GRANDPA [R4]. *(Rises.)* Five hundred, a thousand, two thousand easy. Yep, a good supply. Pick 'em easy, boys, but pick 'em all. A dime for every sack delivered to the press!

DOUG. Hey! Come on, Tom. I'll pick more than you today!

NARRATOR [R1]. Mom opens the front screen door, steps out to stand beside her titan father. (MOM *rises.*) She places a strong, loving hand on the old man's frail shoulder.

MOM [R2]. Dad, are they ready so early?

GRANDPA. Yep. I guess so, daughter. Besides, you think I could hold off those Injuns for another day?

MOM. Boys, boys! Don't work so hard. Leave a few for tomorrow, you know.

TOM. Can't, Mom. There'll never be another day like today.

NARRATOR. And there never is, Doug and Tom. Bend your backs, smiling. Pick the golden flowers, the flowers that flood the world, drip off lawns onto brick streets, tap softly at crystal cellar windows, and agitate themselves so that on all sides lie the dazzle and glitter of molten sun.

MOM. Dandelion . . . it's summer on the tongue.

GRANDPA. Yep, every year they run amuck. I let 'em. A pride of lions in the yard. Stare, and they burn a hole in your eye. Common flower, weed no one sees—but for me, for us, a noble thing, the dandelion. Careful, boys . . . pick 'em easy!

NARRATOR. So plucked carefully, in sacks, the dandelions are carried below. The cellar dark glows with their arrival. Wine press stands open, cold.

GRANDPA. Keep them comin', Injuns. Got the ketchup bottles ready, Daughter?

MOM. They're all cleaned and waiting, Dad.

GRANDPA. Here she comes!

NARRATOR. The golden liquid runs, then gushes from the spout of the press. The essence of the fine, fair month of June flows down, to be crocked, skimmed of ferment, boiled in clean ketchup shakers, then ranked in sparkling rows in the cellar gloom.

DOUG. And labeled! Don't forget we have to label them.

TOM. Label them? What for, Doug?

DOUG. Tom, this is going to be a summer of unguessed wonders. I want it all labeled, so that any time I want to, I can tiptoe down and hold summer in my hand.

NARRATOR. Label the bottles, then, Tom! Put the date of each sparkling day on the cool glass; label, so Douglas Spaulding can peer through the mystery on a winter day and recall June sunshine glowing through a skim of January dust. Label, so Douglas can remember what happened on every day of this summer, forever.

MOM. Summer will be over before it begins, Doug.

NARRATOR. Your words go unheeded, Mom. Tom and Doug are lost in magic!

TOM. Boy, what a swell way to save June, July, and August! Real practical, Doug.

GRANDPA. Better than puttin' things in an old attic you never use again. This way, you get to live summer over for a minute or two here and there, along the way through winter. When the bottles are empty, the summer's gone for good and no regrets and no sentimental trash lying around for you to stumble over forty years from now.

TOM. Clean . . .

MOM. Smokeless . . .

DOUG. Eff—efficient . . .

GRANDPA. (Chuckling.) That's dandelion wine! (GRANDPA, TOM, MOM, and DOUG sit.)

NARRATOR. That's dandelion wine, a bit of summer captured. Even Gran'ma—when snow is falling fast, blinding windows, stealing breath from gasping mouths—will vanish to the cellar for a moment.

Above . . . coughing, sneezing, groans . . . stealthy microbes everywhere. Then, rising from the cellar like a June goddess, Gran'ma with a balm of sun and idle August afternoons. The sounds of ice cream wagons passing on brick avenues . . .

VOICE THREE. The "woosh" of silver skyrockets.

VOICE FOUR. The fountaining of lawn mowers roaming through the July grass.

VOICE TWO. All this in a glass from the cellar.

NARRATOR. A cellar of winter for a June adventure. Mom, Dad, Gran'pa, Gran'ma, or one of the boarders standing in secret conclave with his own spirit and soul . . . communing with the last touch of a calendar long departed and repeating the golden words for every winter in time . . .

VOICE SIX. Dandelion wine . . . (The other voices echo with a chorus-like effect.)

VOICE TWO. Dandelion wine . . .

VOICE THREE. Dandelion wine . . .

VOICE FOUR. Dandelion wine . . .

VOICE FIVE. Dandelion wine . . .

NARRATOR. And so the first harvest of golden wine is complete. Pressed, bottled . . .

DOUG. (Stands.) And labeled!

NARRATOR. Uh . . . yes . . . labeled and stacked in rows upon the shelves. Stand there—in the cellar gloom, Douglas—you and Tom—and shiver a bit. The early June evenings are cool. Or is it altogether the coolness, Doug?

DOUG. (Steps forward.) It's the magic—the magic in the bottles . . .

TOM. (Rises and steps forward.) What'd you say, Doug?

DOUG. It's magic, Tom! . . . Tom . . . I'm alive!

TOM. Heck! That's not new.

DOUG. But thinking about it, down here . . . noticing it . . . that's new. Tom, I walked past old Miss Fern's house yesterday. Do you know there's colored glass in two of her windows?

TOM. Never noticed.

DOUG. I never did either . . . before. But I did yesterday. My gosh, Tom, what else have I never seen before . . . I mean *really* seen?

TOM. I dunno.

DOUG. Well, at least, every time we bottle dandelion wine, we got a whole chunk of 1928 put away, safe. See?

TOM. Nope.

DOUG. Oh, well, gee! See, next winter we come down here, and we look at each bottle—and then we can relive that particular day! We'll remember just what happened; but now we gotta look and *really* see what happens. Each bottle is one whole day of our lives, Tom; and come Labor Day, we'll total up the summer and see what we got. O.K.?

TOM. Yeah—sure, Doug! Sure!

(TOM *and* DOUG *step back and sit. There is a pause while all of the* READERS *change positions to mark a transition in time.*)

Wings of Summer

NARRATOR [R1]. You do not hear them coming. You hardly hear them go. The grass bends down, springs up again. They pass like cloud shadows downhill . . . the boys of summer, running.

DOUG [R3]. *(Rises and steps forward.)* Hey! John Huff! Charlie Woodman! Wait for me.

JOHN [R4]. *(Stands.)* Doug—come on! Doug!

NARRATOR. It's no use. . . . They're gone. The second rite of summer, the dandelion picking, the starting of the wine . . . over. Now the third rite awaits Douglas to make the motions, but he stands very still.

JOHN. Doug! Come on, Doug! (JOHN *sits.*)

NARRATOR. The running boys fade.

DOUG. *(Still standing.)* I'm alive. But what's the use? They're more alive than me. How come? How come?

NARRATOR. You know the answer, Douglas Spaulding. Standing alone there, you know. Look down, Doug. Stare down at your motionless feet . . .

DOUG. It's these shoes . . .

NARRATOR. Late that night, Douglas Spaulding, going home from the two-reeler with your mother and father and brother Tom, you see the *tennis shoes* in the bright store window. Your ankles are seized, feet suspended. The earth spins. Mom and Dad and brother walk quietly forward. You, Douglas, trudge backward, watching the shoes in the midnight window.

DOUG. Dad . . . back there in the window, those creamy-sponge Para Litefoot shoes . . .

DAD [R5]. *(Rises.)* Suppose you tell me why you need a pair of sneakers. Can you do that?

DOUG. Well . . .

NARRATOR. Tell him, Doug. Tell him how they feel like running through summer grass without any shoes on. Like sticking your feet out of hot covers to let cool breezes slip soothingly across them. Tell him how tennis shoes feel like it always feels the first time each year, wading in the slow waters of the clear creek.

DOUG. Dad—it's kind—kind of hard to explain.

DAD. But what's wrong with last year's shoes? Dig *them* out of the closet.

NARRATOR. The people that make tennis shoes seem to know what boys need and want. They must have watched a lot of winds blow the trees and a lot of rivers going down to lakes. Whatever it is, it is in the shoes, and it is summer. Douglas, try to say all this in your words.

DOUG. Don't you see, Dad? I just can't use last year's pair . . .

NARRATOR. They were great last year. But now . . . why, Mr. Spaulding, now they're all dead inside!

DAD. Well . . . we'll see, Doug. *(Meaning "no.")* We'll see. (DAD *sits.*)

DOUG. I just gotta, Dad. I just gotta. Why, with those shoes I could do anything . . . anything at all! (DOUG *sits.*)

NARRATOR. The next morning, old Mr. Sanderson moves through his shoe store as the proprietor of a pet shop must move through his shop where are kenneled animals from every place in the world, touching each one on his way. Brush the shoes in the window . . . some dogs, some cats . . . touch each pair with concern, adjusting laces, fixing tongues . . .

There is the sound of thunder! One moment the door to Sanderson's shoe emporium, empty. Next, Douglas Spaulding standing clumsily in the opening. The thunder had stopped when his shoes stopped. (DOUG *stands.* MR. SANDERSON *rises and remains at left of lectern.*)

SANDERSON [R5]. Don't say a word, Douglas.

NARRATOR. Douglas freezes. All the night before—before he had gone to bed—dreaming of cream-sponge Para Litefoot tennis shoes, he had carefully stacked the nickels, dimes, and quarters of his piggy-bank. He had said to himself . . .

DOUG. Whatever you want, you got to make your own way.

NARRATOR. Now he stands frozen in the doorway, in the bright sunlight of the shoe emporium—frozen, staring down at his leather shoes as if these heavy things could not be pulled up out of the cement.

SANDERSON. *(Moving forward.)* First, I know just what you want to buy.

NARRATOR. Mr. Sanderson's voice reaches Douglas' ears . . . but he cannot respond. He cannot move.

SANDERSON. Secondly, I see you every afternoon at my window. You think I *don't see?* You're wrong. Third, to give it its full name, you want the ROYAL CROWN CREAM-SPONGE PARA LITEFOOT TENNIS SHOES: "Like menthol on your feet!" Fourth, you want credit!

DOUG. *(Moves forward.)* No! I got something better than credit to offer! Before I tell, Mr. Sanderson, you got to do me one small favor. Can you remember when was the last time you yourself wore a pair of Litefoot sneakers?

SANDERSON. Oh, ten, twenty, say thirty years ago. Why?

DOUG. Oh? . . . Well . . . don't you think you owe it to your customers to at least *try* the tennis shoes you sell, so you'd know how they feel?

SANDERSON. You may not have noticed, but I'm wearing shoes.

DOUG. But not sneakers, sir. How can you rave about them if you haven't worn them for thirty years?

SANDERSON. Well, now I . . .

DOUG. Mr. Sanderson, you sell me something, and I'll sell you something just as valuable.

SANDERSON. Is it absolutely necessary to the sale that I put on a pair of the sneakers, boy?

DOUG. I sure wish you would, sir.

SANDERSON. Well . . . *(He sighs and shrugs resignedly.)*

NARRATOR. A minute later, seated, panting quietly, he laces the tennis shoes to his long narrow feet. They look detached and alive down there next to the dark cuffs of his business suit.

DOUG. How do they feel?

SANDERSON. "How do they feel?" he asks. They . . . they feel just fine.

DOUG. Oh, sir! Please don't sit down; kinda rock back and forth, sponge around while I tell you the rest.

NARRATOR. Better sit back, Mr. Sanderson. Sink deep into your shoes, flex your toes. You can't stop this flow of words. A dike has burst. Limber your arches. All the flood will come out in one gigantic inundation of words. So sit back, test your ankles . . . feel the softness on your feet.

DOUG. Mr. Sanderson, I'll give you my money; you give me the shoes. I still will owe you a dollar. But, Mr. Sanderson—soon as I get those shoes on, you know what *happens?*

SANDERSON. What?

DOUG. Bang! I deliver your packages, pick up packages, bring you coffee, burn trash, run to the post office, library . . . you'll see twelve of me in and out every minute. Feel those shoes . . . see how fast they'd take me? Feel all that running inside? You stay in the nice cool store while

I'm jumping all over town! But it's not me, really; it's the shoes. They go like mad down alleys, cutting corners . . . there they go! Whooooooooooosh! . . .

NARRATOR. Feel those shoes, Mr. Sanderson. Douglas is right. Feel how they hush themselves deep into the carpet, sink as in jungle grass, in loam and resilient clay. You should look in a mirror, Mr. Sanderson. How many years has it been since *that* light shown in your face, in your eyes?

SANDERSON. Boy! In five years, how'd you like a job selling shoes in this emporium?

DOUG. Gee, thanks, sir! I don't know what I'm going to be, yet.

SANDERSON. Anything you want to be, son—you'll be it. No one will ever stop you. Find your size and lace 'em up. There's a dozen things you have to do for me today. Finish them, we're even-steven, and you're fired.

DOUG. Thanks, Mr. Sanderson, I'm on my way!

SANDERSON. Stop! . . . How do they feel, boy?

NARRATOR. The boy looks down at his feet in deep rivers, in fields of wheat in the wind, already rushing him out of town. He looks up at the old man; his eyes flame; his mouth moves . . . but no sound comes out.

SANDERSON. Antelopes, son? Gazelles?

NARRATOR. Douglas hesitates, nods a quick yes and vanishes. (DOUG *sits*.) With a whisper he spins around and is gone. The door stands empty. The sound of tennis shoes drifts away on the jungle air. From a long time ago a memory comes to old Mr. Sanderson.

SANDERSON. I remember when I was a boy . . . I remember the sound. Beautiful creatures leaping under the sky, gone through brush, under trees, away. Only the soft echo of their running left behind. Antelopes. Gazelles.

NARRATOR. Mr. Sanderson stoops to pick up the boy's abandoned winter shoes, heavy with forgotten rains and long melted snows. (MR. SANDERSON *sits*.) And across town, out of the blazing sun, Grandpa places another shiny new bottle of dandelion wine on the shelf in the cellar.

(There is a short pause, during which the READERS *shift their positions to denote time passage.)*

The Time Machine

TOM [R5]. *(Rises, moves forward.)* What'cha doin', Doug?

DOUG [R3]. *(Rises, moves forward.)* I'm writin'.

TOM. Yeah, Doug, sure. I can see that. *(After a pause.)* What'cha writin'?

DOUG. Boy! Little brothers can sure be ex—exas—be a bother! *(After another pause.)* Tom, you know summer is rituals, and each one's got its own time and place.

TOM. Like what?

DOUG. Like . . . like the ritual of lemonade or iced-tea making, the ritual of the wine making, shoes or no shoes.

TOM. Oh!

DOUG. What have you got to report, Tom: A new first, a fancy ceremony of some sort—like creek-crab catching or water-strider-spider grabbing?

TOM. Ain't nobody ever grabbed a water-strider-spider in his life. You ever know anyone that did? Go ahead, think, Doug.

DOUG. I'm thinking.

TOM. Well?

DOUG. You're right. Nobody ever did. They're just too fast.

TOM. It ain't that they're fast. They just don't exist. *(After still another pause.)* That's right! They just never did exist at all. Well, that's all.

DOUG. What's that mean?

TOM. Water-strider-spiders don't exist, because you can't catch them. And only the things you can hold and touch . . . and look onto . . . exist.

DOUG. I don't believe you.

NARRATOR [R1]. Can you tell him, Tom? Can you tell him what is just a nucleus of thought in your youthful mind? Can you tell him of the endlessness of time? Of the great circle in which those things that were, and those things that are to be, and those things that never were . . . except in the minds of young boys . . . are all together and a part of . . . and forever are one with time. Can you tell him, Tom?

TOM. Nothing exists except what you can hold and touch.

DOUG. Phoooiii!

(DOUG *and* TOM *return to their stools and sit. There is a slight pause but no shifting of the* READERS' *positions.*)

NARRATOR. The lazy days of July are long and full. The bright warm days are filled to the very brim of being with warm sweet odors of dandelions; and in the cellar of Grandma's house the shelves are filling, day by wonderful day, with ketchup bottles transformed into crystal vessels of dandelion wine. Each day a new, shiny bottle . . . labeled and filled with the events of that day. There's the first harvest . . . and there's the day of the time machine . . .

DOUG [R3]. *(Rises.)* Now, John Huff, what are you feeding me? A time machine?

JOHN [R4]. *(Rises.)* A time machine. Mother's scout's honest Injun's honor!

LUCY [R2]. *(Rises.)* An' it travels in the past and future, too?

JOHN. No, Lucy. Only in the past. But you can't have everything. Here we are.

DOUG. Heck, this is just old Colonel Freeleigh's place.

LUCY. Can't be no time machine in there. He's no inventor.

JOHN. Okay! Be knuckleheads. Sure, Colonel Freeleigh didn't invent it, but he's got prop . . . prop . . . prop—pri-e-tary interest in it. An' it's been here all the time. Come on. (JOHN *and* LUCY *step to the side of their lecterns.*)

NARRATOR. John escorts Lucy in past the screen door. (DOUG *steps out from behind his lectern.*) It does not slam. Douglas catches it and follows Lucy and John into Colonel Freeleigh's house. They peer down a long dark hall toward a room that is like an undersea grotto . . . soft green, dim, and watery.

JOHN. Colonel Freeleigh? *(After a pause.)* He don't hear so good. Colonel!

NARRATOR. No answer . . . only the dust, sifting down and around the spiral stairwell from above. Then a faint stir in that undersea chamber at the far end of the hall. Move carefully, children . . . peer into the room. You will see two pieces of furniture—an old man and a chair. They resemble each other, both so thin you can see how they are put together. The rest of the room . . . naked ceiling and walls and vast quantities of air . . . silent and still.

DOUG. He . . . he looks dead.

JOHN. Naw, he's just dreaming of places to travel. Colonel?

NARRATOR. One of the pieces of brown furniture moves. It's the Colonel —blinking, focusing, smiling a wild and toothless smile.

COLONEL [R5]. *(Rises and steps forward.)* Eh? Oh, Johnnie! Why . . . why, come in, boy! Come in!

JOHN. Colonel, Doug and Lucy are here, too . . .

COLONEL. Eh? Oh, oh, yes! Well, all of you, come in. Come on, now.

LUCY. But where's the . . .

JOHN. Ssssssh!

COLONEL. Where's what?

JOHN. Uh . . . she means . . . but where's the . . . uh . . . point in *us* talking? . . . I . . . uh . . . *you* talk, Colonel. Huh?

COLONEL. *(Laughing.)* Beware, Johnny Huff! Old men lie in wait for people to ask them to talk. Then they rattle on like a rusty elevator wheezing up a shaft.

JOHN. Tell us about Pawnee Bill!

COLONEL. Eh? What?

JOHN. Pawnee Bill . . . the way west!

COLONEL. Ah . . . yes . . . the way west . . . me and Pawnee Bill. (DOUG, JOHN, *and* LUCY *return to their stools and sit.*)

NARRATOR. The Colonel's voice murmurs; it drifts away on serene lake waters.

COLONEL. This is how it was over fifty years ago . . . 1875! People asleep in the small towns of the East . . . or not yet asleep in their beds, and hearing sounds of horses in the night and the creak of the Conestoga ready to go . . . the brooding of oxen under the trees . . . and the small crying of children, old before their time. Sound of arrivals and departures, blacksmiths in red hells through midnight. . . . The smell of bacon and hams ready for travel . . . heavy feel of wagons, ships floundering with goods. . . . Dogs running out to the edge of the wilderness ahead and, fearful, running back with a look of empty space in their eyes. . . . This is how it was, going west so long ago . . . out on the rim of the precipice, on the edge of the cliff of stars . . .

That's how it was in 1875 . . . an' me an' Bill out there, somewhere in that wilderness, on a little rise in the middle of the prairie, waitin'. Bill, he leans over to me—

PAWNEE BILL [R1]. *(Stands.)* Colonel?

COLONEL. Huh? What is . . . ?

PAWNEE BILL. Listen.

COLONEL. The prairie's like a big stage all set for the storm to come. Thunder! Softness in the gloom. Thunder again!

PAWNEE BILL. Out there, Colonel. Look at the size o' that cloud! Yellow —fer az th' eye kin see. Full o' black lightnin' sunk down to earth. Fifty miles wide, twice't as long, an' a mile high.

COLONEL. Lord . . .

PAWNEE BILL. Yellow cloud, Colonel—inch off'n th' groun'—hit's a comin'.

COLONEL. Lord . . . Lord A'mighty, Bill!

PAWNEE BILL. Look at hit, Colonel!

COLONEL. The earth pounding like a heart gone mad. Children . . . a heart gone to panic. Our bones shaking fit to break. The very earth, quivering and shaking, and rumbling.

PAWNEE BILL. That's 'em, Colonel!

COLONEL. Let's git 'em, Bill! (PAWNEE BILL *sits.*) And I shouted again. The veil of dust lifted, and I saw 'em! I swear to God, I saw 'em! The grand army of the prairie: the bison, the buffalo!

NARRATOR. *(After a pause.)* There is thunder and lightning in the Colonel's room. The air is unbreathable with dust; a roar drowns out all sight, all sound.

COLONEL. Heads like giant fists, bodies like locomotives. Twenty, fifty, two hundred thousand iron missiles shooting out of that yellow cloud, flailing cinders from their hooves, eyes a-glowin' with the heat of hell! Six hours . . . six hours it took them to pass away over the horizon toward less kind men than me. I couldn't shoot them. I tried to, but I couldn't do it. Bill was gone. I stood alone on the prairie. But I saw 'em—the great herds of American buffalo. I saw, but couldn't shoot. Six hours it took to pass on over to eternity. I hear them still, roaring like a great wind. I wish you children could have heard—could have seen—the roaring . . . the hot breaths searing the grass. Wish you could have . . . could have . . .

DOUG. *(Stands.)* Is—is he asleep?

JOHN. *(Stands.)* No . . . he's just recharging the batteries.

LUCY. *(Stands.)* But where's the time—?

JOHN. My gosh, Lucy. You're sure dumb. (LUCY *sits.*)

COLONEL. Antietam . . . Bull Run . . . Shiloh . . .

DOUG. Gee! Does he know about the Civil War, too? *(In the background, a voice softly sings "The Battle Hymn of the Republic.")*

JOHN. Do you remember the Civil War, sir? (JOHN *sits.*)

COLONEL. Do I remember the—? Oh, yes . . . I do, I do! Everything! Except . . . which side I fought on . . .

DOUG. The color of your uniform. (DOUG *sits. The singing stops, but a humming begins.*)

COLONEL. Colors begin to run on you. It's gotten hazy. I see soldiers with me, but a long time ago I stopped seeing color in their coats or caps. *(Humming stops.)* Born in Illinois . . . raised in Virginia . . . married in New York . . . built a house in Tennessee, an' now—very late— here I am, good Lord, back in Greentown. . . . The *soldiers* are there, but the colors run an' blend.

NARRATOR. The light is dimming in the western sky, children. The time machine is running down. Hurry! Ask him about Bull Run! Ask him about Shiloh! John Huff, ask the time machine which side of the hills he fought on!

JOHN. Did the sun rise on your left or right? Did you march toward Canada or Mexico?

COLONEL. Seems some mornings the sun rose on my good right hand, some mornings over my left shoulder. . . . Son, we marched *all* directions. It's almost seventy years since—

NARRATOR. Seventy years since Chattanooga and Lookout Mountain, since Gettysburg. You forget suns and mornings and directions *that* long past. But a battle, Colonel—a battle won somewhere?

A VOICE. *(Singing softly.)* "Oh, I wish I was in the land of cotton! Old times there are not forgotten . . . " *(The singing stops, but a humming begins.)*

COLONEL. No. I don't remember anyone winning . . . anywhere . . . any time. *(Humming stops.)* War's just not a winning thing. You lose—all the time—and the ones who lose last asks for terms. All I remember is a lot of losing and sadness and nothing good at the end of it all. Ah! The end of it. *That* was a winning . . . but a winning all to itself and had nothing to do with the guns. But that ain't a winning you want me to talk about, is it, young'uns?

LUCY. *(Rises.)* What about Antietam?

COLONEL. I was there.

DOUG. *(Rises.)* Bull Run!

COLONEL. I was there.

JOHN. *(Rises.)* Shiloh? Were you at Shiloh, Colonel?

COLONEL. A beautiful name, Shiloh. What a shame to see it only on battle records!

JOHN. Shiloh, then? Fort Sumter? (LUCY, DOUG, *and* JOHN *sit again.*)
COLONEL. I saw the first puffs of powder smoke. So many things come
back . . . oh, so many things . . . soldiers lying peacefully near the
Potomac . . . dreaming. Tents in the clear autumn moon. Watchfires
gleaming . . . no sound save the rush of the river . . . and the dew falls
softly on the faces of the dead . . . the picket's off duty forever! . . .
After the surrender . . . there stands Mr. Lincoln on the White House
balcony. What's that he's sayin'? . . . Did he say, "Will the band play
'Dixie'"? *(A voice hums "Dixie," continuing through the* COLONEL'*s
speech.)* Late at night I feel my mouth move . . . singing the songs back
in another time . . . the songs . . . I remember the songs . . . singing!
*(The humming stops, and various voices sing snatches of Civil War
songs.)*
VOICE TWO. "Look away, look away, look away, Dixie Land . . . "
VOICE ONE. "Mine eyes have seen the glory of the coming of the Lord."
VOICE FOUR. "He is trampling out the vintage where the grapes of wrath
are stored."
VOICE TWO. *(To the tune of "The Yellow Rose of Texas.")* "Ye cavaliers
of Dixie, who guard the southern shores . . . "
VOICE ONE. "When the boys come home in triumph, with the laurels they
shall gain . . . "
COLONEL. So many songs, sung on both sides, blowing north, blowing
south on the high winds . . .
VOICE ONE. "We are coming, Father Abraham, three hundred thousand
more . . . "
VOICE FOUR. "Tenting tonight, tenting tonight, tenting on the old camp
ground . . . "
VOICE TWO. "Hurrah, hurrah, we bring the Jubilee. . . . Hurrah, hurrah,
the flag that makes us free."
COLONEL. *(Singing.)* "Hurrah, hurrah, we bring the Jubilee . . . "

(There is a long pause. The COLONEL *steps back to his stool but does not
sit.* JOHN *rises and steps to the side of his lectern.)*

JOHN. Well! Is he or isn't he? (LUCY *and* DOUG *rise and step to the side
of their lecterns.)*
LUCY. He sure is!
COLONEL. Huh? I sure am *what?*
DOUG. A time machine, a time machine.
COLONEL. Is that what you call me?
JOHN. Yes . . . yes, sir, Colonel.
DOUG. Well, I guess we'd better go . . .
LUCY. Yes—uh—thank you, Colonel.
COLONEL. What? Oh . . . oh, so long, children.
NARRATOR. Quietly . . . ever so quietly the children tiptoe out of the room
and down the long hall. (LUCY, JOHN, *and* DOUG *step back from their lec-*

terns but remain standing.) Colonel Freeleigh does not see them go. In the street they are startled as someone shouts from a first floor window above.

COLONEL. *(With a step forward.)* Hey!

JOHN. Yes, sir, Colonel?

COLONEL. You're right! Why didn't I think of that? A time machine, by God. I *am* a time machine.

LUCY. Yes, sir.

DOUG. *(At the same time.)* You sure are, sir.

COLONEL. So long children . . . and . . . and come aboard any time. *(He steps back to his lectern and sits.)*

LUCY, JOHN, DOUG. *(All together.)* Yes, sir! We will! Good-bye!

NARRATOR. And you will go aboard many times this summer, Douglas and Johnny and Lucy. You're riding a very special train.

DOUG. The Colonel . . . well, he's been down the track before, and he knows. And now here we come, you and me, along the same track, but further on. . . . We need old Colonel Freeleigh to shove us and say "Look alive" so we remember every second! So when kids come around when *we* are old, we can do for them what the Colonel once did for us. That's the way it is. We all got to go visit him a lot and listen . . . we got to go far-traveling with him as often as we can!

JOHN. Far-traveling?

LUCY. Far-traveling. You make that up, Doug?

DOUG. Maybe . . . maybe no.

LUCY. Far-traveling . . .

DOUG. Yes, one thing I am sure of . . . *(His voice hollow, fading out— and into an echo effect.)* . . . far-traveling—it sure sounds lonely.

(LUCY, DOUG, *and* JOHN *sit. There is a long pause, during which all of the* READERS *shift their positions slightly to mark the passage of time. Then* DOUG *rises and steps forward.*)

II. THE REALIZATION: THE SORROWS OF SUMMER

A Game of Statues

DOUG [R3]. People shouldn't be in such a hurry. People are always running. I put that down in my nickel tablet. "People shouldn't run." Because if you run, time runs. You yell and scream and race and roll and tumble, and all of a sudden the sun is gone and the whistle is blowing.

JOHN [R4]. *(Rises, steps forward.)* I'm leaving you, Douglas Spaulding. Going away.

DOUG. John! Say that again.

JOHN. You heard me the first time, Doug.

DOUG. Did you say you were—going away?

JOHN. Got my train ticket here in my pocket. Whoo-whoo-clang! Sush-sush-sush-sush . . . whoooooooooo . . . going tonight.

DOUG. Tonight! But, my gosh! Tonight we're playing "Red-Light—Green-Light." And "Statues"! How come all of a sudden?

JOHN. It's my father. He's got a job in Milwaukee.

DOUG. Going away—gee! Summer sure is changing.

JOHN. Changing?

DOUG. Why, John, I just realized this summer I was alive. And now things are happening too fast. I—I—I—thought everything would go on forever: the perfection, the sound of a good friend whistling like an oriole . . .

VOICE ONE. Pegging the softball . . .

VOICE FIVE. Key-jingling the dusty path . . .

VOICE SIX. All of it complete . . .

VOICE TWO. Everything can be touched.

VOICE SIX. Things stay near . . .

VOICE ONE. Things are at hand and will remain.

DOUG. *(After a pause.)* People shouldn't run. The only way to keep things slow is to watch everything and do nothing! You can maybe stretch a day—a night—into three days, three nights. Sure . . . just by watching! And everything stays as it is forever!

JOHN. Doug?

DOUG. Yes?

JOHN. I got time, time for maybe one game of "Statues," then I got to go home. The train leaves at eight. Who's going to be "it"?

DOUG. Me! I'm "it"! Start running!

VOICE ONE. Boys scatter, yelling . . .

VOICE SIX. John backs away, then turns . . .

VOICE TWO. Begins to lope.

VOICE SIX. Douglas counts slowly.

VOICE FIVE. Let them run far . . .

VOICE ONE. Spread out . . . separate . . . each to his own small world.

VOICE TWO. Momentum up!

VOICE FIVE. Almost out of sight! . . .

DOUG. Statues! Everyone, freeze!

NARRATOR [R1]. Very quietly, Douglas moves across the lawn to where John Huff stands like an iron deer in the twilight.

DOUG. John, now—don't you move so much as an eyelash. I absolutely command you to stay here and not move at all for the next—*three hours!*

JOHN. Doug . . .

DOUG. *(Commandingly.)* Freeze!

JOHN. *(In a small whisper.)* I've got to go.

DOUG. Not a muscle. It's the game.

JOHN. I've got to go home now.

VOICE SIX. Now the statue moves . . .

VOICE TWO. Takes its hands down out of the air . . .

VOICE FIVE. Moves its head to look at Douglas.

NARRATOR. The two boys stand looking at each other.

JOHN. We'll play one more round. But this time, I'll be "it." Run!

VOICE SIX. The boys run.

JOHN. Freeze!

VOICE TWO. The boys freeze, Douglas with them.

JOHN. Not a muscle . . . not a hair! Doug, this is the only way to do it.

DOUG. John . . .

VOICE FIVE. Douglas feels John walking around him . . .

VOICE ONE. Even as he had walked around John a moment before.

VOICE SIX. He feels John sock him on the arm once—not too hard.

JOHN. So long, Doug. (JOHN *moves back to his stool and sits.*)

VOICE ONE. Then there is a rushing sound . . .

VOICE TWO. The sound of boys running in summer.

VOICE FIVE. He knows there is nobody behind him. (*There is a pause, and* VOICE FOUR *vocalizes the sound of a faraway train whistle.*)

VOICE FOUR. Whoo-whoo-oooo . . .

DOUG. (*After another pause.*) So long, John Huff, so . . . long.

VOICE ONE. Statues are best.

VOICE TWO. They are the only things you can keep on your lawn.

VOICE FIVE. Don't ever let them move.

VOICE SIX. Once you do, you can't do a thing with them.

DOUG. John? John! John, you're my enemy, you hear? You're no friend of mine. Don't come back now, ever! Get away! Enemy! You hear me? That's what you are. It's all off! Now you're dirt . . . (*crying*) . . . John, you hear me? *John?*

VOICE ONE. Doug stands on the porch.

VOICE TWO. The sky darkens like a wick down a notch.

VOICE SIX. He looks at his fist pointed down the street . . .

VOICE TWO. He looks at his fist . . .

VOICE FIVE. And it dissolves . . .

VOICE ONE. The world dissolves beyond it.

DOUG. I'm mad, I'm angry, I hate him, I'm mad, I'm angry, I hate him, I'm mad, I'm angry, I hate him! Hate—hate—hate . . .

(DOUG *returns to his stool and sits. There is a long pause as the* READERS *change positions to mark the transition.*)

The Closing Window

(*As successive* READERS *speak the following lines, each rises and moves to a position in front of his lectern.*)

VOICE SIX. There's the day of the new tennis shoes . . .

VOICE TWO. There's the day of the first dandelion harvest . . .

VOICE FOUR. And the day a god left Greentown, and the world dissolved.

VOICE ONE. And then there comes the day when, all around, you hear the dropping of apples . . .

VOICE FIVE. One . . . by one . . . from the trees.

NARRATOR [R1]. Falling like horses' hoofs in the soft, darkening grass . . .

VOICE THREE. And *you* are the last apple on the tree.

NARRATOR. You wait. Wait for the wind to work you slowly from the tree—from your hold upon the sky . . .

VOICE TWO. To drop you down . . .

VOICE THREE. Down . . . to fall into darkness . . .

VOICE SIX. From the light of perpetual day . . .

NARRATOR. To the coldness and blackness of eternal night. (READERS THREE, FOUR, *and* SIX *return to their stools and sit.*)

COLONEL [R5]. (*Steps forward.*) No! No, not like that! Please, God—not like that.

TELEPHONE OPERATOR [R2]. Colonel Freeleigh? Colonel Freeleigh, here is your call. Mexico City, Erickson 3-8-9-9.

NARRATOR. Now far away but infinitely clear . . . (MIGUEL *rises and steps to the right side of his lectern.*)

MIGUEL [R4]. Bueno.

COLONEL. Miguel?

MIGUEL. Señor Freeleigh! Again? Thees cost you much money.

COLONEL. Let it cost! You know what to do, Miguel?

MIGUEL. Sí, señor. The window?

COLONEL. Yes, Miguel . . . and hurry. Hurry!

MIGUEL. Sí. Un minuto, señor.

NARRATOR. Thousands of miles away, in a southern climate, the sounds of footsteps move away from a telephone receiver. Then can be heard the grate of a window opening.

COLONEL. Ahhh. Yes—yes. I can hear . . . all the sounds.

VOICE SIX. The sounds of Mexico City on a hot, yellow noon . . .

VOICE TWO. Sounds rising through an open window into a waiting phone . . .

VOICE ONE. A man named Miguel holding the mouthpiece out into the bright day.

MIGUEL. Señor? (MIGUEL *sits.*)

COLONEL. No! No, please . . . let me listen.

NARRATOR. Listen to hooting metal horns . . .

VOICE SIX. Squealing brakes . . .

VOICE TWO. The call of vendors selling red-purple bananas and jungle oranges . . .

VOICE FOUR. Tires ripping on hot pavements . . .

VOICE SIX. Eyes shut tight, and the vision of meat hanging in great slabs . . .

VOICE TWO. The smell of stone alleys, wet with the morning rain.

VOICE SIX. The clean feeling of a hot sun burning on brown straight shoulders.

VOICE FIVE. Young—twenty-five—no more wheelchair, no more failing heart . . . but twenty-five, and walking . . . alert . . . looking, seeing . . .

VOICE SIX. Drinking all colors and all smells.

NARRATOR. A rap on the door. The old man quickly hides the phone under his lap robe.

VOICE TWO. The nurse enters. (THE NURSE *rises and stands at the right of her lectern.*)

NURSE [R6]. Hello. Have you been good?

COLONEL. Yes.

NARRATOR. It is an effort . . . mechanical. He can hardly see. The shock of a simple rap on a door is such that part of him is still in another city far removed. He waits for his mind to rush home—it must be there to answer questions, act sane, be polite.

NURSE. I've come to check your pulse.

COLONEL. Not *now!*

NURSE. You're not going anywhere, are you?

NARRATOR. He looks steadily at the nurse.

COLONEL. I haven't been anywhere for ten years.

NURSE. Give me your wrist.

VOICE TWO. Fingers, hard and precise, search like a pair of calipers for the sickness in his pulse.

NURSE. What have you been doing to excite yourself?

COLONEL. Nothing!

VOICE TWO. Her gaze shifts and stops on the empty phone table.

NURSE. Why do you do this? You promised you wouldn't. That's how you hurt yourself in the first place—getting excited, talking too much, those children in here jumping around . . .

COLONEL. They sat quietly and listened, and I told them things they'd never heard before. The buffalo, I told them. It was worth it. I was in a pure fever. I was alive. It doesn't matter if being alive kills a man. Now give me the phone. I can at least talk to someone outside this room!

NURSE. I'm sorry, Colonel. Your grandson will have to know about this. I prevented his having the phone taken out last week. Now it looks like I'll have to let him have his head.

COLONEL. This is my house, my phone! I pay your salary!

NURSE. To make you well. Not to allow you to get yourself excited. To bed with you now, young man.

NARRATOR. From the bed he looks back at the phone and *keeps* looking at it.

NURSE. I'm going to the store for a few minutes. And just to be sure you don't use the phone again, I'm hiding your wheelchair in the hall. (*The* NURSE *sits.*)

VOICE TWO. She wheels the empty chair out the door.

NARRATOR. He hears her pause in the downstairs entry and dial the extension phone.

COLONEL. Mexico City? She wouldn't dare!

VOICE TWO. The front door shuts.

NARRATOR. He thinks of the last week here, alone, in his room . . . of the secret, narcotic calls across the continents, an isthmus, whole jungle countries of rain forests, blue orchid plateaus, lakes, hills . . .

COLONEL. Talking . . . talking . . . to Buenos Aires . . . and Lima . . . Rio de Janeiro.

NARRATOR. He lifts himself in the cool bed. Tomorrow . . . the phone gone.

COLONEL. What a greedy fool I've been!

NARRATOR. He slips his brittle ivory legs down from the bed, marveling at their desiccation.

COLONEL. They seem to be things that were fastened to my body one night when I slept—my younger legs taken off and destroyed in the cellar furnace.

NARRATOR. Over the years, they had destroyed all of him, removing hands, arms, and legs.

COLONEL. Leaving me with substitutes as delicate and useless as chess pieces.

NARRATOR. And now they are tampering with something more intangible —the memory.

COLONEL. They're trying to cut wires leading back into another year!

NARRATOR. He crosses the room in a stumbling run. Grasping the phone, he takes it with him as he slides down the wall to sit upon the floor.

COLONEL. Must get the long-distance operator.

NARRATOR. Heart pounding—exploding within—faster and faster—a blackness in the eyes.

COLONEL. Hurry, hurry!

MIGUEL [R4]. (After a pause, rising.) Bueno?

COLONEL. Miguel, we were . . . cut off.

MIGUEL. We must not phone again, señor. Your nurse called me. She says you are very ill. I must hang up.

COLONEL. No, Miguel! Please. One last time, listen to me. They're taking the phone out tomorrow. I can never call again. (After a short, tense pause.) For the love of God, Miguel! For friendship . . . the old days. I haven't moved in ten years.

NARRATOR. He drops the phone and has trouble picking it up, his chest thick with pain.

COLONEL. Miguel, you are still there, aren't you?

MIGUEL. Thees weel be the last time?

COLONEL. I promise.

NARRATOR. The phone is laid on a desk thousands of miles away. Once more, the footsteps, the pause, and—at last—the raising of a window.

VOICE TWO. From somewhere drifts across the silent air flamenco music.

COLONEL. Listen!

NARRATOR. And he hears a thousand people in another sunlight—

VOICE SIX. The faint tinkling music of a guitar . . .

VOICE FOUR. The people in the city of early siesta . . .

VOICE ONE. Shops closing . . . little boys crying, "Lotería, nacional para hoy!"

VOICE FOUR. "Lotería, nacional . . .!" (*The voice becoming an echo.*) "Lotería, nacional para hoy!"

NARRATOR. And at last, the clearest, most improbable sound of all . . .

COLONEL. The sound of a . . . a green trolley car going around a corner . . .

VOICE ONE. A trolley burdened with a brown, alien, and beautiful people.

VOICE SIX. And the sound of other people running and calling out with triumph as they swing aboard . . .

VOICE TWO. Vanishing around a corner on shrieking rails and borne away in a sun-blazed distance.

COLONEL. Hurry . . . hurry! The people . . . places . . . are falling . . . falling away . . . (*The* COLONEL *sits.*)

NARRATOR. Long before you hit the grass, you will have forgotten there ever was a tree, or other apples, or a summer, or dandelion wine, or green grass below. You fall into a darkness.

VOICE TWO. (*After a pause.*) And above the static of two thousand miles, a strange sound. From two thousand miles away, the closing of a window.

(*There is a longer pause during which all of the* READERS *shift positions slightly to mark the passage of time.*)

NARRATOR. Tom sits on the Civil War cannon in the courthouse square.

TOM [R5]. (*Rises and steps forward.*) Boom! Boom! Boom!

VOICE ONE. Douglas, in front of the cannon, clutches his heart and falls down on the grass. But he doesn't get up; he just lies there, his face thoughtful.

DOUG [R3]. (*Rises and steps forward.*) Tom, it just hit me!

TOM. What?

DOUG. Yesterday the Civil War ended right here in this town forever! Yesterday Mr. Lincoln died right here, and so did General Lee and Grant and a hundred thousand others facing north and south. And yesterday afternoon, at Colonel Freeleigh's house, a herd of buffalo as big as all Greentown, Illinois, went off a cliff into nothing at all. Tom, it's awful! Yesterday a whole lot of dust settled for good. I never dreamed so many people could die so fast.

TOM. They sure did, though. They sure did . . . when Colonel Freeleigh died.

DOUG. You know, Tom, I'm worried.

TOM. 'Bout what?

DOUG. 'Bout the way God runs the world.

TOM. He's all right, Doug. He tries!

(TOM *and* DOUG *step back and sit. There is a pause; all of the* READERS *change their positions slightly to denote a transition in time and place.*)

A Sum in Arithmetic

NARRATOR [R1]. She was a woman with a broom or a dustpan or a mixing bowl in her hand, Great-Grandma was.

GREAT-GRANDMA [R6]. *(Rises.)* In a few hours I shall be dead.

NARRATOR. She strolled but twice in any garden, and flowers bloomed in the warm air.

GREAT-GRANDMA. I'm not afraid.

NARRATOR. And walking, she touched people like pictures, setting the frames a little straighter.

GREAT-GRANDMA. *(Steps forward.)* When you have lived as long as I have, you put away the fear. I never liked lobster in my life, and mainly because I never tried it. On my eightieth birthday, I tried it. Can't say as I am greatly excited over it; but still, I have no doubt as to its taste.

NARRATOR. Death will be a lobster, too.

GREAT-GRANDMA. And I can come to terms with it.

DOUG [R3]. *(Rises.)* Gran'ma . . . Great-Gran'ma . . .

NARRATOR. Now the huge sum in arithmetic is almost completed.

GREAT-GRANDMA. I've stuffed turkeys, chickens, men, and boys. I've washed ceilings, walls, invalids, and children . . .

NARRATOR. Look back now, Sara Spaulding . . . look back on thirty billion things started, carried, and finished and done. It all sums up, totals out. The last decimal placed, the final zero is swinging into place on the line.

GREAT-GRANDMA. I've drawn shades, pinched candles, turned switches . . . and grown old.

NARRATOR. You finished the arithmetic, Sara Spaulding. Now stand back from life a silent hour before reaching for the eraser.

DOUG. Great-Gran'ma . . . ?

GREAT-GRANDMA. *(Very weak.)* Let me see now. Let me see . . .

MOTHER [R2]. *(Choking.)* Great-Gran'ma . . .

GREAT-GRANDMA. Here now, here! All of you here? Well, just let me lie. I'm sleepy . . . so sleepy. I'm ninety-two years old . . . and I'm tired . . .

GRANDPA [R4]. *(Rises.)* Mother, now you listen to me. What you're doin' is no better than breakin' a lease. This house will fall down without you. You gotta give us a year's notice! (GRANDPA *sits.*)

GREAT-GRANDMA. No, son. I can't wait so long, I'm afraid. . . . Is Doug here?

DOUG. Yes, Gran'ma.

GREAT-GRANDMA. I'm so like you sometimes, Doug . . . sittin' through Saturday matinees until your father has to come down after you.

DOUG. I'm sorry . . . I . . .

GREAT-GRANDMA. No, no, child. . . . Doug, when the time comes that the same cowboys are shootin' the same Indians on the same hill, then it's time to fold back the seat and head for home, with no regrets . . . so I'm just leavin' while I'm still happy and still entertained. (DOUG *cries.*) Doug . . . ? Doug, are you cryin' . . . ?

DOUG. Y—yes . . .

GREAT-GRANDMA. What are you cryin' for, child?

DOUG. Be—because you won't be here tomorrow.

GREAT-GRANDMA. Why, honey, I'm not *dying* today. Look in the mirror with me, Doug. Tomorrow morning, I'll get up at seven and wash behind my ears; I'll go to church with Charlie Woodruff; I'll picnic at Electric Park; I'll swim, run barefoot, fall out of trees, chew spearmint gum. . . . Douglas . . . Douglas, for shame! You cut your fingernails, don't you, Douglas?

DOUG. *(Sniffs.)* Yes'm.

GREAT-GRANDMA. And you don't yell when your body makes itself over every seven years or so . . . old cells dead and new ones added to your fingers and your heart. You don't mind that, do you?

DOUG. No'm.

GREAT-GRANDMA. Well, consider then, boy. Any man saves fingernail clippings is a fool. You ever see a snake bother to keep his peeled skin?

DOUG. No . . .

GREAT-GRANDMA. That's about all you got here today in this bed. Fingernails and snake skin. One good breath would send me up in flakes. *(After a pause.)* Important thing is not the me that's lying here, but the me that's downstairs gettin' supper or outside in the backyard tinkerin' with the old car . . . or in the parlor readin'. Why, Douglas, bless you, child! I'm not dying today. No person ever did die that has a family. I'll be around a long time. *(After another pause.)* The world's goin' on . . . and since the part of me which is called—for convenience—Great-Gran'ma won't be here to step it along, all the *other* parts of me—the parts called Uncle Bert and Tom, Mother and Pa, and Douglas and all the other names . . . they'll have to take over, each to his own.

DOUG. Yes, Gran'ma.

GREAT-GRANDMA. So . . . now don't you all worry over me. All of you go . . . go and let me get my work *all* finished . . . (*There is a pause.* DOUGLAS *steps back to his stool but does not sit.*)

NARRATOR. They're all gone now, Sara Spaulding.

GREAT-GRANDMA. Well, that's better. Alone.

A GIRL'S VOICE [R2]. *(Singing.)* "Yes, we'll gather at the river, the beautiful, the beautiful river . . ."

VOICE ONE. No regrets, Sara Spaulding . . .

A GIRL'S VOICE. *(Continuing to sing.)* "Yes, we'll gather at the river . . ."

GREAT-GRANDMA. *(Breaking in on the song.)* No. No regrets. Death's fitting and proper. Like everything else in life, it's fitting.

A GIRL'S VOICE. *(Finishing her song.)* "That flows by the throne of God!"

(GREAT-GRANDMA *sits. There is a pause; the* READERS *shift their positions; and, again, there is a transition in time and locale.)*

The Fever Dream

DOUG [R3]. Here it is, all written down in my nickel tablet: "You can't depend on things, because . . .

VOICE ONE. Like machines . . . they fall apart or rust or run down.

VOICE TWO. Like tennis shoes, you can run so far, so fast, and then the earth's got you again.

VOICE FIVE. Like wine presses. Presses, big as they are, always run out of dandelions, and squeeze, and squeeze to a halt."

DOUG. "You can't depend on people, because . . .

VOICE FOUR. They go away . . .

VOICE TWO. Strangers die . . .

VOICE FIVE. People you know die . . .

VOICE ONE. Friends die . . .

VOICE SIX. Your own folks can die."

DOUG. So . . . *(With a big breath.)* . . . so . . .

VOICE ONE. So if wine presses and friends and near-friends can go away for awhile or go away forever,

VOICE TWO. Or rust,

VOICE SIX. Or fall apart,

VOICE FIVE. Or die,

DOUG. And if . . . if someone like Great-Gran'ma . . .

VOICE FOUR. Who was going to live forever . . . can die . . .

DOUG. Then . . .

VOICE TWO. Then you, Douglas Spaulding, someday must . . .

DOUG. Then I, Douglas Spaulding, someday must . . . no!

VOICE ONE. Colonel Freeleigh . . .

VOICE FIVE. Dead!

VOICE ONE. Great-Gran'ma . . .

VOICE SIX. Dead!

DOUG. Me! No, they can't kill me!

VOICE FOUR. Yes.

VOICE TWO. Yes.

VOICE SIX. Yes!

VOICE FIVE. Yes, anytime they want to . . .

VOICE ONE. No matter how you kick or scream . . .

VOICE TWO. They just put a big hand over you,

VOICE FIVE. And you're still.

DOUG. I don't want to die!

VOICE SIX. You'll have to, anyway.

VOICE ONE. You'll have to, anyway.

VOICE SIX. Write it in your notebook, Douglas:

VOICE FOUR. I, Douglas Spaulding—someday—must . . .

DOUG. "I . . . Douglas Spaulding . . . someday . . . must . . . must . . . (*very small*) . . . die." (DOUG *sits. There is a short pause.*)

TOM [R5]. (*Stands.*) Mom! Mom! Mom!

MOM [R2]. (*Stands.*) Tom, yes, Tom? What's the matter, boy?

TOM. It's Doug, Mom! He's sick. Terribly sick! He's gonna die, Mom! He's gonna die! (TOM *and* MOM *slowly reseat themselves.*)

VOICE ONE. Noon:

VOICE FOUR. Sun smashing Doug to the ground. Doctor arrives . . .

VOICE ONE. One o'clock:

VOICE SIX. Doctor exits house, shaking head. He doesn't know . . .

VOICE ONE. Two o'clock:

VOICE TWO. Mother and Tom carry ice packs to Doug's face and body . . .

VOICE ONE. Inside redness, inside blackness . . . Doug, listen to the dim piston of your heart, the muddy ebb and flow of the blood in your arms and legs.

VOICE FIVE. (*Slowly and heavily.*) Thoughts . . . heavy and barely ticking . . .

VOICE SIX. Like seed pellets falling in an hourglass . . .

VOICE FOUR. Slow . . . one by falling one.

VOICE ONE. *Tick* . . .

VOICE FOUR. Chug-a-chug-ding! Woo-woooooooo! (*The "Woo-woooooooo!" is echoed; the scene begins to build, to pick up speed.*)

VOICE TWO. Boy on rooftop—a boy locomoted, pulling an invisible whistle string . . .

VOICE SIX. Then freezing into a statue.

DOUG. John! John Huff—you! Hate you . . . John! John, we're pals, we're pals! Don't hate you, no . . . (*The pace slows down momentarily.*)

VOICE ONE. *Tick* . . .

VOICE FOUR. John falls down an elm-tree corridor . . .

VOICE TWO. Down an endless summer well . . . dwindling away.

VOICE ONE. *Tick* . . .

DOUG. John Huff . . .

VOICE ONE. *Tick* . . .

VOICE FOUR. Sand pellet dropping . . .

VOICE ONE. *Tick* . . .

DOUG. (*Stands.*) John . . .

VOICE ONE. *Tick! Tick* . . .

VOICE FIVE. *(Stands.)* Colonel Freeleigh leans out of the face of a clock . . .

VOICE FOUR. *(Stands.)* Buffalo dust springs down the street . . .

VOICE ONE. *Tick! Tick! Tick* . . .

VOICE FIVE. And buffalo dust clears, whirls, forms shapes . . .

VOICE ONE. *Tick!*

VOICE SIX. *(Stands.)* Fingernails and a heart—a flake upon a white bed . . . (READER TWO *stands and sings in a voice that becomes increasingly wild and off-key.*)

VOICE TWO. "Shall we gather at the river . . . river? Shall we gather at the river . . . river . . . river . . . ?"

DOUG. Gran'ma! Great-Gran'ma!

VOICE TWO, VOICE FOUR, VOICE FIVE. *(Climactically.)* "River . . . river . . . !"

VOICE SIX. Soft . . . soft . . .

VOICE TWO. *(Fading out.)* River . . . *(All of the* READERS *sit.)*

VOICE ONE. *(Slowly; in a low pitch.)* Five o'clock in the afternoon:

VOICE FOUR. Flies dead on the pavement . . .

VOICE SIX. Dogs wet mops in their kennels . . .

VOICE ONE. Six o'clock in the afternoon:

VOICE FIVE. Shadows herded under the trees . . .

VOICE SIX. Downtown stores shut up and locked.

VOICE ONE. Seven o'clock:

VOICE TWO. Greentown resembles a vast hearth . . .

VOICE FIVE. Shudderings of heat move again and again from the west.

VOICE ONE. Seven-thirty: *(The tempo of the scene accelerates again as it builds anew.)*

VOICE SIX. A slight breeze from the east . . .

VOICE ONE. Seven forty-five:

DOUG. Burning . . . burning up . . . an ash . . . a cinder . . . water . . . please . . . Tom? . . . water . . . Mom?

VOICE ONE. Eight o'clock:

VOICE TWO. Far away, barely audible . . .

VOICE FIVE. Thunder.

DOUG. Someday, I, Douglas Spaulding, must die!

VOICE FIVE. Thunder . . .

VOICE TWO. Closer now . . .

VOICE FIVE. Thunder!

VOICE SIX. *(The climax.)* Summer rain—begins light—*(hope begins now)*—increases—and falls heavily!

VOICE TWO. A scent of cool night and cool water . . . and cool white snow . . .

VOICE SIX. And cool green moss and cool silver pebbles lying at the bottom of a quiet river . . .

VOICE ONE. And Douglas—inside like a fall of snow in his bed—turns and opens his eyes to the freshly falling sky . . .

DOUG. Someday *I*, Douglas Spaulding, must die . . . and . . . *(rises)* . . . and someday . . . someday I will.

TOM [R5]. *(Also rises.)* Mom! Mom! It's Doug. He's all right! He's all right! He's not going to die, Mom! Mom! He's alive!

(DOUG *and* TOM *sit. There is a pause. The* READERS *vary their positions slightly, effecting another transition.)*

The Last Ritual

VOICE ONE. Then, quite suddenly, summer is over.

VOICE TWO. Doug knows it first when walking downtown.

VOICE SIX. Tom grabs his arm and points, gasping, at the dime-store window.

TOM [R5]. *(Rises and steps forward.)* Pencils, Doug—ten thousand pencils!

DOUG [R3]. *(Also rises and steps forward.)* Oh, my gosh!

VOICE ONE. Nickel tablets, dime tablets . . .

VOICE FOUR. Notebooks, erasers . . .

VOICE SIX. Water colors, rulers, compasses . . .

DOUG. A hundred thousand of them!

TOM. Don't look. Maybe it's a mirage.

DOUG. No. It's school! School—straight on ahead.

TOM. They've ruined what's left of vacation. Why did they go and do that?

DOUG. Don't know. Didn't make the world. *(After a pause.)* Though sometimes I feel like I did . . . like I got every bit of it right here inside me, Tom.

TOM. You and two zillion other people, I bet.

DOUG. Come on . . . race you home. Bet Gran'pa's in the cellar puttin' up the last of the dandelion wine.

TOM. Come on! (DOUG *and* TOM *quickly return to their stools and sit.)*

VOICE ONE. Down in the cellar, they all look at the summer they have shelved there in glimmering, motionless streams, the bottles of dandelion wine. Numbered from one to ninety-odd, there in ketchup bottles, most of them full now, burning in the cellar twilight—one for every living summer day.

DOUG. *(Rises.)* There's the first day of summer.

VOICE TWO. *(Rises.)* The new-tennis-shoes day . . .

DOUG. There's the day I found out I was alive. Why isn't it a bit brighter?

VOICE FOUR. *(Rises.)* There's the day John Huff fell off the edge of the world.

VOICE SIX. *(Rises.)* The day the part of us called Great-Grandmother quit working.

VOICE FIVE. *(Rises.)* There's the day Colonel Freeleigh fell six feet into the earth.

VOICE FOUR. Seems like it ought to be different—just a speck, mebbe, of buffalo dust or something. But it's just like all the others.

VOICE ONE. As he climbs the stairs from the golden cellar to the real world upstairs, Douglas breaks a spider's web with his face. A single invisible line on the air touches his brow and snaps without a sound.

DOUG. I'm alive. *(In a whisper.)* I am *alive*.

VOICE ONE. *(After a pause.)* Move slowly, Douglas, to your sorcerer's tower . . . dark, secret tower . . . alive with the distant thunders and visions. Move to the portal of glass through which the stars are blinking. Lift slowly your finger and perform the last magic ritual.

DOUG. *(Steps forward.)* Everyone, clothes off! *(After a pause.)* Brush teeth. *(After another pause.)* Climb into bed. *(After a final pause.)* Now, out with the lights.

VOICE SIX. And the town winks out its lights, sleepily, here and there.

DOUG. *(Steps back, still standing.)* The last ones now . . . there . . . there.

VOICE ONE. *(After a long pause.)* He lies in his bed now . . . the town dark . . . and around him his family, his friends, the old people and the young.

VOICE FIVE. And the people . . .

VOICE FOUR. And the world . . .

VOICE SIX. And all of time are in you—*are* you, Douglas Spaulding . . .

VOICE TWO. Never to fade away—never to die . . .

VOICE FIVE. But to go on, as Colonel Freeleigh goes on.

VOICE FOUR. As John Huff . . .

VOICE SIX. As Great-Grandma goes on . . .

DOUG. *(Triumphantly.)* Never to die—but to go on forever.

VOICE ONE. And so thinking, Douglas, sleep; and sleeping, put an end to summer, 1928.

BY STEPHEN LEACOCK

Behind the Beyond

A short story adapted for Readers Theatre by Melvin R. White

Mr. Leacock's tale tosses delightful fun at the English drawing-room comedy of the late nineteenth century, directing deftly barbed attention to the "dram-ah" of the period: stock characters, stock situations, the overdone and artificial style of acting—and not overlooking the theatre audiences of the era.

CAST OF CHARACTERS

Four Men, Three Women, and a Narrator—either Man or Woman.
The roles of the Valet and Postal Clerk may be read by one Man.

NARRATOR. *An enthusiastic storyteller with a mature, pleasing voice*

SIR JOHN. *Pompous, stuffy, dull; middle-aged or older*

VALET. *The frozen-faced English butler*

LADY CICELY. *Young, beautiful—the ingénue type; quite saccharine sometimes*

JACK HARDING. *"A narrow young man with a handsome but weak face"; not a very good actor—in an accomplished sort of way*

MRS. HARDING. *Still beautiful at forty-five*

POSTAL CLERK. *Distinguished by a marked French accent*

THE FRENCH MAID. *Extremely French and lovely*

APPAREL

Behind the Beyond can be costumed in accordance with the period, with frock coats for the men and long dresses for the women. However, it is sufficient for the readers to wear items of clothing which will merely suggest the characters. For instance: SIR JOHN: dark business suit; LADY CICELY: frilly, feminine dress, very "ingénue"—possibly pastel; JACK HARDING: handsome "leading-man" type suit—a bit too smart, perhaps; MRS. HARDING: dark dress, decidedly matronly; VALET: black suit and tie, white shirt; POSTAL CLERK: business suit with "uniform" cap of some kind; FRENCH MAID: bright-colored dress, probably a bit too tight and a bit too short.

THE PHYSICAL ARRANGEMENT OF THE SCENE

The suggested approach for presenting this Readers Theatre adaptation is to exaggerate the very formal and highly artificial atmosphere of the story. The seven readers, seated in a row of chairs parallel to the back wall, upstage, are provided with four lecterns centered well forward in the downstage area. On cue, the reader-character rises from his chair, moves forward to the designated lectern, places his script upon it, and thus "enters the scene." The NARRATOR stands at a lectern at far DR.

The focus is always offstage; the characters never look at each other on the stage. To heighten the humor, however, the readers follow or enact the descriptions given by the narrator as he unfolds the story. For example, if he reads that LADY CICELY falls into a fit of coughing, she does so; if he says there is a hunted look on MR. HARDING's face, MR. HARDING assumes a hunted look. In short, although the readers work from behind

FIGURE 11. *Behind the Beyond* floor plan

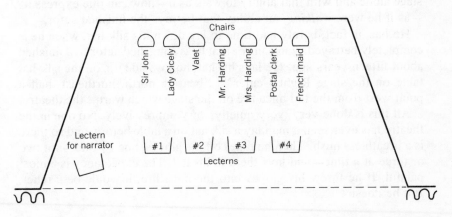

the lecterns, very seriously and formally, they use as much action and reaction as possible, playing it all straight front, facing the audience, and "seeing" the characters to whom they are speaking offstage in the realm of their imagination—and that of the spectators. This should be overdone to add to the artificiality of this period story. Throughout the script are suggestions which, it is hoped, will not only prove useful to the director and his readers but which may also suggest to them further possibilities for humorous elaboration.

Parenthetical directions concerning possible entrances, exits, positions and movements of the readers are offered on the basis of the physical arrangement in the diagram.

(As the presentation begins, the NARRATOR *stands at his lectern at DR and speaks directly to the audience.)*

NARRATOR. *(Impressively.) Behind the Beyond* . . . in Three Acts . . . and Two Drinks . . . by Stephen Leacock. *(Pauses, then resumes descriptively.)* As the curtain rises, the ushers of the theatre are still moving up and down the aisles. There is a buzz of brilliant conversation, illuminated with flashes of opera glasses and the rattle of expensive jewelry.

Then suddenly—in fact, just as if done by machinery—the lights all over the theatre, except on the stage, are extinguished. Absolute silence falls. Here and there is heard the crackle of a shirt front. But there is no other sound. Then, in this expectant hush, a man in a checked tweed suit walks onto the stage: only one man, one single man . . . (SIR JOHN *stands and walks to Lectern #1, as the* NARRATOR *continues.)* . . . Because if he had been accompanied by a chorus, that would have been a burlesque; if four citizens in togas had been with him, that would be Shakespeare; if two Russian soldiers had walked after him, that would have been melodrama. But this is a problem play. So he steps onto the stage alone and with that ability to walk as if—how can one express it? —as if he were *walking,* an ability that betrays the finished actor.

He has, in fact, barely had time to lay down his silk hat, when he is completely betrayed: you can *see* that he is a finished actor . . . finished about fifteen years ago. He lays his hat, hollow side up, on the silk-hat table on the stage Right Center . . . bearing north, northeast, half a point west from the red mica fire on the stage which warms the theatre.

All this is done very, very quietly, very impressively. No one in the theatre has ever seen a man lay a silk hat on a table before, and so there is a breathless hush. Then he takes off his gloves, one by one—not two or three at a time—and lays them in his hat. The expectancy is almost painful. If he threw his gloves into the mica fire, it would be a relief. But he doesn't.

The man on the stage picks up a pile of letters. There are a great many of these letters, because all of his business correspondence, as well as his private letters, are sent here by the government post office. Getting his letters in this way at night, he is able to read them like lightning. Some of them he merely holds upside down for a fraction of a second. Then at last he speaks.

SIR JOHN. So Union Pacific's risen two . . . hmmmm . . . Copper down again . . . Moreby anxious. "Better sell for half a million.". . . Hmmmm . . .

NARRATOR. *(Always to the audience.)* Did you get that? Half a million, and he takes it just as quietly as that!

SIR JOHN. "Lady Gathorne . . . dinner . . . Thursday the ninth." "Lunch with the Ambassador . . . Friday the tenth."

NARRATOR. And mind you, this is just patter. The Ambassador and Lady Gathorne are just put in to let the people in the cheaper seats know the kind of thing they're up against. Then the man steps across the stage and presses a button. Even before the bell begins to ring, a cardboard door swings aside . . . (VALET *rises and walks to Lectern #2.*) . . . And a valet enters. He says:

VALET. *(His face expressionless.)* Did you ring, Sir John?

NARRATOR. There is a rustle of programs all over the house. You can hear a buzz of voices say: *(Entire cast "buzzes," with one voice projecting the following line.)*

VOICE. He's Sir John Trevor!

NARRATOR. They're all on to him. When the valet says:

VALET. Did you ring, Sir John?

NARRATOR. He ought to answer:

SIR JOHN. No, I merely knocked the bell over to see how it would sound.

NARRATOR. But he misses it and doesn't say it.

SIR JOHN. Has Lady Cicely come home?

VALET. Yes, sir.

SIR JOHN. Has anyone been here?

VALET. Mr. Harding, sir.

SIR JOHN. Anyone else?

VALET. No, sir.

SIR JOHN. Very good.

NARRATOR. The valet bows and goes out through the cardboard door . . . (VALET *bows stiffly and sedately returns to his chair.*) . . . And everybody in the seats worth over a dollar knows there's something strange in the relations of Lady Cicely and Mr. Harding. You notice? Mr. Harding was here and no one else was here. In a problem play, that's enough. The double door at the back of the stage, used only by the principal characters, is opened . . . (LADY CICELY *rises and slinks down to Lectern #2.*) . . . And Lady Cicely Trevor enters. She is young and very beautiful, and wears a droopy hat and long slinky clothes which she drags across the stage. She throws down her feather hat and her crepe de what-you-call-it boa on the boa stand. Sir John says to Lady Cicely:

SIR JOHN. Shall I ring for tea?

NARRATOR. And Lady Cicely says:

LADY CICELY. *(Wearily, as if very bored.)* Thanks, no . . .

NARRATOR. In a weary tone. This shows they are the kind of people who can have tea at any time. Tea in a problem play is the same as whisky in a melodrama. Then there ensues a dialogue to this effect: Sir John asks Lady Cicely if she has been out. He might almost have *guessed* it from her coming in wearing a hat and cloak, but Sir John is an English baronet. Lady Cicely says:

LADY CICELY. *(Still bored.)* Yes, the usual round . . .

NARRATOR. And bats out a few details about duchesses and princesses for the general good of the audience. Then Lady Cicely says to Sir John:

LADY CICELY. *(Without turning her head—using her eyes only—to look at him.)* You are going out?

SIR JOHN. *(Stuffily.)* Yes. Immediately.

LADY CICELY. *(Bored with it all.)* To the House, I suppose.

NARRATOR. This doesn't mean, as you might think, the Workhouse, or the White House, or the Station House. It is the name given by people of Lady Cicely's class to the House of Commons.

SIR JOHN. Yes. I am extremely sorry. I had hoped I might ask to go with you to the opera. I fear it is impossible. . . . an important sitting . . . the Ministers will bring down the papers . . . the Kafoonistan business. *(Growing excited over the prospect.)* The House will probably divide in committee. Gatherson will ask a question. We must stop it at all costs. *(Climactically.)* The fate of the party hangs on it.

NARRATOR. Sir John has risen. His look is altered. You can see him alter it. The technical details given above have gone to his head. He can't stop. He goes on:

SIR JOHN. *(Continuing to build.)* They will force a closure on the second reading, go into committee, come out of it again, re-divide, subdivide, and force us to bring down the estimates.

NARRATOR. While Sir John speaks, Lady Cicely's manner has been that of utter weariness. (LADY CICELY *covers her mouth daintily as she yawns.)* She has picked up the London *Times* and thrown it aside; taken up a copy of *Punch* and let it fall with a thud to the floor; looked idly at a piece of music and decided, evidently, not to sing it. (LADY CICELY *repeats her yawn.)*

The dialogue has clearly brought out the following points: Sir John is in the House of Commons. Lady Cicely is not. Sir John is twenty-five years older than Lady Cicely. He doesn't see it. *(Confidentially.)* Isn't he a fool, when everybody in the gallery can see it? . . . Doesn't he see that his parliamentary work is meaningless to her, that her life is insufficient? Lady Cicely is being "starved." All that she has is money, position, clothes, and jewelry. These things starve any woman. They cramp her. That's what makes problem plays. Lady Cicely speaks, very quietly.

LADY CICELY. *(Too casually.)* Are you taking Mr. Harding with you?

SIR JOHN. Why?

LADY CICELY. Nothing. I thought perhaps I might ask him over for tea.

NARRATOR. What would a problem play be without tea?

LADY CICELY. I might ask him to the opera. Puffi is to sing.

SIR JOHN. Do, pray do. Take Harding with you, by all means. Poor boy, do take him with you.

NARRATOR. Sir John pauses. He looks at Lady Cicely very quietly for a moment. (SIR JOHN *uses the pause to put a troubled look on his face.*)

SIR JOHN. Do you know, Cicely, I've been rather troubled about Harding lately. There's something the matter with the boy, something wrong.

LADY CICELY. Yes? (LADY CICELY'S *face registers "Have I been found out?"*)

SIR JOHN. He seems abstracted, moody. I think . . . in fact I'm sure . . . that the boy is in love. (LADY CICELY *reveals fear with her eyes, and perhaps with a gesture to her breast.*)

NARRATOR. Lady Cicely has turned slightly pale. The weariness is out of her manner. (LADY CICELY, *no longer languid, straightens up.*)

SIR JOHN. *(Somewhat smugly.)* Trust the instinct of an old man, my dear. There's a woman in it.

NARRATOR. Remarkable deduction.

SIR JOHN. We old parliamentary hands are very shrewd, you know, even in these things. Someone is playing the deuce with Jack . . . with Harding. (LADY CICELY *is perturbed.*)

NARRATOR. He cannot see the change in Lady Cicely's face. He is not meant to see it. But even the little girls in the tenth row of the gallery are wise. He goes on:

SIR JOHN. Talk to Harding. Get it out of him. You women can do these things. Find out what the trouble is and let me know. *(With determination.)* I must help him.

NARRATOR. A pause. Sir John is speaking almost to himself . . . and the gallery.

SIR JOHN. I promised his mother when she sent him home, sent him to England, that I would.

NARRATOR. Lady Cicely speaks:

LADY CICELY. *(A note of suspicion in her voice.)* You knew Mr. Harding's mother very well?

SIR JOHN. Very well.

LADY CICELY. That was long ago, wasn't it?

SIR JOHN. Long ago.

LADY CICELY. Was she married then?

SIR JOHN. No, not then.

LADY CICELY. Was it here in London?

SIR JOHN. *(With forced levity.)* Yes, in London. I was only a barrister then, with my way to make, and she was a famous beauty.

NARRATOR. Sir John is speaking with a forced levity that doesn't deceive even the ushers.

SIR JOHN. She married Harding, of the Guards. They went to Afghanistan. And there he spent her fortune . . . and broke her heart.

NARRATOR. Sir John sighs. (SIR JOHN *sighs, one very deep sigh.*)

LADY CICELY. You have seen her since?

SIR JOHN. Never. (SIR JOHN *emphasizes this with at least one good negative shake of his head.*)

LADY CICELY. She has never written you?

SIR JOHN. Only once. She sent her boy home and wrote to me for help. That was how I took him as my secretary.

LADY CICELY. *(With dawning understanding.)* And that was why he came to us in Italy two years ago, just after our marriage.

SIR JOHN. Yes, that was why.

LADY CICELY. Does Mr. Harding know that you . . . *(making much of this next word)* . . . knew his mother?

NARRATOR. Sir John shakes his head.

SIR JOHN. *(Doing so.)* I have never talked with him about his mother's early life.

NARRATOR. The stage clock on the mantelpiece strikes four or five, and Sir John says:

SIR JOHN. There! Eight o'clock! I must go. I shall be late at the House. Good-bye.

NARRATOR. He moves over to Lady Cicely and kisses her. (SIR JOHN *almost smiles.*) There is a softness in his manner . . . such softness that he forgets the bundle of parliamentary papers that he had laid down. Everybody can see that he has forgotten them. Sir John goes out. (SIR JOHN *returns to his chair.*) Lady Cicely, looking fixedly at the fire, speaks to herself.

LADY CICELY. How his voice changed! Twenty-five years ago . . . so long as that. *(Musingly.)* I wonder if Jack knows.

NARRATOR. There is heard the ring of a bell off the stage. *(Use sound effect if desired.)* The valet enters. (VALET *rises and comes down to Lectern #1.*)

VALET. Mr. Harding is downstairs, my lady.

LADY CICELY. Show him up, Ransome. (VALET *bows and returns to his chair.*)

NARRATOR. A moment later, Mr. Harding enters. (MR. HARDING *rises and comes to Lectern #3. His characteristic expression is somewhat dead-pan.*) He is a narrow young man in a frock coat. His face is handsome but weak. It has to be. Mr. Harding is meant to typify weakness.

Lady Cicely walks straight to him. She puts her two hands on his shoulders, looks right into his face, and speaks with passion.

LADY CICELY. *(With passion.)* My darling . . .

NARRATOR. She says. Just like that. You can feel the thrill of it run through the orchestra chairs. All the audience point opera glasses at Mr. Harding. They can see that he is just the sort of ineffectual young man that a starved woman in a problem play goes mad over. Lady Cicely repeats:

LADY CICELY. My darling . . .

NARRATOR. Several times . . .

LADY CICELY. My darling, my darling, my darling . . .

NARRATOR. Mr. Harding says:

MR. HARDING. *(Looking slightly pained.)* Hush . . .

NARRATOR. And tries to disengage himself. She won't let him. He offers to ring for tea. She won't have any.

LADY CICELY. Oh, Jack . . .

NARRATOR. She says . . .

LADY CICELY. I can't go on any longer. I can't. When first you loved me, I thought I could. But I can't. It throttles me here . . . *(Clutches her heart area.)* This house, this life *(with a broad gesture)* . . . everything . . .

NARRATOR. She has drawn him to a sofa and has sunk down in a wave at his feet.

LADY CICELY. Do you remember, Jack, when first you came to me, in Italy, that night, at Amalfi, when we sat on the piazza of the palazzo?

NARRATOR. She is looking rapturously into his face. (LADY CICELY *suits her actions to the words*.) Mr. Harding says that he does. (MR. HARDING *shakes his head up and down once*.)

LADY CICELY. And that day at Fiesole, among the orange trees . . . and Pisa and the Capello de Terisa and the Mona Lisa? . . . Oh, Jack, take me away from all this! Take me to the Riviera, among the contadini, where we can stand together with my head on your shoulder just as we did in the Duomo at Milano, or on the piaggia at Verona. *(Gesturing broadly.)* Take me to Corfu, to the Campo Santo, to Civita Vecchia, to Para Noia . . . *anywhere!*

NARRATOR. Mr. Harding, smothered with her kisses, says:

MR. HARDING. *(With his usual dead-pan face.)* My dearest, I will, I will.

NARRATOR. Any man in the audience would take her to Honolulu. While she is speaking, Sir John's voice has been heard off the stage.

SIR JOHN. *(From his chair.)* No, thank you, Ransome. I'll get them myself; I know just where I left them. (SIR JOHN *rises, walks halfway to Lectern #1, and stops*.)

NARRATOR. Sir John enters hurriedly, advances and picks up his papers on the table . . . turns . . . and stares. He sees his wife's attitude and hears her say:

LADY CICELY. Riviera, Amalfi, Orangieri . . .

NARRATOR. He drops the parliamentary papers. They fall against the andirons with a crash. The lovers turn.

(LADY CICELY *and* MR. HARDING *turn their eyes to right as* SIR JOHN *moves on to Lectern #1; then all three stare straight front.*)

All three look at one another. For a moment they make a motion as if to ring for tea. They then stand petrified.

LADY CICELY. *(Gasps.)* You . . .

NARRATOR. Gasps Lady Cicely. Everybody says afterward that it was just splendid when she said:

LADY CICELY. You!

NARRATOR. Sir John stands gazing in horror.

SIR JOHN. Him! *(Corrects his grammar.)* He!

NARRATOR. Mr. Harding says nothing. He looks very weak. (MR. HARD-ING *looks weak*.) Lady Cicely breaks out, speaking through her nostrils:

LADY CICELY. *(With passion.)* Yes, I love him! I love him! I'm not ashamed of it. What right have you to deny it me? You gave me nothing. You made me a chattel, *a thing!*

NARRATOR. At this, you can feel the rustle of indignation through the house. To make a woman a thing is the crowning horror of a problem play.

LADY CICELY. You starved me here. *(Begins to throttle herself.)* You throttled me.

NARRATOR. Lady Cicely takes herself by the neck and throttles herself a little to show how.

LADY CICELY. *(Repeating her gestures.)* You smothered me! I couldn't breathe! . . . And now I'm going! Do you hear? . . . Going away, to life, to love . . . *(with a very broad gesture)* . . . behind the beyond!

NARRATOR. Aha! That's where the title came from . . . BEHIND THE BEYOND. She gathers up Mr. Harding—practically—and carries him passionately away. He looks back weakly as he goes. (LADY CICELY *and* MR. HARDING *return to their chairs.*) Sir John stands as if stunned. His face is set.

SIR JOHN. Jack . . .

NARRATOR. He mutters . . .

SIR JOHN. Jack!

NARRATOR. While he still stands there, the valet enters with a telegram on a tray. (VALET *rises and walks to Lectern #2.*)

VALET. A telegram, sir.

NARRATOR. Sir John is dazed and tries to collect himself.

SIR JOHN. What?

VALET. A telegram, Sir . . . a cablegram. (VALET *pantomimes handing Sir John the telegram, bows, and returns stiffly to his chair.*)

NARRATOR. Sir John takes it, opens it, and reads aloud:

SIR JOHN. "He is dead . . . my duty is ended . . . I am coming home . . . Margaret Harding." *(Stunned.)* Margaret . . . coming home! It only needed *that* . . . my God!

NARRATOR. As he says it, the curtain falls—slowly, deliberately. The lights flick up. There is a great burst of applause. The curtain rises and falls. Lady Cicely . . . (LADY CICELY *rises quickly and comes forward.*) . . . And Mr. Harding . . . (MR. HARDING *rises quickly and joins* LADY CICELY.) . . . And Sir John . . . (SIR JOHN *joins the other two, and the three join hands and bow to each other and to the audience.*) . . . All come out and bow charmingly, holding one another's hands. (LADY CICELY, MR. HARDING, *and* SIR JOHN *return to their chairs.*)

Then the curtain falls, and the orchestra breaks out into a Winter Garden waltz. The boxes buzz with discussion. Some of the people think that Lady Cicely is right in claiming the right to realize herself; others think that before realizing herself she should have *developed* herself. But everybody feels that the subject is a delicious one. Those people who have seen the play before very kindly explain how it ends, so as to help the rest to enjoy it. But the more serious-minded of the men have risen, very gently, and are sneaking up the aisles. Their expression is stamped with deep thought, as if pondering over the play. But their step is as that of leopards on the march, and no one is deceived as to their purpose.

Soon the leopards come stealing back. The orchestra boils over in a cadence and stops. The curtain silently lifts, and it is: Act II. Six months later! The programs rustle. The people look to see where the next act takes place. And they find that it is an apartment in Paris. Notice that this place, which is used in every problem play, is just called "An Apartment." Even if it were "A Apartment," it would feel easier. But "An Apartment"! The very words give the audience a delicious shiver of uncomfortableness.

When the curtain rises, it discloses a French maid moving about the stage in four-dollar silk stockings. (*The* FRENCH MAID *rises and comes to Lectern #4.*) She is setting things on a little table, evidently for supper. She explains this in French as she does it, so as to make it clear.

FRENCH MAID. Bon! la serviette de monsieur! bon! la serviette de madame, bien . . . du champagne, bon! . . . langouste aux champignons, bien, bon! . . .

NARRATOR. This is all the French she knows, poor little thing. But "langouste aux champignons" beats the audience, so she is all right. As the maid moves about, there is a loud knock at the cardboard door of the apartment. (*Use sound effect if desired.*) A man in official clothes sticks his head in. (POSTAL CLERK *rises and walks to Lectern #3.*) He is evidently a postal special messenger because he is all in postal attire with a postal glazed hat.

POSTAL CLERK. Monsieur Arrding? . . .

NARRATOR. He says.

FRENCH MAID. Oui.

POSTAL CLERK. Bon! Une lettre.

FRENCH MAID. Merci, monsieur.

NARRATOR. He goes out. (POSTAL CLERK *returns to his chair.*) The audience feels a thrill of pride at having learned French. The maid lays the letter on the supper table. Just as she does it, the door opens; and there enter Mr. Harding and Lady Cicely. (LADY CICELY *and* MR. HARDING *stand. She crosses to Lectern #4.*) Yes, them. The audience catches it like a flash. They *live* here. There is great gaiety in Lady Cicely's manner. Her face is paler. There is a bright spot in each cheek. Her eyes are very bright. There follows the well-known supper scene. Lady Cicely is very gay. She pours champagne into Mr. Harding's glass. They both drink from it. She asks him if he is a happy boy now. He says he is. (MR. HARDING *shakes his head yes.*) She runs her fingers through his hair. He kisses her on the bare shoulder. Lady Cicely rattles on about Amalfi and Fiesole. She asks Mr. Harding if he remembers that night in the olive trees at Santa Clara, with just one thrush singing in the night sky. He says he remembers the very thrush. (MR. HARDING *again shakes his head yes.*) At times, Lady Cicely falls into a fit of coughing . . . (LADY CICELY *coughs dramatically*) . . . and presses her hand to her side. *(She does so.)* Mr. Harding looks at her apprehensively. She says:

LADY CICELY. It is nothing, silly boy. It will be gone . . . *(repeats her artificial cough)* . . . in a moment.

NARRATOR. It is only because she is so happy. Then, quite suddenly, she breaks down and falls at Mr. Harding's knees.

LADY CICELY. Oh, Jack, Jack, I can't stand it! I can't stand it any longer. *(Gestures to her throat.)* It is choking me!

MR. HARDING. My darling, what is it?

LADY CICELY. This, all this, it is choking me . . . this apartment, these pictures, the French maid—all of it! I can't stand it! I'm being suffocated! Oh, Jack, take me away . . . take me somewhere where it is quiet! Take me to Norway, to the great solemn hills and the fjords . . .

NARRATOR. Then suddenly Mr. Harding sees the letter in its light blue envelope lying on the supper table. (MR. HARDING *sees the letter and reacts to it.*) It has been lying right beside him for ten minutes. Everybody in the theatre could see it and was getting uncomfortable about it. He seizes it and tears it open. There is a hunted look on his face as he reads. (MR. HARDING *assumes a hunted look.*)

LADY CICELY. Jack! What is it?

MR. HARDING. My mother . . . good gracious, she is coming! She is at the Bristol and is coming *here!* What can I do?

NARRATOR. Lady Cicely is quiet now.

LADY CICELY. Does she know?

MR. HARDING. Nothing, nothing.

LADY CICELY. How did she find you?

MR. HARDING. I don't know. I can't imagine. I told the solicitors . . . curse them! . . . to keep the address secret.

NARRATOR. Mr. Harding paces the stage, giving an imitation of a weak man trapped. He keeps muttering:

MR. HARDING. What can I do? What can I do? What can I do?

NARRATOR. Lady Cicely speaks very firmly and proudly.

LADY CICELY. Jack. There is only one thing to do. Tell her.

NARRATOR. Mr. Harding, aghast:

MR. HARDING. *(Aghast.)* Tell her?

LADY CICELY. Yes, tell her about our love, about everything. I am not ashamed! Let her judge me!

NARRATOR. Mr. Harding sinks into a chair. He keeps shivering and saying:

MR. HARDING. I tell you, I can't. I can't! She wouldn't understand.

NARRATOR. The letter is fluttering in his hand. He does it splendidly. Lady Cicely plucks the letter from his fingers. She reads it aloud, her eyes widening as she reads:

LADY CICELY. *(Holding up one page of her manuscript.)* "Hotel Bristol. My darling Boy: I have found you at last! Why have you sought to avoid me? God grant there is nothing wrong. He is dead—the man I taught you to call your father—and I can tell you *all* now. I am coming to you this instant. Margaret Harding."

NARRATOR. Lady Cicely advances to Mr. Harding and grips his hand.

LADY CICELY. What does it mean, Jack? Tell me, what does it mean?

MR. HARDING. Good God, Cicely, don't speak like that!

LADY CICELY. This . . . these lines . . . about your father.

MR. HARDING. I don't know what it means. . . . I don't care. . . . I hated him, the brute. I'm glad he's dead. I don't care about that. But she's coming! Here! Any minute! And I can't face it.

NARRATOR. Lady Cicely, more quietly:

LADY CICELY. Jack, tell me. Did my . . . did Sir John Trevor ever talk to you about your father?

MR. HARDING. No. We never spoke of him.

LADY CICELY. Did he know him?

MR. HARDING. Yes . . . I think so . . . long ago. But they were enemies. Trevor challenged him to a duel . . . over some woman. But he wouldn't fight. . . . The cur.

NARRATOR. Lady Cicely, dazed and aghast: (LADY CICELY *is dazed and aghast, but speaks with dawning comprehension.*)

LADY CICELY. I . . . understand . . . it . . . now.

NARRATOR. She recovers herself and speaks quickly:

LADY CICELY. *(Speaks quickly.)* Listen! There is time yet. Go to the hotel! Go at once! Tell your mother nothing. Nothing, you understand. Keep her from coming here. Anything, but not that. *(Calls.)* Ernestine!

NARRATOR. She calls to the maid, who reappears for a second. *(The* FRENCH MAID *stands, but remains at her chair.)*

LADY CICELY. A taxi . . . at once! *(The* FRENCH MAID *curtseys and resumes her seat.)*

NARRATOR. The stage is full of bustle. If the play is really well put on, you can presently hear the taxi buzzing outside. Mr. Harding goes to Lady Cicely and tries to kiss her. She puts him from her in horror and hastens him out. (MR. HARDING *returns to his chair.)* She calls the maid. *(The* FRENCH MAID *rises and comes to Lectern #4.)*

LADY CICELY. Ernestine, quick! Put my things—everything—into a valise.

FRENCH MAID. Madame is going away?

LADY CICELY. Yes, yes, at once!

FRENCH MAID. Madame will not eat?

LADY CICELY. No, no!

FRENCH MAID. Madame will not first rest?

NARRATOR. The slow comprehension of these French maids is something exasperating.

FRENCH MAID. Madame will not await Monsieur?

LADY CICELY. No, no . . . *quick,* Ernestine! Bring me what I want. Summon a taxi. I shall be ready in a moment. *(The* FRENCH MAID *curtseys, but remains at Lectern #4.)*

NARRATOR. Lady Cicely passes through a side door into an inner room. (LADY CICELY *hurries to her chair and sits.)* She is scarcely gone when Mrs. Harding enters. (MRS. HARDING *rises and comes to Lectern #3.)* A woman about forty-five, she is still very beautiful. She is dressed in deep black. The play is now moving very fast. You have to sit tight to follow it all. She speaks to Ernestine.

MRS. HARDING. It is Mr. Harding's apartment?

FRENCH MAID. Yes, madame.

MRS. HARDING. Is he here?

NARRATOR. She looks about the room. (MRS. HARDING *looks about the room.)*

FRENCH MAID. No, madame, he is gone this moment in a taxi . . . to the Hotel Bristol, I heard him say.

NARRATOR. Mrs. Harding, faltering:

MRS. HARDING. Is . . . anyone . . . here?

FRENCH MAID. No, madame, no one. Milady was here a moment ago. But she, too, has gone out.

NARRATOR. This is a lie, but of course the maid is a French maid.

MRS. HARDING. Then it *is* true. There *is* someone . . .

NARRATOR. She is just saying this when the bell rings . . . *(sound effects of bell if desired)* . . . the door opens and there enters . . . Sir John Trevor. (SIR JOHN *rises and walks to Lectern #2.)*

MRS. HARDING. You! . . .

NARRATOR. Says Mrs. Harding.

SIR JOHN. *(Gasps.)* I am too late! . . .

NARRATOR. Gasps Sir John. She goes to him tremblingly.

MRS. HARDING. After all these years . . .

NARRATOR. She says. She takes his hands and looks into his face as she goes on speaking:

MRS. HARDING. I have thought of you so often in all these bitter years! It sustained me even at the worst. . . . And I knew, John, that it was for my sake that you had never married.

NARRATOR. Then, as she goes on talking, the audience realizes with a thrill that Mrs. Harding does not know that Sir John married two years ago—that she has come home, as she thought, to the man who loved her. And more than that, they get another thrill when they realize that Lady Cicely is learning it, too! (LADY CICELY *rises and comes part of the way downstage to the left of* MRS. HARDING.) She has pushed the door half open and is standing there unseen, listening. She wears a hat and cloak; there is a folded letter in her hand, and her eyes are wide. (LADY CICELY *pointedly widens her eyes.*)

MRS. HARDING. And now, John, I want your help. Only you can help me; you are so strong. . . . My Jack—I must save him!

NARRATOR. She looks about the room. (MRS. HARDING *looks about the room.*) Something seems to overcome her.

MRS. HARDING. Oh, John, this place . . . his being here like this . . . it seems a judgment on us! (MRS. HARDING *may cry a little.*)

NARRATOR. The audience is getting it fast now. And when Mrs. Harding speaks of . . .

MRS. HARDING. Our awful moment of folly . . . the retribution of our own sins . . .

NARRATOR. They grasp it and shiver with the luxury of it. After that, when Mrs. Harding says:

MRS. HARDING. *(With great fervor.)* Our wretched boy! We must save him! . . .

NARRATOR. They all know why she says "our." She goes on more calmly:

MRS. HARDING. I realized . . . I knew . . . he is not alone here.

NARRATOR. Sir John's voice is quiet, almost hollow.

SIR JOHN. *(Speaks hollowly.)* He is not alone.

MRS. HARDING. *(Earnestly.)* But this woman . . . can you not deal with her . . . persuade her . . . beg her for my sake . . . bribe her to leave my boy?

NARRATOR. Lady Cicely steps out. (LADY CICELY *comes to Lectern #4.*)

LADY CICELY. *(In a martyred tone.)* There is no bribe needed. I am going. If I have wronged him . . . and you . . . it shall be atoned.

NARRATOR. Sir John has given no sign. He is standing stunned. (SIR JOHN *does.*) She turns to him.

LADY CICELY. I have heard, and I know now. I cannot ask for pity. *(Tragically.)* But when I am gone . . . when it is over . . . I want you to give him this letter. . . . And I want you—you two—to be as if I had never lived!

NARRATOR. She lays the letter in his hand. Then without a sign, Lady Cicely passes out. (LADY CICELY *makes a tragic "exit" to her chair and sits.*) There is a great stillness in the house. Mrs. Harding has watched Lady Cicely and Sir John in amazement. Sir John has lowered his head almost to his chest. Now Mrs. Harding breaks out:

MRS. HARDING. *(Excitedly.)* John, for goodness sake! What does it mean? . . . This woman? . . . Speak! . . . There is something awful I must know.

SIR JOHN. Yes, you must know. It is fate. Margaret . . . two years ago I married . . .

MRS. HARDING. But this woman! *(Beginning to comprehend.)* This woman . . . ?

SIR JOHN. She is . . . she *was* . . . my wife.

NARRATOR. And at this moment, Harding breaks into the room. (MR. HARDING *rises and comes part way down toward Lectern #4.*)

MR. HARDING. Cicely! Cicely, I was too late . . .

NARRATOR. He sees his mother . . .

MR. HARDING. Mother . . . (MR. HARDING *completes his trip to Lectern #4.*)

NARRATOR. He says in agony. Then he sees Sir John—and is taken aback even further!

MR. HARDING. And *you!* . . . *(Glancing wildly about.)* Where is Cicely?

NARRATOR. He looks frantically about.

MR. HARDING. Where is she? What is happening? I must know!

NARRATOR. Sir John, as if following a mechanical impulse, has handed Harding the letter. He tears it open and reads:

MR. HARDING. "Dearest, I am going away, to die. It cannot be long now. The doctor told me today. That was why I couldn't speak or explain it to you and was so strange at supper. But I am glad now. Good-bye."

NARRATOR. Harding turns upon Sir John with the snarl of a wolf.

MR. HARDING. *(With the snarl of a wolf.)* What have you done? Why have you driven her away? *(Beginning to build toward a climax.)* What right have you to her, you devil? I loved her . . . she was mine!

(From here to "My God" all of the readers, including the NARRATOR, *build swiftly toward the climactic zenith of the scene.)*

NARRATOR. He has seized a pointed knife from the supper table. His shoulders are crouched . . . he is about to spring on Sir John. Mrs. Harding has thrown herself between them.

MRS. HARDING. Jack, Jack, you mustn't strike!

MR. HARDING. Out of the way, I say! I'll—

MRS. HARDING. Jack, Jack, you mustn't strike! Can't you understand?

Don't you see . . . *what* . . . *who* he is?

MR. HARDING. What do you mean? Stand back from me!

MRS. HARDING. Jack, he . . . is . . . your . . . *father!*

NARRATOR. The knife clatters to the floor.

MR. HARDING. My God! *(Staggered by this revelation, the* READERS *return to their chairs.)*

NARRATOR. And then the curtain falls. There's a burst of applause. And, in accordance with all the best traditions of the stage, one moment later Lady Cicely . . . (LADY CICELY *rises and comes forward.)* . . . And Mrs. Harding . . . (MRS. HARDING *rises and quickly joins* LADY CICELY.) . . . And Sir John . . . (SIR JOHN *rises and hastens to join* LADY CICELY *and* MRS. HARDING.) . . . And Mr. Harding . . . (MR. HARDING *rises and hurries down to join his fellow* READERS, *as do the* FRENCH MAID *and the* POSTAL CLERK.) . . . And the French Maid and the Postal Clerk are all bowing and smiling like anything. *(The entire cast take their bows, return to their chairs, and sit.)* Then the orchestra plays, and the leopards sneak out, and the people in the boxes are all talking gaily to show that they're not in the least affected. And everybody is wondering how it will come out, or rather how it can possibly come out at all, because some of them explain that it's all wrong. And just as they are making it clear that there shouldn't be any third act, the curtain goes up and it's: Act III. Three months later. The curtain rises on the drawing room in Mrs. Harding's house in London. (MRS. HARDING *rises and comes to Lectern #2.)* Mrs. Harding is sorting out parcels. There is a great air of quiet about the scene. The third act of a problem play always has to be very quiet. Does Mrs. Harding start to talk about Lady Cicely and Jack, and Paris? Not a bit. She is simply looking over the parcels and writing names on them and talking to herself so that the audience can get the names.

MRS. HARDING. *(Speaks nobly.)* For the Orphan's Home . . . poor little things. For the Foundlings' Protection Society . . .

NARRATOR. Another parcel . . .

MRS. HARDING. For the Lost Infants' Preservation League . . .

NARRATOR. A deep sigh . . .

MRS. HARDING. *(Sighs deeply.)* Poor, poor children!

NARRATOR. Now, what is all this about? What has this to do with the play? Why, don't you see? The storm is over, and there is nothing in Mrs. Harding's heart but pity. Don't you see that she is dressed in deeper black than ever? And don't you get that air on her face . . . that third-act air . . . that resignation? Don't you see that the play is really all over? They're just letting the wind out of it. A man announces:

VALET. *(Stands at his chair.)* Sir John Trevor! (VALET *bows and seats himself.* SIR JOHN *walks tragically to Lectern #1.)*

NARRATOR. Mrs. Harding goes to meet him with both hands out.

MRS. HARDING. *(In rich, sad tones.)* My dear, dear friend . . .

NARRATOR. She says in rich, sad tones. Sir John is all in black. He is much aged, but very firm and very quiet. You can feel that he's been spending the morning with the committee of the Homeless Newsboys' League or among the Directorate of the Lost Waifs' Encouragement Association. In fact, he begins to talk of these things at once. The people who are not used to third acts are wondering what it is all about. The real playgoers know that this is atmosphere.

MRS. HARDING. *(In sorrowful tones.)* Tea? . . .

NARRATOR. Says Mrs. Harding.

MRS. HARDING. Shall I ring?

SIR JOHN. *(Also speaks tragically.)* Pray do . . .

NARRATOR. Says Sir John. He seats himself with great weariness. (SIR JOHN *sighs deeply*.) The full melancholy of the third act is on him. The tea which has been made for three acts is brought in. They drink it, and it begins to go to their heads. The "atmosphere" clears off just a little; but the sad and tragically hollow tones persist.

MRS. HARDING. You have news, I know . . .

NARRATOR. Says Mrs. Harding.

MRS. HARDING. You have seen him?

SIR JOHN. I have seen him.

MRS. HARDING. And he is gone?

SIR JOHN. Yes, he has sailed . . .

NARRATOR. Says Sir John.

SIR JOHN. He went on board last night, only a few hours after my return to London. I saw him off. Poor Jack! Gatherson has been most kind. They will take him into the embassy at Lima. There he can begin life again. The Peruvian ambassador has promised to do all in his power.

NARRATOR. Sir John sighs deeply and is silent. (SIR JOHN *sighs deeply*.) This is to let the fact soak into the audience that Jack has gone to Peru. Any reasonable person would have known it. Where else could he go to?

MRS. HARDING. *(Bravely, not really convinced.)* He will do well in Peru . . .

NARRATOR. Says Mrs. Harding. She is imitating a woman being very brave.

SIR JOHN. Yes, I trust so . . .

NARRATOR. Says Sir John. There is silence again. In fact, the whole third act is diluted with thirty per cent of silence. Presently, Mrs. Harding speaks again in a low tone.

MRS. HARDING. You have other news, I know.

SIR JOHN. Yes. I have been to Switzerland. I have seen the curé . . . a good man. He has told me all there is to tell. I found him at the hospice, busy with his travails de bienfaisance. (SIR JOHN *pauses, and then says tragically*.) He led me to her grave.

NARRATOR. *(Aghast.)* Lady Cicely dead? Everybody in the theatre gasps.

Dead! But what an unfair way to kill her! To face an open death on the stage, in fair hand-to-hand acting, is one thing; but this new system of dragging off the characters to Switzerland between the acts and then returning and saying that they are dead is quite another! *(Pauses, then resumes quietly.)* Presently, Mrs. Harding speaks again, very softly:

MRS. HARDING. And you? You will take up your work here again?

SIR JOHN. No. I am going away.

MRS. HARDING. Going . . . ?

SIR JOHN. Yes, far away. I am going to Kafoonistan.

NARRATOR. Mrs. Harding looks at him in pain.

MRS. HARDING. To Kafoonistan?

SIR JOHN. Yes. To Kafoonistan. There is work for me to do there.

NARRATOR. There is silence again. Then Sir John speaks.

SIR JOHN. And you? You will settle down here in London?

MRS. HARDING. No, I am going away.

SIR JOHN. Going away?

MRS. HARDING. Yes, back to Balla Walla. I want to be alone. I want to forget. I want to think. I want to try to realize.

SIR JOHN. You are going alone?

MRS. HARDING. *(Feeling somewhat noble.)* Yes, quite alone. But I shall not feel alone when I get there. The Maharanee will receive me with open arms. And my life will be useful. The women need me; I will teach them to read, to sew, to sing.

SIR JOHN. *(With emotion.)* Mrs. Harding . . . Margaret . . . you must not do this. You have sacrificed your life enough. You have the right to live!

NARRATOR. There is emotion in Sir John's tone. It is very rough on him to find his plan of going to Kafoonistan has been outdone by Mrs. Harding's going to Balla Walla. She shakes her head.

MRS. HARDING. *(Shakes her head.)* No, no. My life is of no account now. But you, John, you are needed here. The country needs you. Men look to you to lead them.

NARRATOR. Mrs. Harding would particularize if she could, but she can't just for the moment remember what it is Sir John can lead them *to*. Sir John shakes his head.

SIR JOHN. *(Shakes his head.)* No, no. My work lies there in Kafoonistan. There is a man's work to be done there. The tribes are ignorant, uncivilized.

NARRATOR. This dialogue goes on for some time. Mrs. Harding keeps shaking her head and saying that Sir John must not go to Kafoonistan, and Sir John says she must not go to Balla Walla. He protests that he wants to work, and she claims that she wants to try to think clearly. But it is all a bluff. They are not going. Neither of them. And everybody knows it. Presently, Mrs. Harding says sadly:

MRS. HARDING. *(Sadly.)* You will think of me sometimes?

SIR JOHN. I shall never forget you.

MRS. HARDING. I'm glad of that.

SIR JOHN. *(Dramatically.)* Wherever I am, I shall think of you! . . . Out there in the deserts, or at night, alone among the great silent hills, with only the stars overhead, I shall think of you. Your face will guide me wherever I am!

NARRATOR. He has taken her hand.

SIR JOHN. And you . . .

NARRATOR. He says . . .

SIR JOHN. You will think of me sometimes in Balla Walla? *(Not to be "out-acted" by* SIR JOHN, MRS. HARDING *"hams" it up a bit, too.)*

MRS. HARDING. Yes, always. All day while I am with the Maharanee and her women, and at night . . . the great silent Indian night . . . when all the place is asleep and there is heard nothing but the sounds of the jungle, the cry of the hyena and the bray of the laughing jackass, I shall seem to hear your voice.

NARRATOR. She is much moved. She rises, clenches her hands, and then adds:

MRS. HARDING. I have heard it so for five and twenty years.

NARRATOR. He has moved to her.

SIR JOHN. *(With much intensity.)* Margaret!

MRS. HARDING. *(Matches his intensity.)* John!

SIR JOHN. *(Builds a big climax.)* I cannot let you go! Your life lies here . . . with me . . . next to my heart. I want your help, your love . . . here . . . *inside* the beyond! (MRS. HARDING *and* SIR JOHN *return to their chairs.)*

NARRATOR. And as he speaks and takes her in his arms, the curtain sinks upon them, rises, falls, rises, and then sinks again—asbestos and all—and the play is over. The lights are on, the audience rises in a body and puts on its wraps. All over the theatre you can hear the words:

VOICES. *(Entire cast speaking.)* Perfectly rotten! Utterly untrue . . .

NARRATOR. And so on. The general judgment seems to be that it is a perfectly rotten play but very strong. The audience are saying this as they surge out in great waves of furs and silks, with black crush hats floating on billows of white wraps among the foam of gossamer scarfs. Through it all is the squawk of the motor horn, the call of the taxi drivers and the inrush of the fresh night air. *(He makes a complete change of tone, his voice becoming very personal, confidential, knowing.)* But just inside the theatre, in the office, is a man in a circus waistcoat adding up dollars with a blue pencil . . . and *he* knows that the play is all right.

BY MARK TWAIN

The Diaries of Adam and Eve

Adapted for Readers Theatre by Leslie Irene Coger

Excerpts from the private and intimate journals of the world's first male
and female are amusingly juxtaposed and movingly meshed in such a way
as to lay bare their innermost yearnings, to contrast their shrewd and
often conflicting estimations of each other's foibles and frustrations,
their fragilities and fortitudes as the pair come to live—and eventually
to love—in that Never-To-Be-Rediscovered Garden . . . and later . . .
after the Fall.

CAST OF CHARACTERS

One Man and One Woman

ADAM. *The first man*

EVE. *The first mate*

THE PHYSICAL ARRANGEMENT OF THE SCENE

In the Beginning, we are told, was a void . . . and probably a darkness
all about. Let there be light, however, upon the face of Eternally Feminine EVE and on the somewhat worried countenance of ADAM, The Man
in Her Life and the Fellow Who Started It All. As it is nearing the end
of the week—Saturday, to be exact—it is appropriate that these two
mortals have a place to rest: two simple stools, with or without lecterns,
in the center of the stage. And since both are writing entries in their
respective diaries, it is also appropriate that they make known the day of
the week on which the entry is being made.

EVE. *Saturday:* I am almost a whole day old now. I arrived yesterday. That is as it seems to me. And it must be so for if there was a day-before-yesterday, I was not there when it happened, or I should remember it. I feel like an experiment. I feel exactly like an experiment.

ADAM. *Monday:* The new creature with the long hair is a good deal in the way. It is always hanging around and following me about. I don't like this; I am not used to company. I wish it would stay with the other animals. . . . Cloudy today, wind in the east; think we shall have rain. . . . *We?* Where did I get that word? . . . I remember now—the new creature uses it.

EVE. *Tuesday:* I followed the other Experiment around yesterday afternoon, at a distance, to see what it might be for—if I could. But I was not able to make out. I think it is a man. I had never seen a man, but it looked like one, and I feel sure that that is what it is. I realize that I feel more curiosity about it than about any of the other reptiles. It has no hips; it tapers like a carrot; when it stands, it spreads itself apart like a derrick; maybe it is architecture.

I was afraid of it at first, and started to run every time it turned around, for I thought it was going to chase me; but by-and-by I found it was only trying to get away, so after that I was not timid any more, but tracked it along, several hours, about twenty yards behind, which made it nervous and unhappy. At last it was a good deal worried and climbed a tree. I waited a while, then gave it up and went home.

ADAM. *Sunday:* Pulled through. This day is getting to be more and more trying. It was selected and set apart last November as a day of rest. I already had six of them per week, before. This morning found the new creature trying to clod apples out of that forbidden tree.

EVE. *Tuesday:* It is up in the tree again. Resting, apparently. It looks to me like a creature that is more interested in resting than in anything else.

ADAM. *Sunday:* Pulled through.

EVE. *Wednesday:* It has low tastes . . . and is not kind. When I went there earlier this evening in the gloaming, it had crept down from the tree and was trying to catch the little speckled fishes that play in the pool, and I had to clod it to make it go up the tree again and let them alone. One of the clods took it back of the ear, and it used language. It gave me a thrill, for it was the first time I had ever heard speech, except my own. I did not understand the words, but they seemed expressive.

When I found it could talk, I felt a new interest in it, for I love to talk; I talk all day, and in my sleep, too.

ADAM. *Wednesday:* I wish it would not talk; it is always talking right at my shoulder, right at my ear, and I am used only to sounds that are more or less distant from me.

EVE. *Next Sunday:* All week I tagged around after him and tried to get acquainted. I had to do the talking, because he was shy, but I didn't mind it. He seemed pleased to have me around, and I used the sociable *we* a good deal, because it seemed to flatter him to be included.

ADAM. *Thursday:* She told me she was made out of a rib taken from my body. This is at least doubtful, if not more than that. I have not missed any rib. . . .

EVE. *Monday:* This morning I told him my name, hoping it would interest him. But he did not care for it. It is strange. If he should tell me his name, I would care. I think it would be pleasanter in my ears than any other sound.

ADAM. *Monday:* The new creature says its name is Eve. That is all right. I have no objections. Says it is to call it by when I want it to come. I said it was superfluous, then. This word evidently raised me in its respect; and indeed it is a large, good word and will bear repetition. It says it is not an It; it is a She. This is probably doubtful; yet it is all one to me; what she is were nothing to me if she would but go by herself and not talk.

EVE. *Tuesday:* No, he took no interest in my name. I tried to hide my disappointment, but I suppose I did not succeed. I went away and sat on the mossbank with my feet in the water. It is where I go when I hunger for companionship, someone to look at, someone to talk to. It is not enough—that lovely white body painted there in the pool—but it is something, and something is better than utter loneliness.

ADAM. *Sunday:* Pulled through.

EVE. *Wednesday:* We are getting along very well indeed now, and getting better and better acquainted. He does not try to avoid me any more, which is a good sign, and shows that he likes to have me with him.

ADAM. *Friday:* She has taken to beseeching me to stop going over the Falls. What harm does it do? Says it makes her shudder. I wonder why.

I went over the Falls in a barrel—not satisfactory to her. Went over in a tub—still not satisfactory. Swam the Whirlpool and the Rapids in a fig-leaf suit. It got much damaged. Hence, tedious complaints about my extravagance. I am too much hampered here. What I need is change of scene.

EVE. *Wednesday:* During the last day or two I have taken all the work of naming things off his hands, and this has been a great relief to him, for he has no gift in that line, and is evidently very grateful. He can't think of a rational name to save him, but I do not let him see that I am aware of his defect. Whenever a new creature comes along, I name it before he has time to expose himself by an awkward silence. The minute I set eyes on an animal, I know what it is.

When the dodo came along, he thought it was a wildcat—I saw it in his eye. But I saved him. I just spoke up in a quite natural way with pleased surprise—not as if I was dreaming of conveying information—and said, "Well, I do declare if there isn't the dodo!"

ADAM. *Wednesday:* I get no chance to name anything myself. The new creature names everything that comes along, before I can get in a protest. And always that same pretext is offered—it *looks* like the thing. There is the dodo, for instance. Says the moment one looks at it, one sees at a glance that it "looks like a dodo." Dodo! It looks no more like a dodo than I do.

EVE. *Friday:* My first sorrow. Yesterday he avoided me and seemed to wish I would not talk to him. I could not believe it, and thought there was some mistake, for I loved to be with him and loved to hear him talk, and how could it be that he could feel unkind toward me when I had not done anything? But at last it seemed true, so I went away and sat lonely in the place where I first saw him the morning that we were made and I did not know what he was and was indifferent about him; but now it was a mournful place, and every little thing spoke of him, and my heart was very sore. I did not know why very clearly, for it was a new feeling; I had not experienced it before, and it was all a mystery, and I could not make it out.

But when night came, I could not bear the lonesomeness and went to the new shelter which he has built, to ask him what I had done that was wrong and how I could mend it and get back his kindness again; but he put me out in the rain, and it was my first sorrow.

ADAM. *Friday:* Built me a shelter against the rain, but could not have it to myself in peace. The new creature intruded. When I tried to put it out, it shed water out of the holes it looks with, wiped it away with the back of its paws, and made a noise such as some of the other animals make when they are in distress.

She has taken up with a snake now. The other animals are glad, for she was always experimenting with them and bothering them; and I am glad, because the snake talks, and this enables me to get a rest.

EVE. *Sunday:* It is pleasant again, now, and I am happy; but those were heavy days; I do not think of them when I can help it. I tried to get him some of those apples, but I cannot learn to throw straight. I failed, but I think the good intention pleased him. They are forbidden, and he says I shall come to harm; but so I come to harm through pleasing him, why shall I care for that harm?

ADAM. *Wednesday:* About an hour after sunup, as I was riding through a flowery plain where thousands of animals were grazing, slumbering, or playing with each other, according to their wont, all of a sudden they broke into a tempest of frightful noises, and in one moment the plain was in a frantic commotion, and every beast was destroying its neighbor. I knew what it meant—Eve had eaten that fruit, and death was come into the world. . . . I looked up, and there was Eve. I was not sorry she came, for there are but meagre pickings here, and she had brought me some of those apples. I was obliged to eat them, I was so hungry. It was against my principles, but I find that principles have no real force except when one is well fed. . . . She came curtained in boughs and bunches of leaves; and when I asked her what she meant by such nonsense, and snatched them away and threw them down, she tittered and blushed. I had never seen a person titter and blush before, and to me it seemed unbecoming and idiotic. She said I myself would soon know why it was thus. This was correct. Hungry as I was, I laid down the apple, half-eaten—certainly the best one I ever saw, considering the lateness of the season—and arrayed myself in the discarded boughs and branches, and then spoke to her with some severity and ordered her to go and get some more and not make such a spectacle of herself. She did it. And afterward, we crept down to where the wild-beast battle had been, and collected some skins; and I made her patch together a couple of suits proper for public occasions. They are uncomfortable, it is true, but stylish; and that is the main point about clothes. . . . I find she is a good deal of a companion. I see I should be lonesome and depressed without her. Another thing, she says it is ordered that we work for our living hereafter. She will be useful. I will superintend.

EVE. *Friday:* I tried once more to persuade him to stop going over the Falls. That was because the fire which I had discovered had revealed to me a new passion—quite new, and distinctly different from love, grief, and those others which I had already discovered—fear. And it is horrible!

ADAM. *Friday:* Perhaps I ought to remember that she is very young, a mere girl, and make allowances. She is all interest, eagerness, vivacity, the world is to her a charm, a wonder, a mystery, a joy; she cannot speak for delight when she finds a new flower; she must pet it and caress it and smell it and talk to it, and pour out endearing names upon it. And she is color-mad: brown rocks, yellow sand, gray moss, green foliage, blue sky, the pearl of the dawn—none of them is of any practical value, so far as I can see; but because they have color and majesty, that is enough for her, and she loses her mind over them. If she could but quiet down and keep still a couple of minutes at a time, it would be a reposeful spectacle. In that case, I think I could enjoy looking at her; indeed, I am sure I could; for I am coming to realize that she is a quite remarkably comely creature—lithe, slender, trim, rounded, shapely, nimble, graceful; and once when she was standing marble-white and sun-drenched on a boulder, with her young head tilted back and her hand shading her eyes, watching the flight of a bird in the sky, I recognized that she was beautiful.

EVE. *After the fall:* When I look back, the Garden is a dream to me. It was beautiful, surpassingly beautiful, enchantingly beautiful; and now it is lost, and I shall not see it any more.

The Garden is lost, but I have found *him,* and am content. He loves me as well as he can; I love him with all the strength of my passionate nature, and this, I think, is proper to my youth and sex. If I ask myself why I love him, I find I do not know. I love certain birds because of their song; but I do not love Adam on account of his singing—no, it is not that; the more he sings, the more I do not get reconciled to it! Yet I ask him to sing, because I wish to learn to like everything he is interested in. His singing sours the milk, but it doesn't matter. I can get used to that kind of milk.

It is not on account of his gracious and considerate ways and his delicacy that I love him. No, he has lacks in these regards, but he is well enough just so, and is improving.

It is not on account of his chivalry that I love him—no, it is not that. He told on me, but I do not blame him; it is a peculiarity of sex, I think, and he did not make his sex. Of course, I would not have told on him; I would have perished first; but that is a peculiarity of sex, too; and I do not take credit for it, for I did not make my sex.

Then why is it that I love him? *Merely because he is masculine,* I think.

At bottom he is good, and I love him for that, but I could love him without it. If he should beat me and abuse me, I should go on loving him. I know it. It is a matter of sex, I think.

He is strong and handsome, and I love him for that, and I admire him for that, and I am proud of him, but I could love him without those qualities. If he were plain, I should love him; and I would work for him, and slave over him, and pray for him, and watch by his bedside until I died.

Yes, I think I love him merely because he is *mine* and is *masculine.* There is no other reason, I suppose. This kind of love is not a product of reasonings and statistics. It just *comes*—none knows whence—and cannot explain itself. And doesn't need to.

It is what I think. But I am only a girl, and the first that has examined this matter, and it may turn out that in my ignorance and inexperience I have not got it right.

ADAM. *Ten years later:* After all these years, I see that I was mistaken about Eve in the beginning; it is better to live outside the Garden with her than inside it without her. At first I thought she talked too much, but now I should be sorry to have that voice fall silent and pass out of my life. Blessed be the goodness of her heart and the sweetness of her spirit!

EVE. *Forty years later:* It is my prayer, it is my longing, that we may pass from this life together—a longing which shall never perish from the earth, but shall have place in the heart of every wife that loves, until the end of time; and it shall be called by my name.

But if one of us must go first, it is my prayer that it shall be I; for he is strong, I am weak, I am not so necessary to him as he is to me—life without him would not be life; how could I endure it? This prayer is also immortal, and will not cease from being offered up while my race continues. I am the first wife, and in the last wife I shall be repeated.

ADAM. *At Eve's grave:* Wheresoever she was, *there* was Eden.

BY KENNETH GRAHAME

The Reluctant Dragon

A children's book adapted for Readers Theatre by Linda Glynn and Leslie Irene Coger

Children take a special delight in experiencing Mr. Grahame's colorful and skillfully spun story of a sensitive, peace-doting dragon who would rather compose sonnets and contemplate the ancient countryside than venture forth from the serenity of his cave to terrorize the local peasantry and engulf valiant knights in the fury of his fiery breath. In particular, young audiences readily identify themselves with the shepherd's son—a key character and a bold lad who knows what fairy tales are all about.

CAST OF CHARACTERS

Four Men, One Woman, and One Narrator, who may be read by either a Man or a Woman

THE NARRATOR.

THE SHEPHERD. *A practical man who lives on the edge of the Downs of England*

THE WIFE. *His sensible spouse*

THE SON. *A young lad who is widely read in fairy tales*

THE DRAGON. *A vain but friendly beast*

ST. GEORGE. *An idealist*

THE VILLAGERS. *Whose voices are provided by the foregoing readers*

Adapted from *The Reluctant Dragon* by Kenneth Grahame, with illustrations by Ernest H. Shepherd. Copyright 1938 by Holiday House, Inc. Published by Holiday House, Inc. **Notice:** This adaptation may be presented without payment of a royalty fee.

The DRAGON occupies a high stool on a platform at C. To his right, on a lower stool on the same platform, sits ST. GEORGE; on a stool of similar height, to the left of the DRAGON, sits the Shepherd's SON. Seated on stools near DL, at the stage level, are the SHEPHERD and his WIFE. The NARRATOR rests on a stool at DR. Thus, in effect, the arrangement is a pyramid, with the DRAGON at the top.

(In the beginning there is music; then, as the NARRATOR *speaks, the music fades out.)*

NARRATOR. Long ago . . . in a cottage half way between an English village and the shoulder of the Downs, a shepherd lived with his wife and their little son.

SHEPHERD. The shepherd spent his days . . . and at certain times of the year his nights, too . . . up on the Downs with only the sun and the stars and the sheep for company.

WIFE. He had a very nice wife. She would cook fine meals for him and would hardly ever henpeck the shepherd. She was a very sensible woman.

SON. Their little son, when he wasn't helping his father—and often when he was, as well—spent most of his time buried in big volumes that he had borrowed from the friendly gentry and interested parsons of the country round about.

NARRATOR. What the boy chiefly dabbled in was natural history and fairy tales; and he just took them as they came, in a sandwichy sort of way, without making any distinction.

One evening the shepherd came bursting into the room where his wife and son were peacefully employed.

SHEPHERD. *(Very frightened.)* It's all up with me, Maria! Never no more can I go up on them there Downs.

WIFE. Now don't you take on like that. Just tell us whatever it is as has given you this shake-up, and then you and me and our son here—we ought to be able to get to the bottom of it.

SHEPHERD. It began some nights ago. . . . You know that cave up there . . . well, for some time past there's been faint noises coming from that cave . . . noises like heavy sighings, with grunts mixed up in them and— sometimes—a snoring. Of course, I was terribly frightened; yet somehow I couldn't keep away. So this very evening, before I come down, I took a cast 'round by the cave, quietly. And there I saw him at last, as plain as I see you!

WIFE. *(Sharing his nervous terror.)* Saw who?

SHEPHERD. Why, *him,* I'm a-telling you! He was as big as four cart-horses, and all covered with shiny scales . . . deep blue scales at the top of him, shading off to a tender sort o' green below. He had his chin on his paws, and I should say he was meditating about things. Yes, a peaceable sort o' beast enough, and not ramping or carrying on or doing anything but what was quite right and proper. I admit all that. And yet, what am I to do? Scales, you know, and claws and a tail for certain! *(The* SON *looks up from the book in which he has been absorbed.)*

SON. *(Yawning.)* It's all right, Father. Don't you worry. It's only a dragon.

SHEPHERD. Only a *dragon?* What do you mean—sitting there, you and your dragon? Only a dragon indeed! And what do you know about it?

SON. 'Cos it is, and 'cos I do know. Look here, Father. You know we've each of us got our line. You know about sheep and weather and things; I know about dragons. Just leave this all to me. I'll stroll up tomorrow and have a talk with this dragon, and you'll find it'll be all right. Only, please, don't you go worrying around there without me. You don't understand dragons a bit, and they're very sensitive, you know.

WIFE. He's quite right, Husband. As he says, dragons is his line and not ours. He's wonderful knowing about bookbeasts. If the beast ain't quite respectable, our boy'll find it out quick enough.

NARRATOR. Next day, after he'd had his tea, the boy strolled up the chalky track that led to the summit of the Downs; and, sure enough, there he found the dragon stretched lazily on the sward in front of his cave.

SON. Hullo, Dragon!

(At first, the DRAGON *makes an effort to rise courteously; but then, seeing that his visitor is but a boy, he sets his eyebrows severely.)*

DRAGON. Now, don't you hit me, or bung stones or squirt water, or anything. I won't have it, I tell you.

SON. Silly Dragon, I'm not goin' to hit you; I'm just goin' to sit on the grass 'side you. I've simply looked in to ask how you were and all that sort of thing; but if I'm in the way, I can easily clear out. No one can say I'm in the habit of shoving myself in where I'm not wanted.

DRAGON. *(Hastily.)* No, no, don't go off in a huff! Fact is, I'm as happy up here as the day's long—never without an occupation, dear fellow, never without an occupation! And yet, between ourselves, it *is* a trifle dull at times.

SON. Going to make a long stay here?

DRAGON. Can't hardly say at present. It seems a nice enough place, but I've only been here a short time, and one must look about and reflect and consider before settling down. *(Confidentially.)* Now I'm going to tell you something! You'd never guess it if you tried ever so! Fact is . . . I'm such a confoundedly lazy beggar.

SON. You surprise me!

DRAGON. It's the sad truth.

NARRATOR. And the dragon settled down between his paws, evidently delighted to have found a listener at last.

DRAGON. I fancy that's really how I came to be here. You see, all the other fellows were so active and earnest and all that sort of thing—always rampaging and skirmishing and chasing knights all over the place, and devouring damsels, and going on generally; whereas I liked to get my meals regular and then to prop my back against a bit of rock and snooze a bit. So when it happened, I got fairly caught.

SON. When *what* happened, please?

DRAGON. That's just what I don't precisely know. I suppose the earth sneezed or shook itself or the bottom dropped out or something. Anyhow, there was a shake and a roar and a general smash, and I found myself miles away underground and wedged in tight as tight. Well, thank goodness my wants are few; and, at any rate, I had peace and quietness and wasn't always being asked to come along and do something. And I've got such an active *mind* . . . always occupied, I assure you!

But time went on, and there was a certain sameness about the life, and at last I began to think it would be fun to work my way upstairs and see what other fellows were doing. So I scratched and burrowed and worked this way and that way, and at last I came out through this cave here. And I like the country and the view and the people—what I've seen of 'em—and, on the whole, I feel inclined to settle down here.

SON. What's your mind always occupied *about?* That's what I want to know.

DRAGON. *(Coloring slightly and looking away.)* Did . . . did you ever . . . just for fun . . . try to make up poetry . . . verses, you know?

SON. 'Course I have. Heaps of it.

DRAGON. *(Very pleased.)* Now, you've got culture and education, you have. I could tell it on you at once. I'm fully pleased to have met you, and I'm hoping the other neighbors will be equally agreeable.

SON. Neighbors? *(Uneasily.)* Now, look here, you're a dragon. And when you talk of settling down—and the neighbors and so on—I can't help feeling that you don't quite realize your position. You're an enemy of the human race, you see!

DRAGON. *(Emphatically, confidently.)* Haven't got an enemy in the world. Too lazy to make 'em, to begin with.

SON. Oh, dear! I do wish you'd try and grasp the situation properly. When the other people find you out, they'll come after you with spears and swords and all sorts of things. You'll have to be exterminated, according to their way of looking at it. You're a scourge and a pest and a baneful monster!

DRAGON. Not a word of truth in it. Character will bear the strictest investigation. *(Dismissing the matter.)* Now . . . here's a little sonnet I was working on when you appeared on the scene. . . .

SON. Oh, if you won't be sensible, I'm going off home! I can't stop for sonnets; my mother's sitting up. *(Earnestly.)* Do try to realize that you're a pestilential scourge, or you'll find yourself in a most awful fix. Good night!

NARRATOR. The boy found it an easy matter to set the minds of his mother and father at ease about his new friend. And many a pleasant night he and the dragon had while the dragon told stories of old times when dragons were quite plentiful.

What the boy had feared, however, soon came to pass. In the village, everyone talked of the real live dragon that sat brooding in the cave in the Downs. All were agreed that this sort of thing couldn't be allowed to go on.

WIFE. *(As the voice of a VILLAGER.)* The dreadful beast must be exterminated!

NARRATOR. *(As the voice of another VILLAGER.)* The countryside must be freed from this pest!

SHEPHERD. *(Also as the voice of a VILLAGER.)* We must get rid of this terror, this destroying scourge!

NARRATOR. The fact was that not even a hen-roost was the worse for the dragon's arrival, but . . . everyone was agreed . . .

ALL. *(Speaking as the VILLAGERS.)* He has to *go!*

NARRATOR. One day the boy, on walking into the village, found everything wearing a festal appearance—an air of festivity which could not be accounted for on the calendar. The boy saw a friend of his own age in the crowd and hailed him.

SON. What's up? Is it the players or bears or a circus or what?

SHEPHERD. *(As the SON's friend.)* He's a-coming!

SON. Who's a-coming?

SHEPHERD. *(As the SON's friend.)* Why, St. George, of course! He heard tell of our dragon, and he's comin' on purpose to slay the deadly beast and free us from his horrid yoke. Oh, my! Won't there be a jolly fight!

NARRATOR. And sure enough, at that very moment St. George appeared.

SHEPHERD. *(As the SON's friend.)* Hurray for St. George!

WIFE. *(As a young girl.)* Oh! Isn't he a brave hero!

ALL. *(As the VILLAGERS.)* He's come to free us from the dragon!

NARRATOR. The boy's heart stood still. The beauty and the grace of the hero were so far beyond anything he had yet seen. His fluted armor was inlaid with gold, his plumed helmet hung at his saddle bow, and his thick fair hair framed a face gracious and gentle beyond expression until you caught the sternness in his eyes. St. George dismounted and went into the inn. The boy took off for the cave just as fast as he could run.

SON. It's all up, Dragon! He's coming! He's here. You'll have to pull yourself together and *do* something at last!

NARRATOR. The dragon was licking his scales and rubbing them with a bit of house flannel the boy's mother had lent him. He shone like a great turquoise.

DRAGON. *(Calmly.)* Don't be violent, boy. Sit down and get your breath and try and remember that the noun governs the verb. And then perhaps you'll be good enough to tell me who's coming.

SON. It's only *St. George* who's coming, that's all! He rode into the village half an hour ago. Of course, you can lick him—a great big fellow like you! But I thought I'd warn you, 'cos he's sure to be 'round early; and he's got the longest, wickedest looking spear you ever did see!

DRAGON. *(Perturbed at last.)* O deary, deary me! This is too awful! I won't see him, and that's flat. You must tell him to go away at once . . . please. Say he can write me if he likes, but I can't give him an interview. I'm not seeing anybody at present.

SON. Now, Dragon, Dragon. Don't be perverse and wrongheaded. You've got to fight him sometime or other, you know, 'cos he's St. George and you're the dragon. Better get it over, and then we can go on with the poems. *(Somewhat accusingly.)* And you might consider *other* people a little, too. If it's been dull up here for you, think how dull it's been for me. We could stand a little excitement.

DRAGON. My dear little man, just understand once and for all: I can't fight, and I won't fight!

SON. But if you don't fight, he'll cut your head off!

DRAGON. Oh, I think not. You'll be able to arrange something. I've got every confidence in you. Just run down, and make it all right. I leave it entirely to you.

NARRATOR. The boy made his way back to the village in a state of great despondency. He found St. George in the principal chamber of the inn . . . alone . . . musing over the chances of the fight.

SON. May I come in, St. George? I want to talk to you about this little matter of the dragon, if you're not tired of it by this time.

ST. GEORGE. Yes, come in, boy. *(Sadly; shaking his head.)* Another tale of misery and wrong, I fear me. Is it a kind parent, then, of whom the tyrant has bereft you? Or some tender sister or brother? Well, it shall soon be avenged. All the villagers have been telling me horrible tales of the many wrongs and evil deeds the dragon has committed.

SON. Sir, I'm afraid that there is a great mistake. Our villagers are known as the best storytellers anywhere. All they want is a fight. But, sir, the most important thing is that this dragon is a *good* dragon. He is most domesticated—a gentleman and a scholar. He even writes poetry.

ST. GEORGE. *(Thinking this over.)* Well . . . I must admit that some of these tales of woe have been rather hard to believe. It could also be that I've misjudged the animal. But what are we to *do?* This monster and I are supposed to be ready to kill each other. Can't you think of something?

SON. That's just what the dragon said . . . leave everything to me. *(Sighs, shakes his head.)* I don't suppose you could be persuaded to just . . . *(hopefully)* . . . go away quietly, could you?

ST. GEORGE. Impossible, I fear. Quite against the rules. You know that just as well as I do.

SON. Well, then . . . would you mind strolling up with me and meeting the dragon and talking it over? It's not far, and any friend of mine will be most welcome.

ST. GEORGE. *(Sighs resignedly.)* Well, it's most irregular, but . . . really it seems about the most sensible thing to do. I'll go.

NARRATOR. So up on the Downs they climbed—the Saint and the boy —to meet the dragon.

SON. Hullo . . . Dragon. I've brought a friend to see you.

NARRATOR. The dragon, who had been sleeping, woke with a start and rubbed his great eyes with his huge claws.

DRAGON. *(Clearing his throat.)* Umm . . . I was just—er—thinking things over. Very pleased to make your acquaintance, sir. Charming weather we're having.

SON. This is St. George.

DRAGON. Ah! St. George! *(Heartily.)* By George!

SON. Dragon, we've got things to discuss. And now, for goodness' sake, do let us have a little straight common sense and get down to some practical, businesslike arrangement!

DRAGON. So glad to meet you, St. George. You've been a great traveler, I hear, and I've always been rather a stay-at-home. But I can show you many antiquities, many interesting features of our countryside, if you're stopping here any time—

ST. GEORGE. *(Interrupting politely but firmly.)* I think that we'd really better take the advice of our young friend here, and try to come to some understanding on a business footing about this—this little affair of ours. Now, don't you think that—after all—the simplest plan would be just to fight it out according to the rules and let the best man win? They're betting on you down in the village, I may as well tell you. But I don't mind that.

SON. Oh, yes, do, Dragon! It'll save such a lot of bother.

DRAGON. *(With some sharpness.)* My young friend, you shut up. St. George, believe me, there's nobody in the world I'd sooner oblige than you and this young gentleman here. But the whole thing's nonsense! Conventionality! Popular thick-headedness! There's absolutely nothing to fight about. Never was—from beginning to end. And anyhow, I'm not *going* to. So that settles it!

ST. GEORGE. But supposing I make you?

DRAGON. You can't. I should only go into my cave and retire for a time down the hole I came up. And as soon as you'd really, really gone away, I'd come up again—gaily. For, I tell you frankly, I like this place; and I'm going to stay here!

NARRATOR. St. George gazed for a while upon the fair landscape around them.

ST. GEORGE. But this would be a beautiful place for a fight. *(Envisioning it all.)* These great bare rolling Downs for the arena, and me in my golden armor showing up against your big blue scaly coils! Think what a picture it would make!

DRAGON. Now you're trying to get at me through my artistic sensibilities, but it won't work. *(A trifle wistfully.)* Not but what it *would* make a very pretty picture, as you say.

SON. We seem to be getting nearer to business. *(Persuasively.)* You must see, Dragon, that there's got to be a fight of *some* sort!

ST. GEORGE. "A fight *of some sort!*" *(Thoughtfully, but with growing enthusiasm.)* Yes. It might be . . . arranged.

DRAGON. Arranged?

SON. Arranged!

ST. GEORGE. I must spear you somewhere, Dragon, of course. But I'd not be bound to hurt you very much. There's such a lot of you—there must be a few spare places somewhere. Here, for instance, just behind your foreleg. It couldn't hurt you much. Like this.

DRAGON. *(Wiggling.)* Now you're tickling, George. *(Giggling.)* No, that place won't do at all. Even if it didn't hurt, it would make me laugh. And that would spoil everything.

ST. GEORGE. Let's try somewhere else, then. Under your neck, for instance . . . all these folds of thick skin . . . if I speared you here, you'd never even know I'd done it.

DRAGON. *(Dubiously.)* Yes, but are you sure you can hit off the right place?

ST. GEORGE. Of course I am. You leave that to me.

DRAGON. It's just because I've *got* to leave it to you that I'm asking. No doubt you would deeply regret any error you might make in the hurry of the moment, but you wouldn't regret it half as much as *I* should! *(Gallantly.)* However, I suppose we've got to trust somebody as we go through life. And your plan seems, on the whole, as good as any.

NARRATOR. The boy was growing a little jealous on behalf of his friend, the dragon, who seemed to be getting all the worst of the bargain.

SON. Look here, Dragon. I don't quite see where you come in. There's to be a fight apparently, and you're to be licked. But what I want to know is what *you're* going to get out of it.

DRAGON. St. George, just tell him, please, what will happen after I'm vanquished in the deadly combat.

ST. GEORGE. Well, according to the rules, I suppose I shall lead you in triumph down to the market place and . . .

DRAGON. Precisely. And then . . .

ST. GEORGE. And then there'll be shouting and speeches and things, and I shall explain that you're converted and see the error of your ways, and so on.

DRAGON. Quite so. And then?

ST. GEORGE. Oh, and then . . . why, and then there will be the usual banquet, I suppose.

DRAGON. Exactly! And that's where I come in. Look here. I'm bored to death up here, and no one really appreciates me. I'm going into Society, I am—through the kindly aid of our friend here, who's taking such a lot of trouble on my account. And you'll find I've got all the qualities to endear me to people who entertain! So now that's all settled. And if you don't mind, I'm an old-fashioned fellow. *(Stifling a yawn.)* Don't want to turn you out . . . *(yawns)* . . . but . . .

ST. GEORGE. Remember, you'll have to do your share of the fighting, Dragon. I mean ramping and breathing fire and . . .

DRAGON. I can ramp all right. As to breathing fire, it's surprising how easily one gets out of practice. But I'll do the best I can. Good night.

ST. GEORGE *and* SON. *(Together.)* Good night, Dragon.

NARRATOR. Next morning, the people began streaming up to the Downs at quite an early hour, wearing their Sunday clothes.

WIFE. Everyone was determined to find a good place to watch the combat.

SHEPHERD. Places were chosen, of course, with a view to a speedy retreat in case of emergency—that is, if the dragon should win.

SON. The boy had picked out a good place up front, well up toward the cave, and was feeling as anxious as a stage manager on opening night. Could the dragon be depended upon? He might change his mind and vote the whole performance rot. Or else, seeing that the affair had been so hastily planned, without even a rehearsal, he might be too nervous to show up.

SHEPHERD. At that moment, St. George's red plumes topped the hill. He rode slowly forth on the great level place which stretched up to the grim mouth of the cave.

WIFE. Very gallant and beautiful he looked, riding his tall war horse, his golden armor glinting in the sun, his great spear held erect.

SHEPHERD. The lines of spectators began to give back a little . . . nervously.

WIFE. And even the boys in front stopped pulling hair and cuffing each other, and leaned forward expectantly.

SON. *(Imploringly.)* Now then, Dragon, come on!

NARRATOR. The boy need not have distressed himself. The dramatic possibilities of this thing had tickled the dragon immensely, and he had been up early preparing for his first public appearance.

WIFE. A low muttering, mingled with snorts, now made itself heard—rising to a bellowing roar that seemed to shake the plain.

SHEPHERD. Then a cloud of smoke obscured the mouth of the cave. And out of the midst of it, the dragon himself—shining, sea-blue, magnificent—pranced splendidly forth!

ALL. Oo-oo-oo!

SHEPHERD. His scales were glittering, his long spiky tail lashed his sides.

WIFE. His claws tore up the turf and sent it flying high over his back.

SHEPHERD. And smoke and fire incessantly jetted from his angry nostrils.

SON. Oh, well done, Dragon! Didn't think he had it in him.

ST. GEORGE. St. George lowered his spear, bent his head, dug his heels into the sides of his horse, and came thundering over the turf.

DRAGON. The dragon charged with a roar and a squeal, a great blue whirling combination of coils and snorts and clashing jaws and spikes and fire.

ALL. Missed! End of Round One!

NARRATOR. The dragon sat down and barked viciously while St. George, with difficulty, pulled his horse around into position.

SON. Oh, how well they managed it! But I hope the Saint won't get excited. I can trust the dragon all right. What a regular play actor the fellow is!

ST. GEORGE. St. George caught the boy's eye and held up three fingers.

SON. It seems to be all planned out. Round Three is to be the finishing one, evidently.

ALL. Time!

NARRATOR. And the combat started with a whirl of scales and the gold shine of St. George's armor.

DRAGON. The dragon sat up on one end and began to leap from one side to the other with huge ungainly bounds, whooping like a red Indian.

NARRATOR. The horse swerved violently.

ST. GEORGE. The Saint only just saving himself by clutching the mane.

NARRATOR. And as they shot past,

DRAGON. The dragon delivered a vicious snap at the horse's tail, which sent the poor beast careening madly over the Downs.

ALL. Hurray for the Dragon!

DRAGON. Hurray for the Dragon!

ALL. End of Round Two!

SON. Jolly fight, St. George! (Confidentially.) Can you make it last a bit longer?

ST. GEORGE. Well, I think I'd better not. Fact is, now that the crowd's begun cheering for your friend, I'm afraid it's going to his head. I'll just finish it off this round. Now, don't you be afraid. I've marked my spot very carefully on his neck. He'll be quite all right.

ALL. *Time!*

NARRATOR. St. George now shortened his spear, bringing the butt well up under his arm. And instead of galloping as before, he trotted smartly toward the dragon, who crouched to meet this new approach, flicking his tail till it cracked in the air like a cart-whip.

ST. GEORGE. The Saint wheeled as he neared his opponent and circled warily 'round him, keeping his eye on the spare place.

DRAGON. The dragon, adopting similar tactics, paced with caution 'round the same circle, occasionally feinting with his head.

NARRATOR. So the two sparred for an opening while the spectators maintained a breathless silence. Though the round lasted for some minutes, the end was a lightning-like movement of the Saint's arm and then a whirl of confusion,

WIFE. And spines,

SHEPHERD. Claws,

SON. Tail,

WIFE. And flying bits of turf.

NARRATOR. The dust cleared away . . .

ALL. Hurray for St. George!

DRAGON. *(Without enthusiasm.)* Yeah, hurray . . .

SON. The boy could see that the dragon was down, pinned to the earth by the spear,

ST. GEORGE. While St. George dismounted and stood astride of him.

SON. It all seemed so genuine that the boy ran up in breathless fear, hoping the dear old dragon wasn't really hurt.

DRAGON. As he approached, the dragon lifted one large eyelid, winked solemnly, and collapsed again.

SHEPHERD. Bain't you goin' to cut 'is 'ead off?

ST. GEORGE. Well, not today, I think. You see, I feel that this poor creature has truly repented of his wrongs and is ready to lead a decent, law-abiding life. But I think we should go down to the village first and have some refreshment.

NARRATOR. At the magic word *refreshment,* everyone started for the village, intent on having a joyous celebration. The dragon was forgiven by everyone and was the most popular person—er—dragon at the party. And he ate more than anyone.

SON. The boy was happy because there had been a good fight; and in spite of it all, his two best friends were on the best of terms.

ST. GEORGE. St. George was happy because he had not had to kill the dragon.

DRAGON. The dragon was happy because he was able to enter society at last.

NARRATOR. Everyone else was happy because there had been a fight, and . . . well, they didn't require any other reason to be happy. *(The music begins softly.)* At last the party was over.

SON. And as the boy had promised, he had waited to take the dragon home.

DRAGON. *(Happily.)* Jolly night it's been. Jolly stars, jolly little place this. *(Sleepily.)* Think I shall stop here . . . don't feel like climbing any old hill. *(Yawning.)* Boy will see me home later. I don't have to worry about it. . . . Boy will take . . . responsibility.

NARRATOR. And with that, the dragon sank down and fell fast asleep.

SON. Oh, get up, Dragon! You know my mother's waiting up, and I'm so tired. You made me promise to see you *home*.

NARRATOR. And the weary boy sank down in the road by the sleeping dragon and cried. St. George, hearing the noise, suddenly stepped out; and he soon saw what the matter was.

ST. GEORGE. *(Comfortingly; to the boy.)* Never you mind. I'll help you see the dragon home. *(Sternly.)* Wake up, Dragon!

DRAGON. What? Oh—just resting my eyes. What a night, St. George!

ST. GEORGE. Come, Dragon. This boy needs to be home in bed.

DRAGON. Right you are. I just need two arms to lean on, and home we'll go.

NARRATOR. So they set off up the hill, arm in arm:

ST. GEORGE. The Saint . . .

SON. The boy . . .

DRAGON. And the dragon . . .

NARRATOR. And as they turned the last corner, I couldn't be certain which of them was singing, but I *think* it was the dragon. *(The music swells and then fades out.)*

BY RUSSELL BAKER

Observer: The Person at Bay

A newspaper column adapted for Readers Theatre by Melvin R. White

Although the characters and the situation in this adaptation are fictive and satiric, the arrangement is basically that of a news documentary.

CAST OF CHARACTERS

> *Four Men, One Woman, and a Narrator-Announcer, who may be played by either a Man or a Woman*

NARRATOR. *Who also serves as the Announcer*

NEWSCASTER ONE.

NEWSCASTER TWO.

HARRY PORTER. *The person at bay*

ALICE PORTER. *His wife*

A FUNCTIONARY. *At the Office of Organization Security*

THE PHYSICAL ARRANGEMENT OF THE SCENE

The NARRATOR stands at a lectern near DR; NEWSCASTER ONE and NEWS-CASTER TWO are seated behind a low table at DL. HARRY PORTER sits in an uncomfortable chair at C, slightly upstage. ALICE, his wife, sits on a stool at his right; a FUNCTIONARY of the Office of Organization Security sits rather severely on a straight-backed chair at Harry's left. In the beginning, there is music with a "flourish" or fanfare which comes to crescendo and stops abruptly.

NARRATOR. *(Dynamically; as an announcer.)* Washington, D.C., March 26, 1966!

BROADCASTER ONE. Russell Baker, writing for *The New York Times* . . .

NARRATOR. *(With vocal fanfare.)* Observer: The Person at Bay!

NEWSCASTER ONE. The United States Government recently ordered Professor H. Stuart Hughes of Harvard shadowed by its gumshoes when he goes to Europe later this year. The Government suspects the professor of harboring unorthodox political views.

NEWSCASTER TWO. In addition, General Motors has just admitted that it ordered gumshoes to investigate the private life of Ralph Nader, a lawyer and writer. Mr. Nader has published unorthodox views of certain General Motors cars; to wit, that they are not as safe as they could be.

NEWSCASTER ONE. Messrs. Hughes and Nader are lucky. The Senate interceded for both of them and was able to find out why they were being "tailed." Most people do not find it quite so easy to obtain an explanation. Take the case of . . .

NARRATOR. *(As the dynamic announcer again.)* Harry Porter, The Organization Man! *(His voice becoming more personal, direct.)* For twenty years, Harry had trained himself to love The Organization and to walk abruptly out of any gathering at which the tiniest mouse of un-Organization thought appeared. He had always praised G.M. cars and the FBI, and his favorite toast was . . .

HARRY PORTER. *(A milquetoast of a man.)* My Organization—right or wrong!

NEWSCASTER ONE. Before marriage, Harry Porter had had Alice, his chosen bride, investigated and certified both loyal and presentable by The Organization.

NEWSCASTER TWO. Harry Porter's children were sent to schools that taught The Organization way of life.

NARRATOR. And so, when Harry noted that he was being "tailed" by men in large squishy shoes, he immediately went to the Office of Organization Security for an explanation. To an inscrutable man with hooded eyes he said:

HARRY PORTER. Surely The Organization, which is the most awesome combine of inhuman forces ever merged into a single insuperable force on this earth, can have nothing to fear from one miserable little human being like me.

FUNCTIONARY. *(Cold, impersonal, dominating.)* Keep talking.

HARRY PORTER. I have never bent, spindled, or folded. I believe that bombs are peace. I hold these truths to be self evident: That man is endowed by The Organization with certain inalienable rights, and among these are expressways, television, and the pursuit of credit.

FUNCTIONARY. *(In almost a ritual chant.)* Are you now, or have you ever been, an associate of anyone, male or female, who wears a beard, jeans, a turtleneck sweater, or refuses to observe The Organization creed of cleanliness?

HARRY PORTER. On my honor, I never speak to anyone whose skin is not soaped twice a day or whose throat, mouth, teeth, and armpits are not gargled, washed, brushed, or sprayed with chemicals.

FUNCTIONARY. Do you believe in the new washday miracle?

HARRY PORTER. Of course. And in the heartier flavor, more smoking pleasure, crispier and crunchier goodness, and faster relief as well.

FUNCTIONARY. *(Sighing, no longer chanting.)* You know, of course, that you're not entitled to an explanation of why you are being investigated.

HARRY PORTER. *(Nodding.)* Oh, yes, of course. But I—

FUNCTIONARY. *(Interrupting.)* The Organization cannot tell you because The Organization's mission is solely to help people. And there are a great many people, Mr. Porter. A great many people.

HARRY PORTER. *(Hopefully.)* But I'm people.

FUNCTIONARY. Correction, Mr. Porter. You are a *person*. The Organization never finds it necessary to investigate people. The Organization *is* people. It loves people. The enemy of people and therefore of The Organization is the person. Like yourself.

HARRY PORTER. *(Blanching.)* Are there a great many persons?

FUNCTIONARY. Far too many still, though we are gradually wearing them down. They form committees to stop The Organization from pouring asphalt over their houses so that people can drive faster. They refuse to have zip code numbers tattooed on their brains so that advertisers can send their junk mail more cheaply. They go about the world raising questions about General Motors' cars and The United States' policies.

HARRY PORTER. *(Despairingly.)* I don't suppose that there is much future in being a person?

FUNCTIONARY. *(Chuckling.)* How many persons' republics can you name offhand?

NARRATOR. Harry admitted none and sorrowfully left the Office of Organization Security. When he arrived home, he told his wife:

HARRY PORTER. It's no use. I'm a person, and I've got to be ground down.

ALICE PORTER. Harry, what are you talking about?

HARRY PORTER. *(Getting a wild idea.)* Listen! Let's cut out. We'll take all the credit cards and see how far we can run before we're caught.

ALICE PORTER. *(Trying to interrupt.)* Harry—

HARRY PORTER. We can probably make it to the Isles of Greece before the machines catch us . . .

ALICE PORTER. *(Trying again to interrupt.)* Harry—

HARRY PORTER. *(Hurrying on.)* And it'll be cheaper for The Organization to leave us there than bring us back.

NARRATOR. Harry's wife, who for years had been a volunteer agent for The Organization gumshoes, etc., promptly made a telephone call:

ALICE PORTER. Office of Organization Security? This is Mrs. Harry Porter . . .

HARRY PORTER. *(Stunned.)* Alice!

ALICE PORTER. *(Continuing.)* My husband, Harry Porter, just came home, and he wants to—

HARRY PORTER. *(Desperately pleading.)* Sweetheart . . .

ALICE PORTER. *(Uninterruptable.)* . . . Take all of our credit cards and cut out, and . . .

HARRY PORTER. *(Even more desperately.)* Darling . . .

ALICE PORTER. *(Continuing.)* . . . And see how far we can run before we get caught.

HARRY PORTER. *(Frantically.)* Alice, Alice, Alice . . .

ALICE PORTER. *(Still ignoring him.)* . . . Maybe to Greece, and . . .

FUNCTIONARY. Mrs. Porter, you are quite right to call me. If your husband runs like that, The Organization will cut off your insurance, foreclose the mortgage, cancel his pension, and hold the entire family up to public ridicule. *(Climactically.)* Put the restraints on him immediately!

NARRATOR. *(After a long pause.)* Nowadays Harry sits in his office writing messages on scrap paper and sailing them out the window. They all say:

HARRY PORTER. Help! I'm a person.

NARRATOR. No one ever comes to help, of course. Who in the world could ever take such a message seriously?

BY GEORGE P. McCALLUM

The Song Caruso Sang

A short story adapted for Readers Theatre by the author, assisted by Melvin R. White

Mr. McCallum's short story first appeared in *The American Magazine* in May, 1955, and in its original form is basically a first-person narrative. In the ensuing script, the story materials have been extensively rewritten for Readers Theatre in dialogue style, with provision for music and sound effects, if desired.

CAST OF CHARACTERS

Nine Men and Two Women. The roles of the Engineer and Mr. Kamp may be read by one Man, if desired.

GIORGIO. *The Narrator; a sensitive teen-ager, somewhat mature for his age; 15 or 16*

ENRICO CARUSO. *The famous tenor; enthusiastic, filled with a love of life and people; has strong Italian accent*

THE STUDIO ENGINEER. *A serious, businesslike young man*

PAPA ESPOSITO. *A wise, kindly father; speaks with a slight Italian accent; middle-aged*

MAMA. *A female copy of Papa; has similar accent; also middle-aged*

ANGELINA. *Their sweet, attractive daughter; has a mind of her own; 19*

BEPPE. *The eldest son; strongly influential in family decisions; 22*

GIOVANNI, ENRICO. *The younger sons; much like Beppe but more impatient to get ahead*

DICK MANTINI. *Angelina's boy friend; ambitious but sincere and helpful; 25*

MR. KAMP. *A balding little man; eccentric, impatient, weary; middle-aged*

THE PHYSICAL ARRANGEMENT OF THE SCENE

Throughout the script, the parenthetical directions concerning the possible positions and movements of the readers are made on the basis of the physical arrangement shown in the diagram. The readers use onstage focus throughout, looking at and reacting to each other on the stage. The narrator, Giorgio, speaks directly to the audience at all times.

(As the presentation begins, GIORGIO *sits on a tall stool behind a lectern slightly upstage of Center. If music is to be used, a recording of Enrico Caruso's "Celeste Aïda" from the opera* Aïda *can be heard in the background.)*

GIORGIO. *(To the audience.)* Hear that? Recognize it? That's Enrico Caruso, the greatest tenor that ever lived. He's singing "Celeste Aïda." I'm sure you've heard recordings before of Caruso singing that great aria by Verdi. But I'll bet you've never heard one quite like this. Let me tell you about it. There isn't another copy of that record in the whole world. Caruso himself gave it to my father many years ago. What happened to the Esposito family as a result . . . well, that's what I'd like to tell you about. That recording was very special, and it

FIGURE 12. *The Song Caruso Sang* floor plan

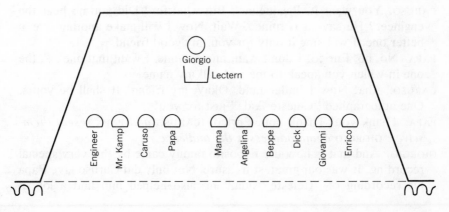

became our proudest possession. It almost became our downfall, too. But I'm getting ahead of the story.

Papa had known Caruso back home in Italy. That was before Mama and Papa came to America and settled in Brooklyn. Caruso had said that if ever Papa came to New York to be sure to look him up. So Papa did. *(The music stops.* PAPA *rises and walks toward Downstage Right as* GIORGIO *continues speaking.)* It was at a recording studio. Caruso was just finishing recording "Celeste Aïda," and as the last notes died away, he looked up and saw Papa. Immediately he called out:

CARUSO. *(Coming from chair DR to left of* PAPA.*)* Eh, Pasquelino! Cumme stai?

GIORGIO. *(To audience.)* He hurried out of the studio and embraced Papa. A few seconds later, one of the engineers came out of the recording room.

STUDIO ENGINEER. *(Stands, comes to left of* CARUSO.*)* Excuse me, Mr. Caruso, but I'm afraid you'll have to do the recording over.

CARUSO. Whatta you say? Do it over? I no understand. I'm a-thinking it's-a pretty good.

STUDIO ENGINEER. Oh, yes, sir. It's excellent. But you see, just as you finished, you called out to your friend here, and—well—it got on the record. Ordinarily we could eliminate something like that, but this comes immediately after the last note, and I'm afraid there's nothing we can do about it.

CARUSO. Okay. You're the boss. We do it over.

STUDIO ENGINEER. Thank you, sir. *(Returns to his chair and sits.)*

PAPA. *(Quickly, eagerly.)* Enrico . . .

CARUSO. Si, Pasquelino?

PAPA. Enrico . . . I am wondering . . . that record . . . the one you—that you spoke to me, called me by name. What will happen to that one?

CARUSO. The engineer says it's-a no good. So in the trash can it must go.

PAPA. Enrico . . . I . . . I . . .

CARUSO. Si, Pasquelino, my friend? What is it?

PAPA. Enrico . . . can I have it?

CARUSO. You want it, Pasquelino? But what for? Did you no hear the engineer? He says it is ruined. Wait. Now I will make another one, a better one. I will sing it only for you, my good friend.

PAPA. No, no, Enrico! I don't want another one. I want that one . . . the one in which you speak to me and call my name!

CARUSO. Aha! Now I understand. Okay, my friend! It shall be yours. One autographed "Celeste Aïda" just for you!

PAPA. Thank you! Thank you, Enrico! (CARUSO *and* PAPA *reseat themselves.* GIORGIO *again addresses the audience.)*

GIORGIO. And that is how the Esposito family came by this very special recording. It was our greatest treasure. Not only did Caruso give Papa his recording of "Celeste Aïda," he also helped him find a job in

Sheeler's Music Store. At first it wasn't much of a job, but even if Papa was only sweeping and mopping the floor, at least he was around music and that was all that mattered. Mr. Sheeler took a liking to Papa and would let him take home records on weekends. Sunday evenings we would all sit in the parlor while Papa played for us the great classics. When he had played the last one, he would say: (*All of the other members of the Esposito family raise their heads and "come alive."*)

PAPA. (*Remaining in his seat.*) Well, my children, that is all for tonight.

THE OTHERS. (*Protesting.*) No, Papa! There is one more!

PAPA. What? One more? But there couldn't be. Look. You see? No, no. That is all for tonight.

ANGELINA. The Caruso record, Papa!

BEPPE. Yes, Papa! "Celeste Aïda." We want to hear it.

PAPA. But I did not bring "Celeste Aïda" tonight. I tell you, this is all.

ANGELINA. Papa! Stop teasing us! You know the one we mean!

MAMA. Si, Pasquelino. Stop teasing the poor children. You know very well what they want to hear.

BEPPE. We want to hear *our* "Celeste Aïda" . . . the best one in the world!

PAPA. Oh! *That* "Celeste Aïda." Now, where is it? Didn't we break it last week?

(*After reacting to Papa's line, all members of the family lower their heads, signifying that they have "disappeared" from the scene.* GIORGIO, *in his role as* NARRATOR, *addresses the audience again.*)

GIORGIO. Sunday evenings in the parlor of the Espositos were always like that. We would ask Papa to play the recording Caruso had given him, and he would pretend to know nothing about it. Then at last he would, with great effort, recall the one we were talking about. We would sit like statues listening to the golden notes and thrill every time when, at the end, Caruso—speaking to our very own father—would call out:

CARUSO. (*From his seat.*) Eh, Pasquelino! Cumme stai?

GIORGIO. Then Papa would remove the record from the machine and carefully put it away until the following Sunday. No one ever touched it but Papa.

The years passed. Each of the Esposito children began to grow . . . even I, Giorgio, the youngest of the six. Beppe, the oldest, got married and moved to another part of the city; but still he and his wife would come every Sunday for dinner and the music in the parlor. Angelina got a secretarial job with an import-export company because she knew both Italian and English and was a good secretary besides. One evening she brought her boss home to dinner. His name was Dick Mantini, and he seemed like a real nice guy. Of course, after dinner we went into the parlor and listened to records from the store. (*The other members of the family "come alive," as does* ANGELINA's *boy friend,* DICK.)

PAPA. Well, that's all for tonight, children.

BEPPE. Not yet, Papa. We have to hear the Caruso record.

ANGELINA. Yes, Papa! "Celeste Aïda."

PAPA. Caruso? "Celeste Aïda"? But I tell you that is all I brought from the store this week.

MAMA. Pasquelino. Don't tease! Tonight we have a guest. He will surely think the Espositos are a foolish bunch.

ANGELINA. You see, Dick, it's a sort of ritual. I know it must sound silly but, as I told you, every Sunday the whole family is together here in the parlor, and we hear records Papa brings from Sheeler's. Then we insist and insist until Papa plays for us his very special recording of "Celeste Aïda" by Enrico Caruso.

DICK. Special? Why is it special?

ANGELINA. You'll see! Play the record for Dick, Papa.

PAPA. Well . . . all right. But only because it is his first time. You see how they pester me, young man? I don't know why. Really, I don't know why they make such a fuss over a record by Caruso. But every Sunday they bother me until I put it on. Well, then, once more . . . and that is definitely all for tonight! Do I make myself clear?

ANGELINA. Papa! Please stop talking so much. Play the record!

GIORGIO. (To audience.) Dick listened politely, but it was obvious he thought we were all out of our minds. Why all this fuss about a record by Caruso? Then came the final notes, and Caruso's words:

CARUSO. (As before.) Eh, Pasquelino! Cumme stai?

DICK. Huh? What was that?

ANGELINA. That was Caruso!

DICK. Yeah, but what was he saying? Who was he talking to?

ANGELINA. He was saying, "Pasquelino! How are you?"

DICK. But who's Pasquelino?

THE OTHERS. That's Papa!

ANGELINA. He was talking to our very own father! Isn't it wonderful? And that's why we like to hear the same record every Sunday.

PAPA. They like to hear Caruso speak to me. Isn't it ridiculous, young man?

ANGELINA. Papa! You love it, too!

DICK. (Genuinely impressed.) Why, that is wonderful! And what a novelty! There isn't another record like it in the world, I'm sure. Enrico Caruso talking right to you, Mr. Esposito.

PAPA. Every time I hear the record I close my eyes and imagine myself there in the studio with him. Many years ago it was, but it is like yesterday.

DICK. You know, I'm surprised you haven't tried to sell the record. You could make a lot of money with something like that. It's a real gimmick. (The members of the family react. DICK continues.) I've no idea what you could get for such a thing, but I have a friend in the recording business. I'd be glad to find out.

202   *Sample Scripts for Readers Theatre*

PAPA. Thank you, young man, but the record is not for sale. It was given to me by my friend, Enrico Caruso. As a matter of fact, I think maybe you are wrong; I doubt that anyone else would have interest in it.

DICK. Excuse me, sir, but I think you're not looking at the total picture. First of all, it's undoubtedly one of the greatest recordings Caruso ever made. That alone makes it valuable. But then, that little touch at the end . . . I tell you, Mr. Esposito, it would sell like hot cakes.

PAPA. Then let the people buy hot cakes. My record is not for sale!

(As GIORGIO resumes his narration, DICK and the various members of the Esposito family lower their heads to indicate they have "disappeared" from the scene.)

GIORGIO. At this point, the others began to get funny looks on their faces. It had never, in all these years, occurred to us that our treasured record could be interesting for anyone but the Espositos. Now here was someone who was convinced it was worth money to us. We were far from a rich family. We were a happy family without money, but it was obvious from the looks on their faces that Beppe and Giovanni and Angelina and Enrico were thinking how much happier we could be *with* money. Even I found myself suddenly thinking about the bicycle in Nussbaum's window. Mama looked around at our faces and decided the subject should be changed. (*The other members of the family raise their heads and become "alive" again.*)

MAMA. Come, everyone. We go to the kitchen and have coffee. Another time you can discuss this if you think you have need to.

PAPA. There is nothing to discuss. The record is not for sale.

BEPPE. But, Papa—

PAPA. (*Sharply.*) Beppe, I said no. That's final!

GIORGIO. (*To audience.*) It wasn't final, though. A week later, after we'd had dinner and the concert and heard the Caruso record, Beppe got up and made a little speech.

BEPPE. (*Stands.*) Papa . . . Mama . . . for a long time now you have dreamed of owning a piece of land out in Jersey where you could have a garden and raise some grapes and fruit trees. Both of you have worked hard, and now it is time for you to take it easy and enjoy yourselves. You deserve it if anyone does. Well, we have been talking—Enrico, Angelina, Giovanni, and I. We talked to Dick again the other night. He saw his friend from the recording company. Papa, it looks like we could get as much as a thousand dollars for the record. Think, Papa, what you could do—Mama and you—with a thousand dollars!

PAPA. I said before and I say again: my record is not for sale. Not for a thousand . . . not for ten thousand dollars. We'll talk about it no more!

BEPPE. But, Papa! Listen! You wouldn't even have to sell your record. You could keep it. Dick's friend said the recording company would pay you just to borrow it and copy it. Think of it, Papa.

PAPA. (*Grudgingly.*) Very well. I will think.

BEPPE. *(Eagerly.)* Does that mean I can find out how to get in touch with the man from the recording company—just in case?

PAPA. I . . . suppose.

BEPPE. Thanks, Papa! You won't be sorry.

(BEPPE reseats himself in his chair, and he and the other members of the family lower their heads. GIORGIO resumes his narration.)

GIORGIO. Beppe shouldn't have added those last words. Before the week was out, Papa was sorry. Mama, too—though she said nothing. I think even I was a little sorry. You see, what happened was that Beppe found out that we would probably get *more* than a thousand dollars for the record.

Suddenly our house became a completely different place. Always before, it had been a happy place . . . crowded and noisy and warm and everything that makes a home what it is supposed to be. And now it wasn't that way at all. The record by Caruso that had been our greatest possession had changed everything.

You see, what happened was this: Every one of us—Beppe, Angelina, Giovanni, Enrico, and—yes, even I—we got to thinking how we ought to spend all the money we were going to get for the record. Giovanni thought we ought to have a car. *(The members of the Esposito family rise and play the ensuing scene in the area DL.)*

GIOVANNI. *(Crossing toward DL.)* Look. We've never had a car. Think how great it would be! We could all pile in and go for long drives on Sunday—clear up to Bear Mountain. And in the summer, we could even take vacations to places like Grand Canyon.

ANGELINA. *(Following GIOVANNI DL.)* No, Giovanni. Mama wouldn't like a car. What she wants, I'm sure, is a house. Look at all the years we've had to live in this little apartment over the Pezzullo fruit store! Mama deserves a nice new house.

ENRICO. *(Heatedly: to ANGELINA and GIOVANNI.)* You are both wrong, Angelina. Did it ever occur to either one of you that Mama and Papa have had one dream since their family has grown up and they can think a little about themselves for a change? A trip back home to Italy! That's what they want . . . to take all of us with them to meet our grandparents and aunts and uncles and—

ANGELINA. Oh, sure! You say that because *you* want a free trip to Italy.

GIOVANNI. And maybe there'll be a little money left over for you to take singing lessons, Enrico.

ENRICO. What do you mean by that, Giovanni?

ANGELINA. He's right, Enrico. Just because you're named after Caruso, you think that—

BEPPE. Quiet! Be still, both of you! You're fighting just like you did when you were in grade school. I don't know where any of you get these crazy ideas. Mama and Papa have talked of only one dream, and that has been a little piece of farmland in Jersey. If they sell the record, that's what they ought to buy with the money.

GIOVANNI. *(Sarcastically.)* Great! Then you and Rosa could take the children there for weekends. Very convenient.

*(The four—*GIOVANNI, ANGELINA, ENRICO, *and* BEPPE*—ad-lib their arguing as they return to their respective chairs and sit. As* GIOVANNI *picks up the narration again, their voices stop; but by the posture of their bodies and the stony-faced silence which they maintain until they lower their heads to "disappear" from the scene, they dramatically convey the hostilities which have been engendered.)*

GIORGIO. So it went, day after day. I must admit even I had dreams about how to spend the record money . . . only my problem was that I changed my mind two or three times a day. *(Sighs, shrugs.)* Well, things moved on. And Beppe arranged for the man from the recording company to come Sunday evening to hear the record. Papa would not allow it out of the house.

By then, nobody in the Esposito family was speaking to anyone. Such long faces had never before been seen in our home as on that evening when we all sat around the table at suppertime. Mama had insisted we all have dinner together as usual. Believe me, it was far from the laughing, talking, eating bunch that usually crowded around the table. It was more like a wake. Just before Mama brought in the soup, Papa stood up to speak. (PAPA *stands, remaining near his chair or stepping around behind it.*)

PAPA. It has been two weeks now since Dick told us we could get a lot of money for our Caruso record. In my bones I felt this was not good. I said my record was not for sale. Then we heard that we didn't have to sell—that we only had to lend. It didn't seem so bad just to let them copy it, so I said nothing. *(Sighs heavily, sadly.)* But it *is* bad. Very bad. I know this now. Ever since we've thought of selling the record, I've been watching this family, and I see we aren't a family any more. Before . . . we were happy, and this house was filled with love and laughter. Now there are only angry faces and sharp words. I used to hurry home from work every night. Now I stay away.

MAMA. *(Sniffling.)* Ay, Pasquelino! Please. The soup is getting cold.

PAPA. No, Mama. I will not stop. Not until I finish what I have to say. The soup can be made hot again. But this family . . . I don't know if it can be made happy again. Not with a big car . . . or a house on Long Island . . . a trip to Italy . . . or a farm in New Jersey.

BEPPE. But, Papa, we were only thinking—

PAPA. Please, Beppe. Let me finish. Why is this? I ask myself. Why is it that in only a few days a family that has been so happy—so very, very happy—can suddenly be so sad? It is because of a record . . . a record by my dear friend Enrico Caruso. Now the thing that for many years is happiness for Pasquelino Esposito is unhappiness. I ask myself, can I buy with money this happiness once again? And I find the only answer is no!

BEPPE. But, Papa, you'd still have your record and the little farm in Jersey with apples and grapes . . .

PAPA. Apples and grapes I can buy at the fruit store of Pezzullo. A family I cannot buy in any place.

GIORGIO. *(To audience.)* With that, Papa left the table without touching his soup and went into the parlor.

(PAPA *reseats himself in his chair and lowers his head to signify that he is disappearing from the scene.* GIORGIO, *meanwhile, continues.*)

Then Mama spoke to us.

MAMA. Beppe . . . Angelina . . . all of you. Please. You must think of all your papa has said. (MAMA *sits and lowers her head.* BEPPE *rises.*)

BEPPE. Papa's right. And it's all my fault.

GIOVANNI. *(Rises, joins* BEPPE.*)* Your fault, Beppe?

BEPPE. Yes, Giovanni. I kept insisting that Papa consider selling the record after he'd made it plain he didn't want to.

GIOVANNI. Don't be stupid, Beppe! You were right to insist. You were just thinking of the good of the family. Once this is all over and the record is copied, Papa will see we did right. He'll have his record and the money, too—like you just said. (ANGELINA *rises and crosses to* GIOVANNI *and* BEPPE.*)*

BEPPE. But the family? *(Worriedly.)* Didn't you hear Papa and see his face just now? And Mama, too? Suddenly, when I looked at them, I realized we stand a chance of losing more than we could buy with a few dollars.

ANGELINA. *(Protesting.)* Beppe, this isn't like you. You've always been the practical one in the family. Now you're becoming a dreamer—just like Papa.

BEPPE. And that's so bad . . . being like Papa?

ANGELINA. That isn't what I mean, and you know it.

GIOVANNI. Well, quit arguing, you two. Any minute now, Mr. Kamp, from the record company, will be here. It's too late to call and tell him not to come. At least we'll have to hear what he has to say.

BEPPE. *(Firmly.)* Anyway, we're not going to sell!

(ANGELINA, GIOVANNI, *and* BEPPE *return to their chairs, reseat themselves, and lower their heads as* GIORGIO *resumes his narration.*)

GIORGIO. I found myself awfully glad about what Beppe had said. Suddenly the bicycle and the electric train and all the other things I dreamed of buying were like nothing at all. I knew now that the last thing I wanted was for us to sell the Caruso record. When it went out of our house, then something terribly important to the Espositos would go with it . . . perhaps forever. *(Pauses, sighs.)* But . . . nevertheless, at exactly seven-thirty, the recording company's representative, Mr. Kamp—a baldheaded little man with a very businesslike manner—knocked at the door.

(All of the Espositos raise their heads and "come alive." By their facial expressions and bodily attitudes, they evidence their feelings of excitement and uneasiness.)

We all went into the parlor and sat down. The room was deadly quiet, like just before a thunderstorm. Papa picked up the record and placed it on the turntable. He seemed nervous, and his hands were shaking as he lowered the needle onto the record. Then, suddenly, he stopped the machine.

PAPA. Excuse me, sir. I put on the wrong record. That was "Vesti la Giubba." How could I have made such a stupid mistake?

MR. KAMP. Very natural, I'm sure, Mr. Esposito. Both records look exactly alike. But may I now hear "Celeste Aïda"? My time *is* limited.

PAPA. Of course, of course. This time I have the right record.

GIORGIO. *(To audience.)* The little man from the recording company leaned forward and stared at the floor as though that was where the sound was coming from. When the recording finished, he nodded and asked to hear it once more. Papa started the record at the beginning again. Then he sat back and gazed around the room as Caruso sang of his love for the beautiful Aida. Following Papa's gaze, I saw Angelina and Beppe and Enrico and Giovanni—all with the same anxious expression, one just like the next. They were not my brothers and sisters at all, nor was this the happy time of the many other Sundays. Finally, "Celeste Aïda" came to its end, and the much-loved Caruso exclaimed, as always:

CARUSO. Eh, Pasquelino! Cumme stai?

MR. KAMP. *(Straightening in his chair.)* Well, Mr. Esposito. You have quite a record there. I'll admit to you frankly that this is the best "Celeste Aïda" I have ever heard. Excuse my immodesty, but I *am* considered one of the best authorities on Caruso. So when I say this is the best, it *is* the best. And that little personal touch at the end . . . absolutely great. That alone would make it a record best seller!

(He laughs at his little play on the word "record"; but when the others fail to join in, he stops and suddenly becomes serious again.)

Yes . . . well, I suppose you want to talk business. And as I said, my time is limited. *(Clears his throat.)* Well, sir, my company will pay you five thousand dollars for all the rights to the use of this recording if it's what we want, and I do not hesitate to assure you that it is.

ANGELINA. Five thousand dollars!

GIOVANNI. Do you hear that, Papa?

ENRICO. We had no idea it would be so much!

BEPPE. Sorry you had to come all the way out to Brooklyn for nothing, Mr. Kamp. Just this afternoon we decided not to sell the record or any rights to it.

MR. KAMP. *(Astounded.)* What's that, young man?

ANGELINA. Beppe! What are you saying?

GIOVANNI. Are you out of your mind? He didn't say *one* thousand—

ENRICO. He said *five* thousand dollars, Beppe!

BEPPE. I heard him. I guess the rest of you forget what we agreed this afternoon. Sorry, Mr. Kamp. I repeat: the record is not for sale.

MR. KAMP. But why? I—I don't understand.

BEPPE. *(Quietly.)* Shall we say . . . for personal reasons.

ANGELINA. Beppe!

MR. KAMP. Well . . . I may as well tell you that my company has authorized me to go as high as six thousand if necessary to—

ANGELINA, GIOVANNI, ENRICO. Six thousand!

MR. KAMP. Yes, six thousand. But not a penny more.

BEPPE. Did you say . . . *six* thousand?

(For a tense moment, all of the Espositos stare in stupefied silence. Then GIORGIO *again speaks to the audience, his voice charged with emotion.)*

GIORGIO. As for me . . . I could not speak. And I had to turn my head away because I didn't want the others to see there were tears in my eyes. Through the blur I could see the record where Papa had put it with the others on the table. I'll never be able to explain—not even to myself—how it happened. But suddenly—sobbing, "No! No!"—I grabbed the record from the table and dashed it to the floor, smashing it into a thousand pieces. Everything in the room stopped dead still. Finally, Mr. Kamp managed to speak.

MR. KAMP. *(Very much upset.)* You're all crazy! And that's for sure! *Good* night! *(He reseats himself in his chair, lowers his head, and "disappears" from the scene as* GIORGIO *continues.)*

GIORGIO. I rushed into the kitchen, no longer able to control my sobs. The others followed. *(Emotion surging into his voice again.)* It was quite a scene, what with everyone crying and hugging me. To tell the truth, I was suddenly embarrassed . . . but mostly I was glad . . . glad I had broken the record. *(All members of the family, except* BEPPE, *rise and play the ensuing scene down front, near C.)*

PAPA. Good boy, Giorgio! This is a family again, and nothing else matters.

GIOVANNI. You had to do it, Giorgio! It was the only way to bring us to our senses.

ANGELINA. It took the baby of the family to make us see it. Otherwise—well, I hate to think how close we came to disaster.

PAPA. Mama! We must have a celebration! Don't you have something for us . . . some coffee at least? Suddenly I'm hungry. I guess it's because I didn't eat any dinner this evening.

MAMA. Si, Pasquelino! I have only to heat it up. And there is the cake that no one touched.

ENRICO. Look at Mama! She's smiling for the first time in two weeks! Mama, you have six children, but you had to have five before you gave birth to an intelligent one.

MAMA. I have the best children in the world . . . from the oldest to the youngest.

GIOVANNI. (Looking around.) Hey! Speaking of the oldest—where's Beppe?

ANGELINA. I think he took Mr. Kamp to the door. (As though from an adjoining room, there can be heard the music and singing of the Caruso recording.)

ENRICO. Listen! (There is a short pause as all listen, their faces filled with wonderment.)

GIOVANNI. It can't be!

ANGELINA. It is! It's "Celeste Aïda"! (BEPPE stands, a happy smile on his face, elation in his voice.)

BEPPE. Yes! Papa's "Celeste Aïda."

ENRICO. Beppe! What is it? What has happened?

BEPPE. I guess we'll have to get a new "Vesti la Giubba." And, Giorgio . . . we'll also have to get you a new pair of glasses! (Laughs.) Seems you couldn't see well enough and grabbed the wrong record off the table!

MAMA. (Happily.) Giorgio! Giorgio has smashed the wrong record!

(All of the Espositos laugh, return to their respective chairs, and reseat themselves as they listen enraptured to the strains of the music while GIORGIO resumes his narration.)

GIORGIO. "Celeste Aïda!" In all the years we had listened to it, it never sounded as beautiful as it did at that moment. We listened as though for the first time. And when at the end, Caruso called out:

CARUSO. Eh, Pasquelino! Cumme stai?

PAPA. Happy again, my friend, very happy!

GIORGIO. And with that answer, Papa spoke for all of us. (Moving around beside his lectern.) Well . . . that's all there is. We're a family again and still have the record. Maybe someday we'll save enough money to move to that farm in Jersey. Right now it's just something nice to dream about. The Sunday evenings are once again as before . . . except that Angelina has married Dick Mantini, and now he is also with us every Sunday. (The members of the family "come alive" and start listening.) And every Sunday, we listen to Caruso and "Celeste Aïda," just as if we'd never heard him say:

CARUSO. Eh, Pasquelino? Cumme stai?

GIORGIO. Only now, Papa always answers, "Happy, my friend Caruso, very happy!"

BY JEAN KERR

The Ten Worst Things About a Man

A humorous essay adapted for Readers Theatre by Leslie Irene Coger

In its original form, a chapter from Mrs. Kerr's book *The Snake Has All the Lines,* the material was expressed entirely by one person—a woman. In this adapted version, a second character—a man—has been added in order to provide an element of contrast and a degree of good-natured conflict to spark the dialogue, thereby converting what was essentially a monologue into a sketch for two people.

CAST OF CHARACTERS

> *One Woman and One Man*

> SHE. *A typical young wife*

> HE. *A typical young husband*

THE PHYSICAL ARRANGEMENT OF THE SCENE

Two stools are provided at or near the center of the stage for the readers; and lecterns may be added, if desired; or the stools may be dispensed with, and the two interpreters may remain standing behind their lecterns. Offstage focus is used throughout. SHE is wearing a uniquely feminine afternoon dress; HE, a solidly masculine business suit; or, if something more glamorous seems in order, SHE may be sheathed in a svelte evening gown and HE in a tuxedo. In the beginning, there might be a bit of appropriate music; but, if so, it quickly becomes indistinct and fades out altogether as SHE begins to speak.

SHE. Actually, I feel a bit of a fraud to be picking on men when I always pretend to be so crazy about them. And, deep down inside, I am crazy about them. They are sweet, you know, and so helpful. At parties, men you've barely met will go back to the buffet to get you a muffin, and they will leap to their feet to tell you that you've got the wrong end of the cigarette in your mouth. Notice that when you are trying to squeeze into a tight parking space, there will always be some nice man driving by who will stick his head out the window and shout:

HE. *(Bawling loudly.)* Lady, you've got a whole mile back there! (SHE *shrugs as a response to his words.*)

SHE. But, charming as men are, we can't honestly pretend they're perfect. It wouldn't be good for them, and it wouldn't be true. Marrying a man is like buying something you've been admiring for a long time in a shop window. You may love it when you get it home, but it doesn't always go with the other things in the house. One reason for this is that most men insist on behaving as though this were an orderly, sensible universe, which naturally makes them hard to live with. The other reason they're hard to live with—and I know this sounds illogical—is that they're so good. Perhaps I can clarify that last statement by allowing one of them to enumerate a few of their more intolerable virtues:

HE. A man will not meddle in what he considers his wife's affairs.

SHE. He may interfere at the office, driving secretaries to drink and premature marriage by snooping into file drawers and tinkering with the mimeograph machine. Back home in the nest, he is the very model of patience. He will stare at you across the dining-room table—as you simultaneously carve the lamb and feed the baby—and announce in tones so piteous as to suggest that all his dreams have become ashes:

HE. *(Piteously.)* Honey, there's no salt in this shaker! *(Her expression says, "What can a wife do with a man like that?")*

SHE. What a wife objects to in this situation is not just the notion that Daddy has lived in this house for thirteen years without discovering where the salt is kept. It's more the implication that only she has the necessary fortitude, stamina, and simple animal cunning to pour the salt into the little hole in the back of the shaker.

HE. *(With impressive self-importance.)* A man remembers important things.

SHE. It really is remarkable the fund of information he keeps at his fingertips:

HE. Why, I can give you the date of the Battle of Hastings, the name of the man who invented the printing press, the formula for water, the Preamble of the Constitution, and every lyric Larry Hart ever wrote.

SHE. *(Smiling indulgently.)* It is obviously unreasonable to expect one so weighted down with relevant data to remember a simple fact like what size shirt he takes, or what grade Gilbert is in, or even that you told him fifteen times that the Bentleys are coming to dinner. A woman just has to go through life remembering for two. As an example of this, I was recently told about a wife who, from time to time, pinned a tag on her husband's coat. The tag read:

HE. *(As if reading from a card.)* "Please don't give me a ride home from the station; I have my own car today."

SHE. However, this technique wouldn't work with *my* husband because he usually forgets and leaves his coat on the train.

HE. *(Changing the subject.)* A man will try to improve his wife's mind.

SHE. Working on the suspicion that women read nothing in the newspapers except bulletins from Macy's and Dorothy Kilgallen, the average man takes considerable pains to keep his scatter-brained wife *au courant* with the contemporary political situation. And we get the following bit of profound dialogue across the dinner table:

HE. Did you read Walter Lippman today on the shake-up in the Defense Department?

SHE. No, what did he have to say?

HE. *(Laconically.)* You should have read it. It was a damn good piece.

SHE. Well, what was the gist of it?

HE. Where's the paper? It should be around here someplace.

SHE. *(Very firmly.)* It's not around here someplace. It went out with the garbage.

HE. That's too bad, because it would have clarified the whole situation for you.

SHE. I'm sure. But what was he saying?

HE. Oh, he was talking about the shake-up in the Defense Department.

SHE. *(Pushing for a definite answer.)* I know that, but what did he *say?*

HE. *(Simply.)* He was against it. (SHE *registers her "What can you do?" response.*)

SHE. A man allows you to make the important decisions because he has such respect for your superior wisdom and technical know-how. He is constantly asking questions:

HE. Does this kid need a sweater?

SHE. Or:

HE. *(Ugh!)* Is this baby wet?

SHE. Personally, I am willing to go down through life being the court of last appeals on such crucial issues as bedtime . . .

HE. Bedtime! *(Surprised.)* Is it?

SHE. Cookies . . .

HE. *(Meaning "Let's be indulgent!")* Can they have another?

SHE. Rubbers . . .

HE. Do they have to wear them?

SHE. And baths . . .

HE. *(In shocked disbelief.)* Tonight? But they just took one last night! (SHE *responds silently but expressively to this unbelievable man of hers.)*

SHE. But just between us, I have no confidence in a man who wanders into the kitchen, peers into the icebox, and asks plaintively:

HE. *(Plaintively and uncertainly.)* Do I want a sandwich?

SHE. A man will give you an honest answer. If you say, "Honey, do you think this dress is too tight for me to wear?" he'll say:

HE. *(Quickly and definitely.)* Yes! (SHE *reacts facially to his lack of tact, but she loves him.*)

SHE. A man takes pride in his personal possessions. A woman will go all her days in the wistful belief that her husband would give her the shirt off his back. Thus, she is in no way prepared for the cries of outrage that will go up should she ever be rash enough to *take* the shirt off his back. It doesn't matter that the shirt in question has a torn pocket, a frayed collar, and has—in any case—been at the bottom of the clothes hamper for three years. It's his, and you wear it at your own risk. My husband will say to me:

HE. *(Incredulously.)* What are you doing in that shirt, for heaven's sake?

SHE. *(Quickly.)* Now he doesn't really want to know what I'm doing. *(Very deliberately.)* He can see what I'm doing. I'm painting the garage doors. He just wants me to know that that shirt was near and dear to him, and now—as a result of my vandalism—it's totally ruined. There are two possible solutions to this problem. You can hire a painter to paint the garage doors, or you can dye the shirt purple so he won't be able to recognize it.

HE. *(Thinking he's changing the subject.)* A man believes in sharing.

SHE. Men are all advocates of togetherness . . . up to a point. They will agree that it is our house, our mortgage, and of course our song. It is interesting, however, to observe the circumstances under which items that once were under joint concern suddenly become your exclusive possession. For instance, a man will return from a stroll in your back yard to tell you:

HE. *(Half-plaintively, half-accusingly.)* Honey, I think your daffodils are getting clump-bound.

SHE. Or on other occasions:

HE. *(As though he has made a discovery.)* I see that the hinge is off your medicine chest.

SHE. In my opinion, this policy of disassociating from anything that is temporarily out of order reaches its ultimate confusion with statements like:

HE. Hey, your man is here to fix the chimney!

SHE. *(Incredulous at his obtuseness.)* My man? I never saw him before in my life!

HE. *(Indulgently.)* A man doesn't want his little woman to worry.

SHE. Since he supposes—and quite correctly—that you worry a great deal about his health, he will go to any lengths to spare you the least alarm about his physical condition. He will say, as though it were the most casual thing in the world:

HE. *(Casually.)* Well, I almost keeled over in Grand Central today.

SHE. Good heavens, what happened?

HE. Nothing, nothing. I leaned against a pillar and didn't actually fall down.

SHE. *(Pressing for information.)* But, honey, what happened? Did you feel faint? You didn't have a terribly sharp pain in your chest, did you?

HE. *(Offhandedly.)* Oh, no . . . no, nothing like that.

SHE. Well, what do you mean—you almost keeled over?

HE. *(Indifferently.)* I almost keeled over, that's all.

SHE. But there must have been some reason.

HE. *(Matter-of-factly.)* Oh, I guess it's that foot again.

SHE. *(Very excitedly.)* What foot again? Which foot?

HE. Oh, I told you about my foot.

SHE. *(Almost beside herself with worry.)* You most certainly did *not* tell me anything about your foot.

HE. The one that's been numb since last summer.

SHE. *(Incredulously; nearly frantic.)* Your foot has been numb since last summer?

HE. Now it's more like the whole leg.

SHE. Good Heavens, let's call a doctor! Let's call this minute!

HE. Why?

SHE. Why? Are you out of your mind? Because there's something the matter with your leg, that's why.

HE. There you go flying off again. I'm sorry I mentioned it. And there's nothing the matter with my leg. Nothing.

SHE. A man idealizes his wife. This is another way of saying that he hasn't really looked at her in fourteen years. To get me the housecoat for my birthday, my husband will make the unthinkable sacrifice of entering Lord and Taylor's, and even penetrate the awesome portals of the lingerie department. There, as I reconstruct the scene later, he selects the slimmest, trimmest, little sales girl on the floor and announces: (HE *thinks it through and sizes up the saleslady.)*

HE. She's about your size.

SHE. Naturally I have to take the thing back and get one four sizes larger. On second thought, I shouldn't complain about that. If you stop and think . . . *(and she does)* . . . it's really rather charming of him. (SHE *turns to her partner and winks.)*

BY AMY LOWELL

The Day That Was That Day

A poem adapted for Readers Theatre by Leslie Irene Coger

The content and basic structure of the piece, as originally written by the poet, lend themselves admirably to the oral interpretive medium. The highly evocative eight-line opening, which may be assigned to three readers, quickly establishes the mood. Rachel Gibbs then sets the stage for her startling and dramatic visit with Minnie Green; and in the ensuing dialogue between the two women, Minnie's plight and problems are probed and adroitly unfolded. At one point, during a natural break in the conversation, the three-reader chorus briefly reinforces the emotional aura; the dialogue is renewed and brought to its culmination; and the chorus provides the concluding commentary.

CAST OF CHARACTERS

Five Women

READER ONE, READER TWO, READER THREE. *Voices in the Chorus*

RACHEL GIBBS. *A country woman; middle-aged*

MINNIE GREEN. *Her friend, middle-aged and despondent*

THE PHYSICAL ARRANGEMENT OF THE SCENE

Five stools should be provided, one for each participant; and a lectern for each may be added if desired. The actual placement of these physical elements will, of course, vary in terms of the director's inclination and ingenuity; for this is a part of the creativity which should be generated

"The Day That Was That Day," by Amy Lowell, in *East Wind,* published by Houghton Mifflin Company, Boston, Mass., 1926. **Important Notice:** This Readers Theatre adaptation of Amy Lowell's poem, "The Day That Was That Day," may not be presented or performed publicly without the written permission of the publisher, Houghton Mifflin Company, 2 Park Street, Boston, Mass., 02107.

by this medium. One director may, for instance, decide to position RACHEL and MINNIE prominently on stools in the center of the stage and arrange the readers in the CHORUS on taller stools behind them. Another director might prefer to place MINNIE and RACHEL at RC, with the CHORUS across from them at LC. The possibilities and variations are limited only by the director's artistic intention and the physical environment in which the reading is to be presented.

READER ONE.   *The wind rose, and the wind fell,*
                And the day that was that day
                Floated under a high Heaven.

READER TWO.   *"Home! Home! Home!"*
                Sang a robin in a spice-bush.

READER THREE.   *"Sun on a roof-tree! Sun on a roof-tree!"*
                Rang thin clouds
                In a chord of silver across a placid sky.

RACHEL. Rachel Gibbs stepped up the path
         To pass the time of day
         With Haywood Green's Minnie.
         My, if she ain't shut th' door!
         An' all th' breeze this side th' house too.
         She must like to stew.

         "Minnie,
         Minnie,
         You ain't gone out have yer?

         I'll skin my knuckles ef I knock agin.
         I wonder did she lock th' door—

         Well, I never!
         Have you gone hard o' hearin'?
         Have you—

         Minnie, child, what's th' matter?
         Why do you look like that?
         What you doin'?
         Speak I tell yer,
         What you hidin' that cup fer?
         God A'mighty, girl, what you doin' with wood-alcohol
         In a drinkin'–cup?
         Here, give it ter me,
         An' I'll set it on th' table.

Set down Minnie dear,
Set right here in th' rocker
An' tell me
What ails yer to be wantin'
To drink stuff like that?

There, there, you poor lamb,
Don't look so scared.
Jest tell me all about it,
An' ease your heart.

Minnie, I'll have to shake yer
Ef you don't stop starin'
In that dretful way.

Poor Dear,
You just lay your head up agin me
An' let me soothe yer.

Poor little thing.
Poor little thing."

MINNIE. "Don't, don't Rachel,
I can't bear it.
I'm a wicked woman,
But I jest couldn't stand no more."

RACHEL. "No more o' what?
Ain't yer Pa good to yer?
What's come over yer, Minnie?
My! I'm jest as sorry as I can be."

MINNIE. "Oh, it ain't nothin' like that.
An' don't be so good to me,
You'll make me want to cry again,
An' I can't cry.
I'm all dried up,
An' it's like squeezin' my heart sick
To want to cry, an' can't."

RACHEL. "But what is it?
Ain't yer never goin' ter tell me?"

MINNIE. "Why ther' ain't nothin' to tell
'Cept that I'm tired."

RACHEL. "Now, look-a-here, Minnie,
No one don't drink poison jest 'cause they're tired."

MINNIE. "I didn't drink it, as it happens."

The Day That Was That Day 217

RACHEL. "No, you didn't, 'cause I come in an' stopped yer.
But I'm mighty afeered you would have.
Lord, it makes me shudder!"

MINNIE. "I guess yer right,
I would have.
An' I wish you'd ha' let me be.
Now it's all to do over agin,
An' I don't know as I'll git th' courage
A second time.
I guess you ain't never been right down tired, Rachel."

RACHEL. "Well, never to th' poison point, no, I haven't.
But what's gone wrong to wear yer out so?"

MINNIE. "The cat's sick."

RACHEL. "Minnie Green, was you takin' poison
'Cause you got a sick cat?
That's down-right foolishness."

MINNIE. "Yes, it does sound so.
But I couldn't face nussin' her.
Look here, Rachel,
I may be foolish, or mad, or jest plain bad,
But I couldn't stan' another thing.
I'm all fretted now
An' more's one too many.
I can't go on!
Oh, God! I can't go on!

I ain't got no more'n most women,
I know that,
But I fuss a lot more.
There's al'ays th' same things
Goin' roun' like th' spokes to a cart-wheel,
Ef one ain't a-top it's another,
An' th' next comin' up all th' time.

It's breakfast, an' dinner, an' supper,
Every day.
An' th' same dishes to wash.
I hate them dishes.
I smashed a plate yesterday
'Cause I couldn't bear to see it
Settin' on th' sink waitin' fer me.

An' when I go up to make Father's bed
I git seasick

218   *Sample Scripts for Readers Theatre*

Thinkin' I'll have to see that old check spread agin.
I've settled it,
An' twitched it this way an' that,
For thirty year,
An' I hate th' sight o' th' thing.
Sometimes I've set an hour on th' stair
Ruther'n go in an' touch it.

Oh my God! Why couldn't yer let me be?
Why'd you have to come interferin'?
Why?
Why?"

RACHEL. "Thank th' Everlastin' Mercy I did!
But, Minnie, how long's this been goin' on?
I never had no idea anythin' was wrong."

MINNIE. "I don't know.
For ever an' ever, I guess.
Rachel, you can't think how hard it is fer me
To set one foot after th' other sometimes.
I hate lookin' out th' winder,
I'm so tired o' seein' th' path to th' barn.
An' I can't hardly bear
To hear Father talkin' to th' horses.
He loves 'em.
But I don't love nothin'
'Cept th' cat,
An' cats is cold things to cling to,
An' now mine's sick!"

RACHEL. "Don't take on so, Minnie.
She'll get well.
There, you rest awhile
You can tell me afterwards."

READER ONE.   *A wind rose, and a wind fell,*
               And the day that was that day
               Hung against a turning sun.

READER TWO.   *The robin sang "Home! Home! Home!"*
               In an up-and-down scale of small, bright notes.

READER THREE. *The clouds rang silver arpeggios*
               Stretched across a pleasant sky.

MINNIE. "I wish I loved somethin', Rachel."

RACHEL. "Bless your heart, Child, don't you love yer Father?"

MINNIE. "I suppose so. But he don't mean nothin' ter me.
He don't say nothin' I want ter hear.
My ears is achin' to hear words,
Words like what's written in books,
Words that would make me all bright like a Spring day.

I lay awake nights
Thinkin' o' hearin' things,
An' seein' things,
I'm awful tired o' these hills,
They crowd in so.
Seems sometimes ef I could see th' ocean,
Or a real big city,
'Twould help.
Kind o' lay my eyes out straight fer a while,
Everythin's so short here
My eyes feel pushed in,
An' it hurts 'em.

I love laylocks,
But I git so tired o' watchin'
Th' leaves come an' th' flowers
Every year th' same,
I'd like to root 'em up.

I've set an' set in th' kitchen evenin's
Awful late,
Fer not bein' able to git up an' light th' lamp
To go ter bed.
I'm all lead somehow.
I guess ef anybody did say anythin'
I'd be deaf
Jest with listenin' so long.
I'm plumb tired out."

RACHEL. "Look-a-here, Minnie,
Why don't you go away
Fer a spell?"

MINNIE. "Me go away!
Oh, no, I couldn't never do that.
I couldn't go no place.
I can't hardly git over to Dicksville
Fer my week with Aunt Abby now.
I'm all wrong away from home.
I can't do nothin'!
Nothin' at all.
I'm so awful tired."

RACHEL. "Minnie, did you ever love anybody?
Any man, I mean?"

MINNIE. "No, Rachel, I never did.
I know that sounds queer, but it's a fact.
I've tried to think I did,
But 'twarn't true.
I hadn't hardly no time fer men-folks,
Mother was sick so long.
An' then ther' was Father.
I never was much account with 'em anyway,
But I s'pose I might ha' had one
Ef I'd fixed my mind so.
But I al'ays waited.
An' now I'm through waitin',
I'm through waitin' fer anythin', Rachel.
It's jest go, go, go,
With never no end,
And nothin' done that ain't to do over agin.

Ther' now it's six o'clock,
An' I must be gittin' supper.
You needn't move that cup, Rachel.
I ain't a-goin' to touch it.
I'll jest keep on now till th' Lord takes me
An' I only hope he'll do it soon."

READER ONE. *The robin flew down from the spice-bush*
And pecked about for worms.

READER TWO. *The clouds were brazen trumpets*
Tumbled along the edge of an apple-coloured sky.

READER THREE. *The shadow of the house*
Fell across the path to the barn
Confusing it with the grass and the daisies.

READER ONE. *A wind rose,*

READER TWO. *And a wind fell,*

READER THREE. *And the day that was that day*
Vanished in the darkness.

PART FOUR

Selected Articles
for Further Study

A Philosophy on Readers Theatre

Keith Brooks, Robert C. Henderhan, Alan Billings

Since the beginning of recorded time, man has thrilled to the wondrous art of the story teller. Man's intellect and emotion alike have been stimulated by the oral communication of literature. That the "play's the thing" which has captured the mood of the times, has moved mobs to act, has made philosophers to contemplate, can be seen in the bards, actors, readers, and jesters of every period of history.

A relatively new phenomenon called Readers Theatre continues the tradition. This art form has excited the interest of performers and spectators from coast to coast. Among the New York productions have been *Don Juan in Hell* with Charles Laughton, Charles Boyer, Sir Cedric Hardwicke, and Agnes Moorehead; *John Brown's Body* with Tyrone Power, Raymond Massey, and Judith Anderson; *The World of Carl Sandburg* with Leif Erickson and Bette Davis; *Brecht on Brecht* with Dane Clark, Anne Jackson, Lotte Lenya, Viveca Lindfors, and George Voskovec; *Dear Liar* with Katherine Cornell and Brian Aherne. College and university groups have included Readers Theatre programs in increasing number, adapting all types of literature (plays, poetry, prose) with particular emphasis on non-dramatic literature. This emphasis has been one of the unique contributions of Readers Theatre: the sharing of literature not usually treated by actors on stage.

This relatively new phenomenon of sharing literature through Readers Theatre has followed a number of forms and methods. The result, understandably, has been vagueness and inconsistency of treatment. On the one hand, there are productions wherein the readers are actors who speak from memory (although attending to their scripts from time to time), movement is much as it would be in a theatrical production, and the literary experience is located

The Speech Teacher, XII, No. 3 (September 1963), 229-232. Reprinted by permission of the authors.

on-stage. On the other hand, productions are seen in which the readers are more dependent on their scripts but familiar enough with the literature to allow for frequent and sustained contact with the realm of the audience, all responsiveness is suggestive in nature, and the literary experience is projected into the realm of the audience. Some productions have combined elements of both.

It is intended herein to present a point of view that may be new to some and, it is hoped, acceptable to most. The point of view is simply that Readers Theatre may utilize the principles of oral interpretation as its guidelines and, if the literature requires, may incorporate selected theatre properties to assist the listener in fulfilling the potential of the literary experience as suggested by the readers.

This philosophy can be illustrated by the statement of three general principles predicated on the notion that a Readers Theatre performance should be evaluated in terms of the ability of the listener to fulfill the potential of the literary experience as suggested by the readers.

1. The readers should not lose their own identities to the extent that they "become" a character or locate the character on-stage; vivid and accurate suggestion (oral and visual cues) remain the readers' function.

2. The function of the listener is to fulfill the suggested potential of the literary experience in his own mind: participating in the re-creative experience rather than witnessing it.

3. The director may heighten or clarify readers' suggestions (if the literature or the readers need such help) through other visual and auditory aids, so long as these aids are kept in the realm of suggestion and do not interfere with the function of the listener.

The third principle is, perhaps, the most controversial because it allows the possibility of staging Readers Theatre. It is important that this principle be properly interpreted. It says "The director may heighten or clarify readers' suggestions (if the literature or the readers need such help). . . ." It is probably less valid to stage Readers Theatre because "the readers need such help." Superior readers are prerequisite to effective Readers Theatre. On the other hand, we need to entertain the judgment that certain literary experiences may be more effectively suggested through the aid of appropriate staging. However, we should be reluctant to entertain the judgment that Readers Theatre is an art form which requires staging. Quite the contrary! This group activity, given expert readers adhering to well established principles of oral interpretation and literature which lends itself to oral interpretation alone, can stimulate listener participation in the writer's literary experience in dynamic fashion.[1]

---

[1]Brooks, Keith. "Readers Theatre: Some Questions and Answers." *Dramatics,* Vol. XXXIV, No. 3 (December, 1962), 14 and 27.

Nevertheless (and this is one of the major points of this article), if it is felt that staging Readers Theatre is an aid to listener participation in re-creating a particular literary experience, that staging must be symbolic and non-illusionistic. Let's develop this "idea" from the standpoint of the readers and the environment of the staged reading.

The readers involved should not be statue-like, holding manuscripts in raised arms. They represent the vibrant medium through which feeling and meaning is shared reciprocally with an audience. Never should a fourth wall be formed between reader and listener for, in theory, both readers and listeners are on the receiving end; receiving stimulation from the literature. In actuality, the listeners are receiving stimulation from the literature through the readers. If this principle is consistently followed by the group in general or by the point of focus at a given time, the director may take certain liberties in both the visual and auditory sphere. Visually, he may have the readers sit or stand and distances between readers may vary to suggest psychological distance between characters, ideas, and emotions. Aurally, he may have the readers employ a natural or imitative voice, or emit any special vocal effects which would enhance the interpretation. The readers should be allowed to offer any symbolic visual or auditory stimulus germane to the mood and meaning which might be helpful to the listeners' function.

The environment of a staged reading will be used in its literal sense as an "aggregation of surrounding things, conditions, or influences."[2] Operating within these bounds, the late Robert Edmond Jones has described the setting for a theatrical production as "an environment for action."[3] This means a physical setting which is generally illusionistic and creates an atmosphere enhancing and aiding the action and interpretation.

It is in this definition that the discrepancy between environment for theatre and environment for a staged reading is evident. That is, the visual and auditory environment for a staged reading must be symbolic or non-illusionistic. The reader serves as an interpreter whose objective is sharing, while the actor attempts to create the illusion of reality. Non-illusionistic or symbolic environment will not, in itself, pull the action on-stage and can, therefore, be consistent with the objectives of Readers Theatre when staged. In this light, it has been found (particularly in the New York productions) that properties, make-up, costumes, sound effects, and notably lighting, are useful as long as the effect is at all times symbolic.

It is possible that dress of a particular cut or color could aid the listener in his participation in re-creating the desired mood. Careful placement of stools or chairs can add to understanding of

---

[2]*The American College Dictionary,* 1st ed., s.v. "environment."
[3]Jones, Robert Edmond, *The Dramatic Imagination.* (New York: *Theatre Arts Books,* 1941), p. 23.

locale. The placement of a carefully selected property might give the feeling of an omnipresent being, as the throne-like chair placed center stage in *The World of Carl Sandburg*. Sound, particularly music, has the capacity to aid in enhancing a mood and to attune the listener to the literary experience; the very abstract quality of certain music lends itself to setting the scene without being literal or illusionistic. The four qualities of light, color, movement, intensity, and direction—can be used to suggest the *feeling* of different locales and moods. A fluid lighting can be used on readers about the stage, dimming on one and accentuating another to give emphasis and focus to the content of the literature. In illusionistic theatre, color must always be carefully and specifically motivated, but in Readers Theatre color should be used for its own psychological impact. The color must always be analogous to the sense and mood of the ideas expressed.

Two words of caution will suffice in the use of imaginative nonillusionistic staging. First, the director must be highly sensitive to the sometimes subtle differences between the symbolic and the literal. If he fails, the result may be abortive theatre instead of effective Readers Theatre. Second, both the director and the technical designer must be careful not to unbalance the production on the side of the environment. If this is done, the result may be a study of costuming, sound, or lighting techniques with accompanying readings. All phases of a staged reading should contribute to the interpretation as an organic whole.

In order to illustrate the preceding, it would be well to consider the effect of this type of staging on at least one production, a cutting of George Orwell's *1984*. Staged recently at the University of Delaware, the production consisted of three readers: a narrator, a man (Winston) and a woman (Julia). To assist in conveying a feeling of the stark, oppressed, hopeless yet hopeful world of 1984, the environment included the following symbolic elements: two plain black stools, a microphone, black sweaters and slacks for the readers, and extensive use of lighting.

The narrator stood down-stage right and was lighted vaguely by a narrow, sharply defined beam. When not reading, the narrator's area was blacked out. In the case of the other readers, lights were raised and dimmed to focus attention and to clarify time sequence. Color was carefully used to accentuate mood and feeling. At times, the readers moved from darkness to light.

In evaluating this Readers Theatre production, two questions were asked: (1) Were the listeners able to fulfill their function? (2) Did the staging at any time interfere with the listeners' function? Empirical evidence seemed to satisfy both questions. At all times the readers communicated directly into the realm of the audience and the environment had apparently served to enhance the communication. When questioned, listeners indicated that the environment had helped them to imagine and that they had not located the situation on-stage.

To determine its relative effectiveness, this staging technique was compared to a more conventional method using the same selection. When symbolic dress and lighting were omitted, the listener response was less definite. When questioned, the listeners expressed interest in the technique but there was a noticeable lacking of comments on the literary experience. This rather subjective evidence seemed to indicate that in the case of this production staging had been helpful in stimulating the desired listener response.

The Group Reading: Expression for Drama of Mental Action

E. Annette Monroe

In the last twenty years, group readings of drama have appeared with ever-increasing frequency in the United States. Since the Readers' Theatre, Inc., production of *Oedipus Rex* in 1945,[1] the professional theatre has undertaken such ventures to its financial gain and to the cultural benefit of audiences in New York, as well as throughout the country.

Group drama readings have not been unique to the professional theatre. Well before 1945 a tradition of public group reading was forming on college campuses. At the turn of the century, an advanced course entitled "Shakespearian Reading," taught by T. C. Trueblood at the University of Michigan, included group readings as class projects.[2] The 1962 annual report on play selection in American colleges and universities belonging to the American Educational Theatre Association gives some indication of the growth of collegiate group readings. Statistics were compiled from 525 schools. Of 3,089 productions of short plays, as differentiated from 2,360 full-length plays, 678 were originals and 421 were public readings. This marks the first time public readings were listed as a separate item in the annual report.[3]

Professional groups have read primarily adaptations of non-dramatic literature, such as *John Brown's Body* by Stephen Vincent Benét, *Pictures in the Hallway* by Sean O'Casey, and miscellaneous selections from prose and poetry in "The Golden Age." Although university readers have chosen all forms of litera-

---

Central States Speech Journal, XV, No. 3 (August 1964), 170-176. Reprinted by permission of the author.
[1] Readers' Theatre, Inc., was the project of a group of directors, including James Light, to "give the people of New York an opportunity to witness performances of great dramatic works which [were] seldom if ever produced." See George Jean Nathan, *The Theatre Book of the Year, 1945-1946* (New York, 1946), p. 234.
[2] Personal letter from R. D. T. Hollister, University of Michigan, March 7, 1962.
[3] Theodore J. Shank, "Conservative Play Selection, 1960-61," *Educational Theatre Journal,* XIV (March 1962), 94.

ture, repertoires of active collegiate reading groups include drama at least as often as prose and poetry.[4]

Little historical, descriptive, and theoretical material have been written concerning the group reading. Recently, attempts have been made to define the nature of this activity.[5] Insight into purpose and mode have been shared, but writers have paid a minimum of attention to choice of material. Neither texts nor articles discuss to any depth specific standards for choice. One suggestion is that all literature is suitable for public reading, although preference would be given to non-dramatic rather than to dramatic literature. According to Brooks, Henderhan, and Billings, "College and university groups have included Readers Theatre programs in increasing number, adapting all types of literature (plays, poetry, prose) with particular emphasis on non-dramatic literature. This emphasis has been one of the unique contributions of Readers Theatre: the sharing of literature not usually treated by actors on stage."[6] If drama be chosen, however, let it be a "talk" play in which physical action is minimal.[7]

Such advice is misleading because it oversimplifies the artistic task of choosing a play. Certainly any selection of literature could be read. But would every selection be suited particularly to the reading form? What is a "talk" play? Is it necessarily correlative with the reading form?

If the group reading is to be an artistic expression of the literature, harmony is necessary among purpose, material, and mode. Since a concept for choice of material has been neglected and since drama has been chosen consistently by collegiate readers, this paper seeks to define at least one type of dramatic literature particularly suited to the reading mode.

The proliferation of labels for the group reading—"staged reading," "concert reading," "Interpreters Theatre," and "Readers' Theatre"—suggests a lack of agreement concerning the nature of the activity. If this discussion of the *suitability* of particular dramas for expression through reading is to be understood, clarification of the term, *reading,* as it is used here, is necessary.

Reading, the term used almost without exception by both professional and university groups, does not have the same connotation for every person. John Mason Brown felt the term to be inadequate because it could apply to both "a painful affair, as

---

[4] See the unpubl. diss. (University of Wisconsin, 1963) by E. Annette Monroe, "The Group Reading of Drama: Its Essence and Aesthetic Principles." The appendices list examples of plays read by group readers from 1900 to 1962.

[5] Leslie Irene Coger, "Interpreters Theatre: Theatre of the Mind," *Quarterly Journal of Speech,* XLIX (April 1963), 157-164; Keith Brooks, Robert C. Henderhan, and Alan Billings, "A Philosophy on Readers Theatre," *Speech Teacher,* XII (Sept. 1963), 229-232.

[6] Brooks, Henderhan, and Billings, p. 229.

[7] Clifford Stuart, "Playreadings," *Drama,* New Series (Autumn 1953), pp. 56-57. See also Leslie Irene Coger, "So You Want to Read a Play," *Dramatics,* XXIX (1957-1958), 9; and Roderick Robertson, "Producing Playreadings," *Educational Theatre Journal,* XII (March 1960), 21.

everyone must recall with a shiver who sat through 'Macbeth' as Dr. Edith Sitwell and her co-vocalists elegantly murdered both Shakespeare and the tragedy," as well as to the First Drama Quartette's "life-giving" reading of *Don Juan in Hell.* According to Brown, reading, in the ordinary theatrical sense, is "understanding and communicating an author's meaning."[8]

But *reading* needs a fuller definition. Webster's *New World Dictionary* defines one who reads as he who "gets the meaning of the printed matter by interpreting its character or signs." The writer has chosen to express his experience of life through language symbols. Therefore the reader studies the language, no matter what the literary genre, in terms of the writer's choice and form. The reader, as himself, attempts then to speak the words in such a way that the author's experience is faithfully imitated. The mode is suggestive in order not to detract from the language, the basic medium. The experience is in the mind's eye, primarily through the physical ear. Amy Lowell believed that the audience at a reading "must see nothing with its eyes which detracts from its mental vision. It must be made to imagine so vividly that it forgets the reader in the thing read."[9]

If the literature contains dialogue, the reader regards the individual speeches in the light of their word choice and construct, as well as in the light of the entire composition's content and form. Characters are suggested from this perspective. The audience listens to what the characters say. Since nothing is to distract from the lines, the mode of delivery is suggestive.[10]

To understand whether any drama can be expressed by the reading form, the nature of this particular literary genre must be reconsidered. Traditionally, *drama* has meant a genre of literature whose basic medium is action. Key words in dramatic theory are "behavior," "man in movement," and "externalized conduct."[11] The word, drama, from the Greek means literally to act or to do. Rather than telling about the action, as in the epic, characters demonstrate the action by moving and speaking. The action, implicit in the literature, is not realized until it is wholly com-

---

[8]John Mason Brown, "What, Shaw Again? Reading of *Don Juan in Hell,*" *Sat. Rev. of Lit.,* Nov. 10, 1951, p. 26.

[9] Amy Lowell, "Poetry as a Spoken Art," *The Dial,* Jan. 25, 1917, pp. 47-48.

[10] For a concept of the purpose and form of delivery in reading, see such texts as: Chloe Armstrong and Paul D. Brandes, *The Oral Interpretation of Literature* (New York, 1963); Charlotte I. Lee, *Oral Interpretation* (Boston, 1952); Wilma H. Grimes and Alethea Smith Mattingly, *Interpretation: Writer, Reader, Audience* (San Francisco, 1961).

[11] Suggested sources for discussion of drama are: Aristotle, *Poetics,* trans. S. H. Butcher in *The Great Critics,* eds. J. H. Smith and E. W. Parks (New York, 1951); George Pierce Baker, *Dramatic Technique* (Boston, 1919), Ch. 1; Cleanth Brooks and Robert B. Heilman, *Understanding Drama* (New York, 1945); Ashley Dukes, *Drama* (London, 1926); Francis Fergusson, *The Idea of a Theater* (Garden City, 1953); John Gassner, *Producing the Play* (New York, 1941); Mordecai Gorelik, *New Theatres for Old* (New York, 1957); Ronald Peacock, *The Art of Drama* (London, 1957); J. L. Styan, *The Elements of Drama* (Cambridge, 1960); Raymond Williams, *Drama in Performance* (London, 1954).

municated by the actor's performance. Characters become focal as they, not the author, directly convey the action. They are the means by which a "living" metaphor, which the audience sees with physical eyes, is presented.

The script or language arises out of the basic action. It results from "the underlying structure of incident and character," according to Fergusson, rather than being either the foundation itself or an independent entity.[12] Non-verbal gesture and sound, as well as words, constitute the language.[13] The intimate intertexture of movement and speech produces the particular genre called "drama."[14]

In the history of drama, there has been a growing tendency to stress *états de l'âme* rather than mere outward situations. As character has become more focal than plot, so, too, have the inward, psychological values of the play. These are conveyed not so much by outer action as by words. Perhaps this accounts for the numerous seeming actionless plays that do not conform to the traditional concept of action. Unless the meaning of *action* can be extended from *doing* to *being,* the definition of drama will be so restrictive as to be limiting. As Floyd so pointedly stated:

> We need to take issue with critics who imply that dramatic action is *external* action in the drama. Isn't it possible—has it not been demonstrated in modern drama—that inner life can be dramatized? Can't states of mind and thoughts of characters be mounted on the stage? . . . I submit that this century's dramatic history offers a long, restless procession of experiments which have attempted to attack the problem: to explore the minds of characters in dramatic terms. . . . [15]

In the nineteenth century Maeterlinck, at the height of his career, theorized on the nature of an inner, seemingly motionless dramatic action.[16] In 1919 Baker termed this particular kind of action, "mental action." He recognized that, although in all plays physical action is to reveal the mental states of the characters, some dramas are more largely focused on mental rather than on physical action. Baker wrote that the "greatest drama of all time, and the larger part of the drama of [the early twentieth century], uses action much less for its own sake than to reveal mental states which are to rouse sympathy or repulsion in an audience. In brief, marked mental activity may be quite as dramatic as mere physical action."[17]

---

[12] Fergusson, pp. 21-22.
[13] Marvin Rosenberg, "The Languages of Drama," *Educational Theatre Journal,* XV (March 1963), 1-6.
[14] Peacock, pp. 167-171.
[15] Information in a speech by Virginia H. Floyd, "'Point of View' in Modern Drama," Interpretation Interest Group, SAA Convention, Cleveland, Ohio, December, 1962.
[16] Maurice Maeterlinck, "The Tragical in Daily Life," *The Treasure of the Humble,* trans. Alfred Sutro (New York, 1909).
[17] Baker, p. 37.

Unless the definition of action can include both the mental and the physical, those plays which imitate the "movement of the psyche"[18] will be excluded. How shall *Prometheus Bound, Oedipus at Colonos, Le Cid, Bérénice, The Way of the World, The Blind, The Master Builder,* and others be categorized in terms of action?

In plays written in the traditional concept of action as *doing,* language is implicitly allied with movement. The basic medium is the speech-gesture. Where mental action becomes more and more the focus, with physical action being minimized, language is more the foundation of the drama; without the text much less of the drama's essence is apparent.

If the reading is to be an artistic means of expressing the drama, a major conflict must be resolved. Language is the medium of the reading; covert action is subsidiary. Action is the medium of the drama; language is subsidiary. If action includes *being* as well as *doing,* in plays where language is the primary means of expressing the mental action of characters, there can be common ground between reading and drama.

The Cocktail Party by T. S. Eliot will serve to demonstrate how the group reading is a suitable mode of expression for drama of mental action. First produced at the Edinburgh Festival in 1949 and later in the United States in January, 1950, *The Cocktail Party* was Eliot's third major play. Together with *South Pacific,* the play won the 1950 Antoinette Perry Award in the United States for "outstanding contribution to the theatre."[19] The London *Times* awarded the play its annual literary prize as "an outstanding contribution to English literature."[20]

The world of *The Cocktail Party* is initially that of the wealthy, sophisticated society whose members patronize the "right" shops, attend the "right" parties, and know the "right" doctor. As one character remarks:

It's not that he regards me as very intelligent,
But he thinks I'm well informed: the sort of person
Who would know the right doctor, as well as the right shops.[21]

Outwardly the play is concerned with the reconciliation of a married couple, Edward and Lavinia. Inwardly, it probes the relationship of man to the community—the relationship of spiritual awareness of ordinary and extraordinary life. Colby synthesizes the focus of the play when he writes that Eliot "dramatizes a moral issue that arises out of a domestic crisis, and the character who represents the paragon of virtue arises from the same society as do the unregenerates of the play, is completely devoid of any

---

[18]Fergusson, p. 161.
[19]"8 Perry Awards to 'South Pacific,'" *The New York Times,* April 10, 1950, p. 14.
[20]"$2,800 Awarded to T. S. Eliot," *The New York Times,* Nov. 6, 1950, p. 33.
[21]T. S. Eliot, *The Cocktail Party* (New York, 1950). All references are to this text.

ecclesiastical trappings, is, in fact, completely unaware of her function and influence over others."[22]

The play is devoid of spectacle. Of course, the Unidentified Guest sings "One-Eyed Riley" in Act I, and drinking is a consistent business throughout the play, whether as an ordinary manifestation of a cocktail party or a symbolic ritual in Dr. Reilly's office. But the physical action is merely drawing-room behavior:

> In the room the women come and go
> Talking of Michelangelo.[23]

According to Williams, it is behavior in the sense that "the words and movement have no direct and necessary relation, but derive, as it were separately, from a conception of 'probable behavior' in the circumstances presented. . . . The speech is prescribed, but the 'acting,' and 'setting,' and therefore the action as a whole, must often be separately inferred, even where the conditions of performance are known."[24] Characters go in and out of rooms; they sit down and get up. The outward action is not the essential. Edward Chamberlayne, like J. Alfred Prufrock, is almost "etherized upon a table." Reilly tells him:

> Stretched on the table,
> You are a piece of furniture in a repair shop
> For those who surround you, the masked actors;
> All there is of you is your body
> And the "you" is withdrawn.

Perhaps because these focal characters are so much like those in Eliot's dramatic monologues, little seems to take place, at least little that is seen.

Instead of physical action, the play rests on mental action. The play is a kind of interlude between the action of the Chamberlaynes' five-year marriage and the action where "every moment is a fresh beginning." The overt action stems from certain insights the characters gain into their lives in terms of good and evil, illusion and reality, and the interdependence of humanity. Characters must be first stimulated to mental action. It is not surprising to find so much of the play, and particularly the last act, devoted to discussion of and meditation over self-identification and the meaning of life.

Language is focal in *The Cocktail Party*. Jones believes that it "is the essential action: first, in the sense it often does what it says, and, secondly, in the sense that it is the most important part of the play, making explicit what is really happening."[25] The poetry, by Eliot's design, seems like ordinary conversation.

---

[22] Robert A. Colby, "The Three Worlds of *The Cocktail Party:* The Wit of T. S. Eliot," *Univ. of Toronto Quarterly*, XXIV (October 1954), 56.
[23] T. S. Eliot, "The Love Song of J. Alfred Prufrock."
[24] Williams, pp. 104 and 111.
[25] David E. Jones, *The Plays of T. S. Eliot* (London, 1960), pp. 7-8.

Critics have considered it "plain" and "natural."[26] Eliot hoped that it would "remove the surface of things," taking the audience unobtrusively from ordinary discourse to moments of greater intensity.[27]

Penetrating the life beneath the surface is achieved through the power of images. Eliot's images are functional rather than decorative. Such casual allusions as Julia's searching for her glasses with one lens missing and the Unidentified Guest's song of "One-Eyed Riley" fit into a concept of darkness and light—of blindness, half-sight, and sight. They particularize the nature of the play's problem:

Edward

* * *

And what is the use of all your analysis
If I am to remain always lost in the dark?

Unidentified Guest

There is certainly no purpose in remaining in the dark
Except long enough to clear from the mind
The illusion of having ever been in the light.

A character's ability to "see" hinges upon his sense of appearance and reality. Eliot's characters first see "as in a glass darkly" and then "face to face." Both Peter and Celia probe which was the dream, which the reality. Peter, referring to his "affair" with Celia, says,

But I must see Celia at least to make her tell me
What has happened, in her terms. Until I know that
I shan't know the truth about even the memory.
Did we really share these interests? Did we really feel the same
When we heard certain music? Or looked at certain pictures?
There was something real. But what is the reality . . .

Celia, referring to her affair with Edward, says that before Lavinia left, she had lived in a happy dream world. But when she learned that Lavinia was gone,

then I suddenly discovered
That the dream was not enough; that I wanted something more
And I waited, and wanted to run to tell you.
Perhaps the dream was better. It seemed the real reality,
And if this is reality, it is very like a dream.

In addition to the images of sight and blindness and of reality and dreams, Eliot uses "the way" and "the journey." Edward

---

[26] Harold Clurman, "Theatre: Cocktail Party," *New Republic*, Feb. 13, 1950, p. 30. See the discussion of this style in Peacock, p. 227.

[27] T. S. Eliot, "Introduction," in S. L. Bethell, *Shakespeare and The Popular Dramatic Tradition* (London, 1944), pp. 8-9. See for Eliot's concept of the poet writing for the theatre.

asks if he has "far to go." Reilly responds that it will be a "long journey." Later, a libation is drunk to those who have to go back in order to go forward and to the one who goes immediately forward into the unknown.

Eliot's thought—his expression of contemporary man's plight—through speech rather than through outer action, is capable of capturing the dramatic imagination of the audience. Through speech the characters' psychological and spiritual readjustment or restoration are clarified. Certainly the group reading is particularly well-suited to reveal this drama of mental action.

The Cocktail Party is not the only drama of mental action. Nearly every period of dramatic literature, from the Greek to the present, offers examples in which the characters' inner or mental action is dominant rather than their outward behavior or physical action.

If the group reading is not to be merely an expedient means of expressing a limited aspect of just any play but an artistic means of expressing the very essence of certain plays, careful consideration must be given to the choice of drama. An interpretation of a play by way of the group reading will be artistic if it passes the following test: the object must be perceived to a greater degree than before. The group reading must not distort the nature of the play; the very medium must enable the audience to have the unique experience of this particular drama.

So long as the group reading of drama continues to be an individual form, it may continue to be artistic. It is individual with its own mode—individual in that language leads to an action of the mind. This form of theatre is yet another way for theatre to effect its high calling. Is not the theatre a place where we are given the sense of the "peculiar power of seeing with the eye of the mind?[28]" The group reading of drama is but another form of theatre seeking to stimulate the mind's eye.

---

[28] Robert Edmond Jones, *The Dramatic Imagination* (New York, 1941), pp. 89-90.

Scene Location in Readers Theatre: Static or Dynamic?

Marion L. and Marvin D. Kleinau

Several essays have reported in speech journals the results of attempts by their authors to analyze and define the nature of a specific kind of oral interpretation known as "Readers Theatre."[1] These essays have been most helpful to those of us who work with Readers Theatre. An attempt to examine critically the form of this kind of theatre production is evident. Yet, the task of analysis is by no means accomplished. Likewise, opinion of the form or the theory underlying it is not unanimous. This essay offers both a closer scrutiny of the theory of scene location in Readers Theatre and a challenge to the theory underlying it.

Readers Theatre: A Definition

Readers Theatre may be defined operationally as two or more readers, each assigned to an individual role and each engaged in the task of presenting a literary work to an audience through the medium of oral interpretation. A single reader may take more than one role, or two or more readers may voice the same lines together. Such a definition, although not entirely comprehensive, presents a functional description of what actually occurs in Readers Theatre; it limits itself to that which is nearly always found and that which can be physically verified. This definition could be extended to include a statement of the effect the readers

---

The Speech Teacher, XIV, No. 3 (September 1965), 193-199. Reprinted by permission of the authors.
[1] Keith Brooks, "Readers Theatre: Some Questions and Answers," *Dramatics Magazine*, vol. 24 (December 1962), p. 14. Dr. Brooks defines Readers Theatre in terms of a definition of oral interpretation advanced by Gertrude Johnson and later clarified and diagrammed by John Dolman. Leslie Irene Coger, "Interpreters Theatre: Theatre of the Mind," *Quarterly Journal of Speech,* vol. 49, no. 2 (April 1963), p. 157. Dr. Coger presented a definition of Readers Theatre, a summation of its history, and an analysis of contemporary productions. Keith Brooks, Robert C. Henderhan, and Alan Billings, "A Philosophy on Readers Theatre," *Speech Teacher,* vol. 12, no. 3 (September 1963), p. 229. In this essay, Readers Theatre is defined in terms of audience response, and an approach to staging is suggested.

expect to have upon the audience. Most definitions include such a statement. Coger stipulated, for example, that the readers " . . . cause an audience to experience the literature."[2] Brooks, Henderhan, and Billings went further in their efforts to evaluate a Readers Theatre performance " . . . in terms of the ability of the listener to fulfill the potential of the literary experience. . . . "[3] Certainly readers are interested in both quality and quantity of audience response, but to date we know very little about it. The attempt to judge a performance in terms of the "abilities" of the audience, as in the case of the second definition, poses an impractical evaluative task. The writers of this essay prefer to discuss the evaluative factor later and to define Readers Theatre only in terms of observable elements in the performance situation.

Scene Location: A Problem in Theory

One line of thought, among others, finds expression in the three essays cited above. It also appears in the very sparse textbook material available on the subject.[4] This line of thought is, namely, that *the scene of action in Readers Theatre must be set in the abstract, or in the minds of the audience, and not in the concrete area of "the stage" as in a full theatrical production.* In making such a positive statement or rule, theorists have, perhaps, failed to consider some pertinent information to be gained from other areas of knowledge. They have, for example, failed to take into consideration the importance of configuration in the perceptual field.

Readers Theatre, as defined above, involves two or more readers located in a somewhat circumscribed area in front of an audience. It is precisely this physical fact which makes dangerous the setting up of rules and criteria for the group reading situation in terms of theory which governs the solo reader. The process of perception by which humans reach an understanding of the visual scene involves not only the object observed, but a perceived relationship between the objects. Often the relationship becomes much more important to understanding than the objects involved in the relationship.[5] The juxtaposition of two human beings standing in reasonable proximity sets up a relationship in the mind of the viewer in terms of a dramatic field of forces with a definite location—the stage or the platform. When these two or more individuals are engaged as units in a larger, unified dramatic experi-

---

[2] Coger, p. 157
[3] Brooks, Henderhan, and Billings, p. 229.
[4] Wilma Grimes and Alethea Smith Mattingly, *Interpretation: Writer, Reader, Audience* (San Francisco: Wadsworth Publishing Company, 1961), p. 331. Chloe Armstrong and Paul D. Brandes, *The Oral Interpretation of Literature* (New York: McGraw-Hill Book Company, 1963), p. 289.
[5] N. L. Gage, "Perception," in *Encyclopedia of Educational Research*, ed., Chester W. Harris (New York: The Macmillan Company, 1960), p. 942.

ence (a story, a play, or even a lyric poem), the relationship and its specific location becomes much stronger.

Techniques used by the solo reader to keep the scene located in the abstract, such as the use of a manuscript, minimal movement, aesthetic distance from role, and, particularly, use of focus, are assumed to work equally well for the group activity, Readers Theatre; and we let the assumption rest at this point. We have not *tested* the theory with regard to group reading. Have we really tested it for the solo reader? Have we tested it sufficiently to lay down hard and fast rules for what *must be?*

The writers of this essay attempt to shed some light upon the problem of critical approach in oral interpretation by a brief exploration into some phenomena basic to one theory: location of the scene of action. In the light of this exploration, the writers seek answers to the following two questions: Is a rigid differentiation between Readers Theatre and full theatrical production in terms of placement of a scene necessary? Would a more flexible approach serve better the literature to be presented?

Perception Theory: A Basis for Scene Location

Two perceptual phenomena appear to be basic to the theory of scene location in oral interpretation. First, a distinct difference exists between a visual space orientation and an aural space orientation. This fact seems to underlie the dictum that the oral interpreter *must* locate the scene in the mind or imagination of each member of the audience. Secondly, a close relationship exists between sensory modalities. This fact makes it *possible* for the interpreter to use one sense modality to stimulate imagination in another or others.

With regard to visual versus aural space, Bartley explained that:

> . . . we can conceive for audition the prime role in dealing with abstract ideas. Hearing is greatly enough divorced from spatial realities or dealing directly and inescapably with the space domain that it can be used for abstract symbolism . . . Vision could not so well carry on this function.[6]

Carpenter and McLuhan made a similar observation in describing the nature of auditory space:

> Auditory space has no point of favored focus. It's a sphere without fixed boundaries; space made by the thing itself, not space containing the thing. It is not pictorial space, boxed in, but dynamic, always in flux, creating its own dimensions moment by moment.[7]

---

[6] Howard Bartley, *Principles of Perception* (New York: Harper and Row, 1958), p. 312.
[7] Edmund Carpenter and Marshall McLuhan, "Acoustic Space," in *Explorations in Communication* (Boston: Beacon Press, 1960), p. 67.

The oral interpreter finds auditory space the natural habitat for the scene he is attempting to recreate in the minds of the audience.

Regarding the second point mentioned above, the close relationship between sensory modalities allows the audience to hear "visually." One view of perception regards the presence of different sensory mechanisms, as well as all diversification of tissue into body organs, as a developmental phenomenon. Concerning this view, Bartley wrote:

> The experience which the adult calls vision, hearing, touch, pain, taste, smell, etc., did not originate as totally different sorts of response and then gradually fuse, but instead, developed from something less separate into the variety of modalities and separate sensory experiences that characterize the adult.[8]

Such a view allows insight into the intricate system of interconnection which exists among the functioning mechanisms of the body.[9] In experimental procedures where both vision and hearing were involved, it was found that a stimulus to one of the two senses had an associative effect upon the other. Further, it was discovered that when more than one sense channel was stimulated simultaneously, subjects were often unable to distinguish which stimulus elicited which experience.[10] A practical illustration of this phenomenon as it occurs in oral interpretation is cited in a recent article by Coger.[11] A western critic, witnessing a professional production of *John Brown's Body*, received such a strong auditory stimulus regarding a white picket fence that he visually placed it on the stage, although no fence was actually there. Further, the image was so real to him that he mentioned it in a critique of the show.

Perception Theory: Its Significance in Scene Location

A three-fold implication exists here for the oral interpreter. First, that one sense (hearing) can stimulate association images in another sense (vision) *allows* the vivid stirring up of images in the imagination of an audience which is elucidated in interpretation theory. Second, the reinforcement of one sense by another suggests the value of the physical presence of the interpreter. The normal person is visually oriented by nature. The infant perceives visual patterns three days after birth[12] and the child learns to understand the visual code before he understands verbal language. It has been demonstrated that neither the auditory nor the visual

---

[8] Bartley, p. 60.
[9] D. O. Hebb, *The Organization of Behavior: A Neuropsychological Theory* (New York: John Wiley and Sons, 1949).
[10] Bartley, p. 64.
[11] Coger, p. 160.
[12] Robert L. Fantz, "Pattern Vision in New Born Infants," *Science*, vol. 80 (April 1963), p. 296.

stimulus alone works as well in direct personal communication as do both working together.[13]

Third, and finally, and most relevant to the present discussion, although a difference exists between visual space orientation and aural space orientation, these two modes of experience are not separated but inter-related. A major problem in oral interpretation theory, especially when applied to Readers Theatre, occurs when we think in terms of an insurmountable barrier between visual and aural orientation. On the other hand, it would seem to be reasonable to believe that the mind can move easily back and forth between these two kinds of attention. Certainly psychological theory supports this view. Similar space changes occur easily in the visual aspect of television and cinema; the picture changes suddenly from a panoramic scene to a focus which forces the attention of the viewer to a specific point, such as the eyes of the actor. Tyrwhitt suggested that "we accept this, because this is the way our eye really works; we can, at will, change its focus and alter its position . . . "[14] We can just as easily move from visual to auditory space orientation and back again, as any daydreamer knows. Writers of contemporary fiction make use of this change in mode of experience as a natural functioning of consciousness when they shift a point of view from contact with outer reality to inner reality and back again many times within a single literary work.

Aural and Visual Cue Relationship: A Dynamic Interaction

When visual cues are eliminated, the audience is released to attend entirely to aural cues. The ultimate attention to aural cues occurs in radio. If the goal is complete auditory attention, we must eliminate the physical presence of the reader and let only his voice communicate. But the oral interpreter uses both body and voice. Thus, the visual sense modality of the audience member is always being stimulated to some degree. Although the reader attempts to use only those visual cues which will reinforce the auditory stimulus, the fact of his physical presence creates duality of orientation which relies upon the interrelationship of the visual and the auditory sense modalities. This duality increases when, as in Readers Theatre, more than one stimulus-giving focal point is placed in the visual field. Kepes attested to the power of the physical presence in terms of the visual arts:

> A human being is more than his own body; he implies those actions which reach out and transform his environment. . . .
> The picture-surface becomes a vital spatial world, not only in

---

[13] Delwin Dusenbury and Franklin Knower, "Experimental Studies of the Symbolism of Action and Voice—II," *Quarterly Journal of Speech*, vol. 25, no. 1 (February 1939), p. 67.
[14] Jacqueline Tyrwhitt, "The Moving Eye," in *Explorations in Communication* (Boston: Beacon Press, 1960), p. 90.

the sense that the spatial forces are acting on it—moving, falling, and circulating—but also in the sense that between these movements the field itself is charged with action. The actual visual elements are only the focal points of this field; they are the concentrated energy.[15]

In this respect, two or more readers become focal points in an action-charged space. That space is located in the visual field of the audience.

What occurs in a Readers Theatre performance with regard to scene location may actually be that the aural stimuli and the visual stimuli interact in such a way as to create for the audience a constantly shifting orientation. We know that the scene is initially restricted to the visual cues presented by the physical arrangement on a stage. It gradually expands under the influence of auditory stimuli into a more highly structured imaginative field where, ideally, it remains throughout the performance. Where this field is located for the auditor we are not sure, but we can hypothesize that he visualizes it somewhere in space between himself and the physical stage. It may be that at certain points in a given production he brings the imaginative field close to himself and that at others he projects it back onto the stage. In all probability the location of scene shifts many times during a single performance, because the complex of visual and aural stimuli varies with the nature of the literary experience being presented. Purely descriptive material, for example, allows an abstract orientation to occur fairly easily. The reader is describing something which is not physically present, and which must, frankly, be imagined. Conversely, in dialogue, when two readers are engaged in a verbal conflict, even though they are not looking directly at one another, the object of each speech is physically present. In the latter case, the viewer is much more likely to tie the scene directly to the source of the stimulus. Thus, audience orientation to scene location may be viewed as a dynamic equilibrium, with a constant shifting of the imaginative field in relationship to the literary experience presented.[16]

The foregoing theory is, of course, hypothetical. But until we secure more objective evidence, any theory of audience reaction, including that found in oral interpretation textbooks, will be hypothetical. The view explained here does, however, seem to be consistent with actual experience and with psychological theory. It not only questions the *possibility* of always keeping the scene off stage, but it questions the desirability of doing so. From such a viewpoint, the problem becomes one of how we can control and use this shifting center of attention created in an audience to the

---

[15] Gyorgy Kepes, *Language of Vision* (Chicago: Paul Theobald and Company, 1944), p. 29.

[16] Robert Kibler, "Communication: Some Thoughts," *Dramatics Magazine*, vol. 34 (May 1963). Dr. Kibler makes a similar observation in relation to communication theory when he stresses the importance of "process."

advantage of the literature presented. It seems reasonable to suppose that some control can be effected through the techniques of the reader. Let us examine briefly one technique, focus, as it functions in the Readers Theatre performance.

Focus as a Technique for Control of Scene Location

Focus, here meaning the physical area toward which the stimulus is directed,[17] is one of the most valuable tools for control of audience attention. As focus is traditionally handled in Readers Theatre, the readers do not look at one another but look out over the heads of the audience, with the lines of focal contact between two readers in a shared scene running almost parallel and perhaps theoretically crossing at a point somewhere toward the back of the room. This tends, psychologically, to place the person addressed somewhere in space behind the audience, rather than in the front position he physically occupies. If we consider this phenomenon in relationship to the visual field of forces created by the presence of more than one reader, we may hypothesize that a tension or conflict in direction is set up between the area of the stage and abstract space. The balance of power may go in either direction, and control of the balance resides to a large extent in the focus of the readers. Any shift in focus can cause an accompanying shift in orientation for the attentive viewer. Thus, if two readers suddenly turn and look directly at one another, the scene orientation immediately travels to the stage.

What a powerful instrument we have in focus. The very fact that, according to the theorist, it can change the location of scene and thus effect the resulting change in audience orientation should indicate its possible usefulness to the director of Readers Theatre. Could it be that the director should sometimes take advantage of the natural tendency of the audience to place the scene specifically on stage with the readers? Should he use focus to direct audience attention where and when he wishes, for a specific purpose as determined by the literature?

These questions are the result of several years' observation of actual Readers Theatre productions in which such techniques have been used, and used successfully. For example, Dr. Elbert Bowen of Central Michigan University, in a production of John Cheever's novel, *The Wapshot Chronicle,* used change of focus to achieve variety in staging, to heighten humor, and to reinforce the author's use of point of view. Throughout the major part of the production, the readers placed the scene visually in the realm of the audience. But in a specific scene, a parody on industrial psychology which consisted of an interview between a doctor and a job applicant, the two characters seated themselves facing each other, and the scene was suddenly on stage. Dialogue at this point

---

[17] This is accomplished by body movement cues, including direction of line of vision.

became more direct, with less intrusion by the author; the directness of contact between the two readers heightened the farcical
elements in the scene.

Another example may be cited from a Readers Theatre production of *Othello,* directed by Dr. Wallace Bacon of Northwestern University. Some of the scenes were deliberately set onstage and some were set off-stage. In the fight between Cassio and
Roderigo, Act V, Scene 1, the readers focused toward the audience; but when Iago wounded Cassio *from behind,* without explanation of the stage business in the lines of the text, Iago actually
ran up behind Cassio to deliver the thrust. *What happened* was
the point here—not what was heard, not what the characters felt
at the moment, but what actually happened. The eye was the
significant witness at the moment; thus the scene was presented
to the eye. Later, in the murder of Desdemona, the director felt
that the significant action was the effect, on Othello, of his own
action—not the deed itself, but what the deed did to the Moor.
The actions were performed—the strangling, Desdemona's
struggle—but the scene was focused toward the audience so that
major emphasis was placed upon Othello's face and thus on his
personal suffering. Here an interesting tension was set up between
physical cues, which tended to draw the scene on stage, and the
readers' focus, which acted to draw the scene into the realm of the
audience. This tension, it may be assumed, acted to reinforce
Othello's own struggle within the audience member.

Finally, in a Readers Theatre version of *Dark of the Moon,*
produced at the University of Wisconsin, Dr. Jean Scharfenberg
used focus to isolate and reinforce one of the main dramatic climaxes of the play. Throughout the production, the lines were
directed forward toward the audience, but at the climactic moment
in question, the two leading characters, Barbara and John, turned
and looked directly at one another for the first time. It was a
moment of awareness and the director used the technique of focus
in a way to make that moment unique.

These productions cannot be termed Readers Theatre if we
adhere strictly to the definitions proposed in the previously mentioned articles. The examples cited defied the prescription that
the scene must always be set in the minds of the audience. They
deliberately made use of the dynamic interrelationship between
eye and ear to emphasize certain values and meanings found
within the literature itself. They were, on the other hand, successful and stimulating. The literature was well-served and the result
was, to these writers, more intriguing than would have been the
more conventional style.

An Approach to Analysis and Definition

The present discussion does not seek to abolish rules and definitions for Readers Theatre. Theoretical restrictions serve a useful

purpose, but let us look carefully at the nature of the limitations we would impose.

In answer to the two questions raised at the beginning of the article, these writers propose that rather than being so concerned in keeping the scene offstage, we should turn our attention to the use of these tools to free the production to serve best the literature in question. It seems to be a far more useful critical approach to speak in terms of techniques and how each technique has been used to serve a given piece of literature. Rather than beginning the criticism of a production with the question, "Is it theatre?" which invariably carries the connotation "bad" or "wrong," we may begin with the question, "What techniques were operative and how did they function?" Such an attitude allows the production to communicate on its own terms, which, we hope, are the terms of the literature being presented. It also allows the critical audience to accept these terms. It pre-supposes that there is more than one way within the scope of Readers Theatre to communicate effectively a given piece of literature.

We have with us a developing form of theatre, experimental and exciting. It is creatively adapting material to its needs, even in some cases beginning to create its own materials. Extending itself in several directions, we do not know exactly how or where it will finally emerge. Critical observation is valuable to the furtherance of any art form, until observations become rigid rules which stultify the artistic impulse. We must attempt to analyze and define this exciting medium, but let us not bind it.

Have You Tried Readers' Theatre?

Margaret Nielsen

"I never did think I'd be acting in a great Greek play."

"You're not acting, Stupe. You're reading."

"Well, it's the next thing to acting when we read like this."

That was the gist of a teenage conversation overheard at a classroom Readers' Theatre rehearsal of *Antigone*. The high school youngsters were impressed by the beauty and power of the Sophocles play and thrilled by their ability to interpret material of such magnitude.

Let me limit my comments to a specific field of Readers' Theatre, for even in this special area of interpretation there are several patterns of performance.

I am dealing with that activity *which involves oral interpretation of a carefully cut script, usually by three to five readers, without memorization, special costume, lighting, props, or sound effects,* portraying their roles by means of vocal and facial expression alone, a narrator possibly providing transitional expository lines for clarification.

Let me stress that I am not referring to an exercise in "reading parts," but to well-planned, well-directed performances of carefully chosen material. The former activity has long been used as a teaching device, even at the elementary level. The latter, Readers' Theatre, is a comparatively recent form of theatrical presentation[1] usable at the secondary level.

Objectives and Advantages

In the first place, the teacher will readily see the infinite possibilities in this simplified form of presentation. Without attention to set, costumes, or special effects, any number of worthwhile, readable plays may come to life in the classroom in a most satisfying

---

Secondary School Theatre Conference News, I, 1 (Winter 1962), 10-12. Reprinted by permission of the author and American Educational Theatre Association, Inc.
[1] Recall! Charles Laughton and his reading quartet.

manner. Often a powerful play, such as Christopher Marlowe's *Dr. Faustus,* completely impractical to produce, conventionally, on the high school stage, may provide a memorable experience for readers and listeners alike through the medium of such group reading.

A class in literature, invited to visit the drama class reading *Antigone,* came away impressed and thoughtful. "Hey, real neat. I thought it would be long-haired and boring."

In the second place, it will be apparent that the entire class may work concurrently and experimentally on such projects (at least, in their early stages) within the confines of the ordinary classroom. A class of 35 may thus be divided into seven working panels, each member actively engaged in the reading-acting assignment. Furthermore, shy, unresponsive students or pupils with limited ability may find themselves drawn readily into participation, when the holding of a book and the group nature of the activity both give psychological support.

Last year my Mephistopheles was played by a withdrawn, sensitive lad, highly idealistic, but somewhat embittered by childhood experiences in Lithuania. I shall never forget the depth of feeling he gave to his lines, almost as if he were pouring out his unhappy past in the grim lines of Mephistopheles, "Why, this is hell, nor am I out of it!" . . . And my Faustus is studying for the ministry! Readers' Theatre provides a challenge to the imagination. Stripped of all visual stage embellishments, it calls upon listeners to imagine for themselves the set, the characters, the situation, the conflict. It calls upon readers to paint pictures upon the minds of their audience by vivid interpretation of lines and characters.

Great attention must be paid to reading skill. While there is no demand, technically speaking, on acting ability, there is great demand on vocal effectiveness and on the accompanying facial expression. Casual, colorless reading will be a waste of time.

A dull, apathetic reading of Antigone's lines from the Sophocles play did not make that young noblewoman emerge at all from the printed page; an inspired, skillful reading made her a truly unforgettable heroine.

Classroom Use

Possibilities for this device as a teaching tool suggest themselves:

(1) Studies in the history of the theatre, enlivened with play readings from each important period: Greek, Medieval, Renaissance, Restoration, Eighteenth Century, etc.

(2) Studies of various types of plays, exemplified by readings from each kind; e.g., *Cyrano de Bergerac, The Cradle Song, On Borrowed Time.*[2]

---

[2]Check on royalty requirements on all plays before inviting guests.

(3) Discussions involving great themes, found in problem plays, historical plays, morality plays; e.g., *A Doll's House, Joan of Lorraine, Everyman.*

Materials

Plays (and stories and poems) of substance seem to lend themselves best to this vehicle, at least from an educational point of view. However, farces and fantasies that have other challenging aspects may also prove worthwhile. Try *Gammer Gurton's Needle* or *The Importance of Being Earnest* or Alice Gerstenberg's *Overtones.*

It goes without saying that plays which are dependent upon visual appeal for their effectiveness are least desirable for Readers' Theatre, and that large casts, requiring much doubling, are too involved.

Cutting

Careful preparation of the script comes next. Which scenes to use, characters to include, and kind of narration to write must all be guided by several factors: (1) time limit of production (2) theme of play (3) significant scenes and lines (4) clarity of plot and characters (5) variety of mood (6) balance in use of readers (7) climactic arrangement.

Narration to be used as transitional bridges should maintain a style appropriate to the play. For the most part, it should be kept at a minimum, but of such wording as will enhance the mood and movement of the whole production.

Occasionally I find a built-in device for this purpose, such as some chorus parts in Greek plays, the part of Christine in *I Remember Mama,* or the Prologue in *Dr. Faustus.*

Personnel

In casting a Readers' Theatre group, the criteria for casting a conventional stage production should be kept in mind, except that in this reading activity there is more leeway, certainly for classroom use. For example, girls may interpret boys' parts with acceptable illusion, and minor parts may be doubled. Of course, specific attention should be paid to distinctive voice quality, much as is done in casting radio plays, since characters are chiefly identified by their voices.

I find that I must not assign the part of the narrator to the weakest, most retiring member of the group, or the whole show will suffer seriously. It is the narrator's responsibility to communicate directly with the audience, catch up any lagging attention, and clarify and intensify each scene. A sensitive, alert reader with a clear, flexible voice will make the best narrator.

Positions most commonly used are as follows:

(1) Readers seated on high stools behind lecterns, rising or facing front for each entrance.
(2) Readers seated behind, and at ends of, a long table, making no changes for entrance.
(3) Readers seated in a modified semi-circle in student chairs, averting their bodies when offstage, facing front when onstage.
(4) Readers standing in a semi-circle, or line arrangement, throughout the performance, with or without lecterns.

Focus of attention must be consistent. The group must decide at the outset of rehearsals whether to look at the characters they are addressing (when they glance up from their script) or at some focal point diagonally front. That technique must then be followed throughout the show.

It is most confusing for me to see one person facing his cast members directly, another fixing his eyes on imaginary people out front, and still another letting his eyes wander all over.

Rehearsal Procedure

If the class has never seen a Readers' Theatre production, the teacher will need to describe what the finished production can be —a theatrical experience of tremendous appeal, perhaps all the more powerful because of its capsular form. Laying the groundwork should be done as carefully as for a conventional show, and rehearsals conducted as thoroughly and painstakingly, to insure a smooth performance. That the cast must make the audience get the theme, follow the plot, visualize the set, sympathize and rejoice with the characters, and gain a final feeling of emotional satisfaction, *all by reading a script*—is quite a challenge!

Take the matter of tempo building. Next to vocal effectiveness, that factor is undoubtedly the most valuable in its training and the most difficult to achieve. But a reading production that has no rhythm, that does not rise and fall in intensity, that reaches no heights nor depths, will leave an audience cold—and the readers, unquestionably, as well. Careful attention must, therefore, be given to the picking up of cues, topping of lines, electric pauses, contrasts, and all the other devices that produce results.

In the Marlowe play, when Mephistopheles and Lucifer have succeeded in enticing Faustus to sell his soul to the devil and come with them to the lower regions, cut the lines short, make them overlap, build energy and pitch by alternating lines, "To hell . . . " "To Hell . . . " "TO HELL . . . , " followed by satanical laughter.

Keep that final objective in mind: a smooth, theatrical production that carries emotional impact.

A successful teacher may wish to expand the use of these productions beyond his classroom; e.g., to guest classes in literature; to assemblies; to festivals and contests; to community entertainment; to poetry and story hours.

Suffice it to say that Readers' Theatre affords a highly flexible and effective vehicle for making good literature come alive; that it affords training in skillful communication and appreciation of good theatre and current trends in staging; and that it has powerful appeal to high school students of drama.

"Like, man, I really dig that stuff!"

The articles, essays, textbooks, dissertations, and theses listed contain information useful to the Readers Theatre interpreter.

AGGERTT, OTIS J., and ELBERT R. BOWEN. Chapter 15, "Suggestions on the Interpretative Reading of Drama," *Communicative Reading,* Second Edition. New York, The Macmillan Company, 1963, 450-463.

ARMSTRONG, CHLOE, and PAUL D. BRANDES. Appendix A, "The Staged Reading," *The Oral Interpretation of Literature.* New York, McGraw-Hill Book Company, Inc., 1963, 289-293.

BACON, WALLACE. Chapter 12, "Group Interpretation: Choric Interpretation, Readers Theatre, Chamber Theatre," *The Art of Interpretation.* New York, Holt, Rinehart & Winston, Inc., 1966, 306-345.

BENTLEY, ERIC. "On Being Read To," *Drama Critique,* VI, No. 3 (Fall 1963), 122-124.

BIRDSALL, MAURICE. "Why Not Tour a Religious Drama?" *Alpha Psi Omega Playbill,* 1958.

BODEN, ANNEKE-JAN. "Original Arrangements of Biblical Literature for Readers' Theatre," unpubl. diss., University of Denver, 1961.

BOYD, LORENZ. "Chamber Drama: Versatile Language Arts Tool," *Scholastic Teacher* (November 2, 1960), 14-15.

BRADLEY, JAMES FRANKLIN, JR. "A Reading Theatre Adaptation of *David Copperfield* for High School Students," unpubl. M.A. thesis, Michigan State University, 1960.

BREEN, ROBERT S. "Chamber Theatre," Chapter V, *Suggestions for a Course of Study in Secondary School Theatre Arts.* Washington, D.C., American Educational Theatre Association, Inc., 1963, 50-52.

BROOKS, KEITH. "Readers' Theatre: Some Questions and Answers," *Dramatics,* XXXIV, No. 3 (December 1962), 14, 27. Also in *Studies in Readers' Theatre,* Coger and White, 12-13.

BROOKS, KEITH, and JOHN E. BIELENBERG. "Readers' Theatre as Defined by New York Critics," *Southern Speech Journal*, XXIX, No. 4 (Summer 1964), 288-302.

BROOKS, KEITH, ROBERT C. HENDERHAN, and ALAN BILLINGS. "A Philosophy on Readers Theatre," *The Speech Teacher*, XII, No. 3 (September 1963), 229-232. Also in *Studies in Readers' Theatre*, Coger and White, 6-8.

COGER, LESLIE IRENE. "Interpreters Theatre: Theatre of the Mind," *Quarterly Journal of Speech*, XLIX, No. 2 (April 1963), 157-164. Also in *Studies in Readers' Theatre*, Coger and White, 1-5.

COGER, LESLIE IRENE. "Let's Have a Readers' Theatre," *Oral Interpretation*. Cincinnati, The National Thespian Society, 1957-1958, 25-27.

COGER, LESLIE IRENE. "Theatre for Oral Interpreters," *The Speech Teacher*, XII, No. 4 (November 1963), 304-307. Also in *Studies in Readers' Theatre*, Coger and White, 29-34.

COGER, LESLIE IRENE, and MELVIN R. WHITE. *Studies in Readers' Theatre*. Brooklyn, N.Y., S & F Press, 1963.

DICKINSON, HUGH. "Time and Interpretation," *Central States Speech Journal*, X, No. 1 (Autumn 1958), 7-13.

DICKINSON, HUGH. "Readers or Rhapsodes," *Quarterly Journal of Speech*, XLV, No. 3 (October 1959), 258-263.

DONHAM, NANETTE. "Production Techniques in Adapting Children's Literature to Chamber Theatre," unpubl. M.A. thesis, Occidental College, 1961.

FRANDSEN, KENNETH D., JAMES R. ROCKEY, and MARION KLEINAU. "Changes in the Factorial Composition of a Semantic Differential as a Function of Differences in Readers' Theatre Productions," *Speech Monographs*, XXXII, No. 2 (June 1965), 112-118.

GEETING, BAXTER M. "Group Performance," *Interpretation for Our Time*. Dubuque, Iowa, William C. Brown Company, Publishers, 1966, 282-291.

GRIMES, WILMA H., and ALETHEA SMITH MATTINGLY. "Readers' Theatre," *Interpretation: Writer, Reader, Audience*. San Francisco, Wadsworth Publishing Company, Inc., 1961, 331-336.

GRIMM, EDGAR C. "A Critical Analysis of Readers' Theatre," unpubl. M.A. thesis, University of Maryland, 1964.

HADLEY, DOROTHY S. "A Readers' Theatre Performance," *Dramatics*, XXXVI, No. 7 (April 1965), 13, 29.

HILE, FREDERIC W., and SHOLIE R. BROWN. "The 49'ers and Three Experiments in Oral Interpretation," *The Speech Teacher*, II, No. 2 (March 1963), 105-108.

JOHNSON, A. RAY. "There Is a Willow," unpubl. Ph.D. diss., University of Denver, 1962.

JONES, ROBERT GRAY. "Readers' Theatre Production: *A Portrait of the Artist as a Young Man,*" unpubl. M.A. thesis, Ohio State University, 1964.

KLEINAU, MARION L., and MARVIN D. KLEINAU. "Scene Location in Readers Theatre: Static or Dynamic?" *The Speech Teacher,* XIV, No. 3 (September 1965), 193-199.

LARSON, WINIFRED A. "An Investigation of Readers' Theatre Production Style," unpubl. M.A. thesis, University of North Dakota, 1964.

LEE, CHARLOTTE I. *Oral Interpretation,* Third Edition. Boston, Houghton Mifflin Company, 1965, "Chamber Theatre," 219-220; "Readers Theatre," 333-335.

LINN, JAMES R. L. "A Historical Study of Oral Interpretation as a Form of Professional Theatre in London, 1951-1962," unpubl. Ph.D. diss., University of Southern California, 1964.

MacARTHUR, DAVID E. "Readers' Theatre: Variations on a Theme," *The Speech Teacher,* XIII, No. 1 (January 1964), 47-51.

MARLOR, CLARK S. "Preparing Plays for Oral Interpretation: A Handbook in Advanced Oral Interpretation," unpubl. Ed.D. diss., New York University, 1961.

MARLOR, CLARK S., ed. "Readers' Theatre Bibliography," *Central States Speech Journal,* XII, No. 2 (Winter 1961), 134-137.

MARLOR, CLARK S., ed. "Readers' Theatre Bibliography," *Central States Speech Journal,* XVII, No. 1 (February 1966), 33-39.

MARTIN, ALBERT P. "New Wine in Old Bottles: Today's Professional Interpreters," *Drama Critique,* VI, No. 3 (Fall 1963), 117-121.

MCCOARD, WILLIAM B. "An Interpretation of the Times: A Report on the Oral Interpretation of W. H. Auden's *Age of Anxiety,*" *Quarterly Journal of Speech,* XXXV, No. 4 (December 1949), 489-495.

MCCOARD, WILLIAM B. "Report on the Reading of *Hiroshima,*" *Quarterly Journal of Speech,* XXXIV, No. 2 (April 1948), 174-176. Also in *Studies in Readers' Theatre,* Coger and White, 24-25.

MONROE, E. ANNETTE. "The Group Reading: Expression for Drama of Mental Action," *Central States Speech Journal,* XV, No. 3 (August 1964), 170-176.

MONROE, E. ANNETTE. "The Group Reading of Drama: Its Essence and Aesthetic Principles," unpubl. Ph.D. diss., University of Wisconsin, 1963.

MOOREHEAD, AGNES. "Staging *Don Juan in Hell,*" *Western Speech,* XVIII, No. 3 (May 1954), 163-166.

NICHOLS, JOSEPHINE. "Readers' Theatre on Tour," *Drama Critique,* VI, No. 3 (Fall 1963), 132-135.

NIELSEN, MARGARET. "Have You Tried Readers' Theatre?" *Secondary School Theatre Conference News,* 1, No. 1 (Winter 1962), 10-12. Also in *Studies in Readers' Theatre,* Coger and White, 9-11.

REYNOLDS, NYDIA J. "A Lively Art," *Today's Speech,* 9, No. 2 (April 1961), 15-17.

ROBERTSON, RODERICK. "Interpreters Theatre," Letter to the Editor in The Forum, *Quarterly Journal of Speech,* XLIX, No. 3 (October 1963), 321-322.

ROBERTSON, RODERICK. "Producing Playreadings," *Educational Theatre Journal,* XII, No. 1 (March 1960), 20-23. Also in *Studies in Readers' Theatre,* Coger and White, 21-23.

ROBINSON, KARL F., and CHARLOTTE I. LEE. "Readers' Theatre," *Speech in Action.* Glenview, Ill., Scott, Foresman and Company, 1965, 466-479.

ROCKEY, JAMES R. "Effects of Directive and Nondirective Criticism on Changes in Semantic Compatibility During the Preparation of a Readers' Theatre Production," unpubl. M.A. thesis, Southern Illinois University, 1964.

SANDOE, JAMES. "A Note or Two about Playreadings," *Western Speech,* 17, No. 4 (October 1953), 225-229. Also in *Studies in Readers' Theatre,* Coger and White, 26-28.

SILL, JOHN THOMAS. "Oral Interpretation of the Letters of Abraham Lincoln with Production Notes on a Group Reading of Lincoln's Letters," unpubl. M.A. thesis, Southern Illinois University, 1958.

STEVENS, PHILLIP B. "Acting and Interpretation: The Reader Faces the Contest," *The Speech Teacher,* XIV, No. 2 (March 1965), 116-122.

STUURMAN, KAY ARTHUR. "Staged Readings of Plays," *Players Magazine,* 18, No. 1 (October 1941), 18-19. Also in *Studies in Readers' Theatre,* Coger and White, 17-18.

SUSAN, SISTER MARY. "Chamber Theatre," *Catholic Theatre,* XVIII, No. 8 (May 1960).

WHITE, MELVIN R. The Mikado *for Readers' Theatre and Stage.* Brooklyn, N.Y., S & F Press, 1964.

WHITE, MELVIN R. "Multiple Readings of Dialogue-Type Poetry," *From the Printed Page (Interpretation Assignment Handbook).* Brooklyn, N.Y., S & F Press, 1964, 13-17.

WHITE, VICKIE SUE. "A Readers' Theatre Presentation of an Adaptation of Stephen Vincent Benét's *Western Star,*" unpubl. M.S. thesis, Kansas State Teachers College, 1964.

WITT, DANIEL M. "A Comparative Analysis of Audience Response to Realistic and Anti-Realistic Drama When Perceived Through Acting, Readers' Theatre, and Silent Reading," unpubl. Ph.D. diss., University of Denver, 1964.

WITT, DANIEL M. "Audience Response to Acting, Readers' Theatre, and Silent Reading of Realistic and Anti-Realistic Drama," *Western Speech,* 30, No. 2 (Spring 1966), 123-129.